THE DANIEL PRESS
&
THE GARLAND OF RACHEL

Emily Daniel with her daughters Rachel and Ruth, in a photograph taken in Oxford during the early 1880s.

The Daniel Press

&

The Garland of Rachel

WILLIAM S. PETERSON AND
SYLVIA HOLTON PETERSON

Oak Knoll Press
NEW CASTLE, DELAWARE

First Edition 2016

Published by
Oak Knoll Press
310 Delaware Street
New Castle, DE 19720, USA

ISBN: 978-1-58456-353-2

© 2016 William S. Peterson and Sylvia Holton Peterson. All rights reserved.

Typesetting & design: William S. Peterson
Set in Garamond Premier Pro

No part of this book may be reproduced without the express written consent of the publisher, except in cases of brief excerpts in critical reviews and articles.

All inquiries should be addressed to Oak Knoll Press, 310 Delaware Street, New Castle, DE 19720.

Printed in the United States of America on acid-free paper meeting the requirements of ANSI/NISO Z39.48-1992 (Permanence of Paper)

Library of Congress Cataloging-in-Publication Data

Names: Peterson, William S., author. | Peterson, Sylvia Holton, author.

Title: The Daniel Press & The garland of Rachel / William S. Peterson and Sylvia Holton Peterson.

Other titles: Daniel Press and The garland of Rachel

Description: First edition. | New Castle, Delaware : Oak Knoll Press, 2016. | Includes bibliographical references and index.

Identifiers: LCCN 2016003509 | ISBN 9781584563532

Subjects: LCSH: Daniel Press--History. | Private presses--England--History--19th century. | Private presses--England--History--20th century. | Oxford (England)--Imprints. | Daniel, C. Henry (Charles Henry) | Garland of Rachel. | English poetry--19th century. | English poetry--19th century--History and criticism.

Classification: LCC Z232.D18 P48 2016 | DDC 686.2--dc23

LC record available at http://lccn.loc.gov/2016003509

CONTENTS

Preface	vii
Abbreviations	ix
1. The Daniels and Their Press	1
2. The *Garland* and Its Contributors	27
3. A Census	55
4. Correspondence	121
5. Bookbinders	175
6. Catalogues	185
Appendix: Text of the *Garland*	197
Index	219

There are nine color illustrations following page 52 and numerous black-and-white illustrations scattered throughout the text.

PHOTO CREDITS

Bodleian Library: Figs. 11, 13, 15.
Philip Bishop: p. 92.
University of Chicago Library: p. 89.
Columbia University Library: p. 75.
University of Delaware Library: p. 99.
Viveca English: p. 29.
Fales Library (New York University): p. 67.
National Portrait Gallery: Fig. 12; pp. 42, 47.
New York Public Library: p. 46.
Newberry Library: Pl. 8.
Private owner/Guild of Handicraft Trust: p. 176.
Penny Tuerk: Frontispiece; Figs. 1, 16, 19, 20; Pls. 1, 2, 3.
Victoria and Albert Museum: pp. 30, 40, 43, 45.
Worcester College Library: Figs. 5, 9, 17, 18.

PREFACE

WHEN we began working on this book, we intended to produce a minor sequel to our *The Kelmscott Chaucer: A Census* (Oak Knoll Press, 2011)—in other words, a detailed inventory of all the known copies of another celebrated English private press book of the late nineteenth century—but this time, we decided, our selected title would be a *small* book with a modest circulation. *The Garland of Rachel*, issued by the Daniel Press in 1881, seemed to fit that description perfectly. Whereas the *Chaucer* had a pressrun of 440 copies, the official figure for the *Garland* was thirty-six. The *Garland* itself seemed comparatively easy to describe: there were no illustrations and few ornaments, the same typeface was used throughout (except for a few words in Greek), and most surviving copies were in identical vellum bindings.

In the end, we succeeded in finding ten contributors' copies and seventeen other copies (for a total of twenty-seven out of thirty-six), and we were able to provide considerable information about some of the unlocated copies as well. Of the ones we located, seven were in private hands and twenty in public institutions. We also identified and described a group of manuscripts of the book, three sets of proofs, and a celebrated facsimile of the *Garland*.

What we gradually discovered, however, is that whereas there is a large body of scholarship and commentary on the Kelmscott Press, remarkably little has been written about the Daniel Press since the publication of Falconer Madan's monumental bibliography in 1921. It became obvious to us that we could not chronicle in isolation merely one book produced by the Daniel Press, even though the *Garland* was certainly its most famous title, but that instead we would have to place that celebrated work in the larger context of the history of the Press as a whole. This is why we decided to write a substantial introductory chapter that tries to reconstruct

PREFACE

the printing activities of the Daniel family over several decades.

In searching for the raw materials of such a history, we found several important archives that shed a great deal of new light on the Daniel Press: in particular, the Daniel family papers in the Worcester College Library, the rich collection of proofs and manuscripts in the Wormsley Library, the largely unknown body of material owned by Rachel Daniel's granddaughter, and the immense archive (now in the Bodleian Library) created by Falconer Madan while preparing his bibliography. We felt that this considerable body of previously unexplored or neglected material justified our decision to take a new look at the Daniel Press.

Many individuals have offered assistance and advice. We must especially mention Penny Tuerk (the granddaughter of Rachel Daniel), Joanna Parker (former Librarian of Worcester College), and Mark Samuels Lasner. Others include Verity Andrews, Lisa Baskin, John Bidwell, Philip R. Bishop, François Bourdillon, Peter Bourdillon, Phil Brown, Anne Buchanan, David Chambers, Meghan Constantinou, Lisa Crane, Hilary Martin Daniel, Christine DeZelar-Tiedman, Mark Dimunation, Viveca English, Colin Franklin, Eric Frazier, Stephen Ferguson, Paul Gehl, Mark Getty, Sarah McCormick Healy, August Imholtz, Diana Ingram, Timothy Johnson, Alan Jutzi, Liz Kay, Julie Anne Lambert, Lisa Long, John Madicott, Bryan Maggs, Eileen Moran, Leslie Morris, Paul W. Nash, Alan O'Day, Richard Oram, Martin Ould, Pam Pryde, John Randle, Anne Rossiter, Julian Rota, Sophie Schneideman, Jane Siegel, Marvin J. Taylor, Philip Weimerskirch, Eric White, Matthew Young, and Timothy Young.

The numerous institutions and collectors to whom we are indebted—especially for permission to quote unpublished documents—are mentioned throughout the book, especially in footnotes.[1] We are grateful to all of them.

---

1. All reasonable efforts have been made to seek permission from rights holders, but information discovered after publication will be included in subsequent editions of this book.

ABBREVIATIONS

Chronicle of… Cruttwell = Cruttwell, Henry Athill. *The Chronicle of Crotall, Curthall, Cruttal, or Cruttwell.* [Camberley: Hickmott, 1933.]

DAB = *Dictionary of American Biography.*

de Ricci = de Ricci, Seymour. *English Collectors of Books and Manuscripts (1530–1930) and Their Marks of Ownership.* Cambridge: Cambridge University Press, 1930.

Dickinson = Dickinson, Donald C. *Dictionary of American Book Collectors.* New York: Greenwood Press, 1986.

Franklin [1] = Franklin, Colin. "Garlands of Rachel." *Book Collector* 30 (Winter, 1981): 479–490.

Franklin [2] = Franklin, Colin. *Poets of the Daniel Press.* Cambridge: Rampant Lions Press, 1988.

Getty = Wormsley Library, private library of Mark Getty.

Grolier 2000 = *Grolier 2000: A Further Grolier Club Biographical Retrospective.* New York: Grolier Club, 2000.

JJC = Falconer Madan's archive for his Daniel Press bibliography (five boxes in the John Johnson Collection, Bodleian Library).[1]

Memorials = *The Daniel Press: Memorials of C. H. O. Daniel, with

---

1. In our references to this archive, the numeral following "JJC" is a box number.

ABBREVIATIONS

a Bibliography [by Falconer Madan] *of the Press, 1845–1919*. Oxford: Printed on the Daniel Press in the Bodleian Library, 1921.

NYU = Fales Collection, New York University.

ODNB = *Oxford Dictionary of National Biography*.

Piehl = Piehl, Frank J. *The Caxton Club, 1895–1995: Celebrating a Century of the Book in Chicago.* Chicago: Caxton Club, 1995.

TLS = *Times Literary Supplement*.

Tuerk = Penny Tuerk (private collection).

Worcester = Worcester College Library.

WWW = *Who Was Who*.

WWW in America = *Who Was Who in America*.

THE DANIEL PRESS
&
THE GARLAND OF RACHEL

1 *Henry Daniel.*

1. THE DANIELS AND THEIR PRESS

HENRY DANIEL was born into a family deeply rooted in England's West Country that had produced generation after generation of Daniel solicitors and Anglican clergymen, all solid, respectable citizens in their communities. His maternal Cruttwell forebears, on the other hand, displayed frequent connections with the worlds of printing and scholarship. William Cruttwell and his brother Richard, for example, were printers/publishers of newspapers in Sherborne and Bath, respectively, and Clement Cruttwell (Henry's great-great-uncle) was even said to have typeset his book *A Concordance of the Parallel Texts of Scripture* (1790) in his own house.[1] Not surprisingly, the Daniels and the Cruttwells—as well as the Olives, the family of Henry's future wife Emily, who was in fact a cousin—intermarried frequently over several generations, so that by the nineteenth century their joint genealogical tree looked like a hopeless tangle.

In 1838 Henry Daniel's parents settled in Frome, a manufacturing town some thirty miles south of Bath, where his father Alfred was installed as the perpetual curate (later the vicar) of the new Holy Trinity Church [*Fig. 2*], which had been explicitly created to serve the needs of an impoverished neighborhood. "The Revd. Daniel and his lady are well fitted by their faith, their mildness and humility for the station assigned them of living with the poor and for the poor," one local citizen, Thomas Bunn, noted in his diary.[2] The family moved into a large, three-storey house [*Fig. 3*] close to the church, Alfred arranged for a school to be built, and soon the

---

1. This anecdote first appeared in Clement Cruttwell's obituary in the *Gentleman's Magazine* 78, part 2 (September 1808): 858, and was duly repeated in the *Dictionary of National Biography*.

2. *Experiences of a 19th Century Gentleman: The Diary of Thomas Bunn of Frome*, ed. Derek J. Gill (Frome: Frome Society for Local Study, 2003), p. 87.

2 *Holy Trinity Church, Frome.*

3 *The Frome rectory in which the Daniel family lived.*

vicarage was humming with high-minded clerical activity. In the 1841 census the household consisted of the Rev. Alfred Daniel, his wife Eliza, their son Henry (whose full name was Charles Henry Olive Daniel), then four years old, two siblings, and two servants. It was a close, devoted, growing family, and Henry Daniel was to maintain close ties with Frome and his brothers and sisters all his life. Nevertheless, it is a mistake to sentimentalize the world of his childhood, for Frome was just then experiencing unusually heavy stress from mid-Victorian religious partisanship. Henry Daniel was not raised in an idyllic village with quaintly old-fashioned customs and ideals; he grew up instead in a community that must have seemed at times like a smaller version of Trollope's Barchester, overrun with feuding, combative clerics.

One of the reasons Holy Trinity Church had been built in the first place was to counteract the exceptionally strong influence of non-Anglican Protestants (known in England as Dissenters or Non-conformists) in Frome. But in 1852 Alfred Daniel was suddenly confronted with a different challenge from the other end of the religious spectrum. The Rev. William Bennett [*Fig. 4*], newly appointed vicar of St. John the Baptist, the town's historic parish church, now arrived in Frome with a national reputation as an ecclesiastical reformer or trouble-maker (depending on one's point of view). At St. Barnabas, Pimlico, in London, he had so energetically introduced ritualistic elements into the services that riots broke out every Sunday morning. Under intense public pressure (including a caricature in *Punch* that linked him with Pugin and Pusey),[1] he was removed from the

4 *The Rev. William Bennett.*

---

1. Eleanor McNees, "'Punch' and the Pope: Three Decades of Anti-Catholic Caricature," *Victorian Periodicals Review* 37 (Spring, 2004): 29.

parish by the Bishop of London, and shortly thereafter he took up his duties in Frome, at which point the Daniel/Cruttwell faction began to circulate petitions and write pamphlets denouncing his views. Bennett of course regarded himself as a loyal servant of the Church of England who was merely recovering valuable lost traditions; Alfred Daniel and others of his persuasion saw Bennett as a Roman Catholic in disguise who was subverting Anglicanism from within.

This poisonous dispute never really resolved itself. Even before Bennett appeared in Frome, the young vicar of Holy Trinity had been conducting lectures on what he called "the Errors of Popery," and now Bennett's presence in town, signaled by countless liturgical innovations at St. John the Baptist, produced full-scale warfare that went on for decades. In 1870 the Church Association, an evangelical pressure-group, managed to have Bennett prosecuted for heresy in the highest ecclesiastical court in England, though he was eventually exonerated and died unrepentant in 1886. His last wish was to be buried in the elaborate priestly vestments that had given such offense to the Daniels and their supporters.

So how did young Henry Daniel respond to this atmosphere of intense parochial strife? In his subsequent career at Oxford it became obvious that he was slowly drifting toward Anglo-Catholicism—not the militant Puseyism of the Rev. Bennett but a tolerant, non-doctrinaire, mainly aesthetic High Church perspective that Pater and others were making fashionable in the latter decades of the nineteenth century. Only on rare occasions did these divisions within the Daniel family come out into the open. After the death of the Rev. Alfred Daniel in 1875, there was a dedication in Frome of an additional burial ground, near Holy Trinity Church, on land donated by the Daniel family. Speeches were, as one might expect, delivered on that occasion by various local clergymen and the Daniels. Henry Daniel, who had returned from Oxford for the dedication, stood up and, according the report in *The Times*, "remarked that he assisted at giving over this ground to the keeping of the National Church with the greater satisfaction, as he saw the time surely approaching for the admission of all, in virtue of a common humanity, to their common resting-place." Then a few minutes

> On Wednesday will be published HYMNS in the Pindaric Style, Arcadian Dialect, by the Berkley Sappho. with emendations. Price Two Pence. for Trinity Ch. Transept
>
> H. DANIEL would be happy to print anything of a small size for either of the under mentioned objects.
> Church Missionary Society | Jews' Society.
> Tr. Ch. Transept Fund.
>
> Transcribed & published by H. Daniel, to whom at his printing office, all correspondence or contributions (for which he will be obliged) must be addressed.

5 Henry Daniel as a child produced a family newsletter, both in manuscript and printed formats, entitled THE BUSY BEE.

later his brother George announced to the gathering that he "felt bound as a good Churchman to express a friendly disagreement on this point, and trusted the Church would retain that which was now in its keeping."[1] It is an illuminating little episode, because it reminds us of the extraordinary ecclesiastical tensions that must have troubled Henry Daniel during childhood and from which be was unable wholly to escape in his Oxford years.

Though one may perhaps harbor the suspicion that Henry Daniel was trapped during his earliest years in an oppressively clerical environment, the Daniel vicarage seems to have been in other respects a comfortable home for an imaginative, bookish child. In 1845 the Daniels offered a perfect Christmas gift for their clever son: an extremely simple little printing device. Immediately Henry and his brothers—and perhaps occasionally their father—began turning out, as a Bath librarian was to phrase it many years later, "coal tickets, notices for services, tickets for Christmas and other

---

1. "In Memoriam," *The Times*, 24 September 1877, p. 9.

6 *A Ruthven press similar to the one used by Henry Daniel in printing* THE GARLAND OF RACHEL. *He replaced it later with an Albion.*

festival teas, labels for prizes and for preserves for the household."[1] Soon the boys were taking on more impressive projects such as a series of small books of poetry (initially written by various Cruttwell relatives). Henry also, in 1851, launched an ambitious family newspaper, *The Busy Bee*, some numbers of which were printed and some in his handwriting. Even the manuscript issues are typographically notable, because they cleverly imitate the appearance

---

1. Elsie A. Russ, "The Daniel Press, Frome," *Bath Weekly Chronicle & Herald*, 4 January 1947, p. 16. The fullest description of these early Daniel productions can be found in David Chambers and Martyn Ould, *The Daniel Press in Frome* (Hinton Charterhouse: Old School Press, 2011).

of English newspapers of that day. "Transcribed & published by H. Daniel, to whom, in his printing office, all correspondence or contributions (for which he will be obliged), must be addressed," reads the notice in No. 2 (15 November 1851) [*Fig. 5*]. He was then fifteen years old.

Henry Daniel's earliest attempts at printing were done with an uncomplicated apparatus that required him to push down, with his thumbs, on a piece of paper laid over the inked type—a primitive technique that is certainly reflected in the poor quality of his first ephemera.[1] The types were scraps that the Daniel boys found at a local printing firm, W. C. & J. Penny.[2] Nevertheless, Henry kept up a brave front, for he sent out a notice to family and friends thanking them "for all the business, upon which they have employed his types and thumb," and he added that he "hopes their patronage will be continued to him, now that he has a more abundant supply, and far greater variety, of types. He, for his part, will strive to do his best, and to satisfy his employers. As he has no press, some allowance must be made for the press work."

The toy wooden press that he acquired a bit later represented an improvement, but not much, and in 1850 Daniel's parents purchased a more sophisticated machine for him, a Ruthven press [*Fig. 6*]. Falconer Madan, incidentally, muddied the waters when he declared in his Daniel Press bibliography that this early press was a small Albion—a claim that has been repeated many times since then—but a Henry Daniel letter of 1895 makes it unmistakably clear that what he now had at this disposal was a Ruthven, not

---

1. The records of printing done during the 1840s and 1850s are hazy, as one might expect, but a letter from Wilson Eustace Daniel to Falconer Madan, 24 October [1920?], makes the sequence of equipment reasonably clear: "The earlier issues of *the Thumb* and *the Toypress* were produced in the School room of the Parsonage, or if I remember rightly the bedroom which my brother [Henry] occupied" (emphasis supplied; JJC 2).

2. Wilson Eustace Daniel to Madan, 30 November [1911] (Bodleian Don e. 227). Madan added this note to the letter: "Mr. Eustace Daniel told me in Feb. 1915 that this waste type which they were allowed to pick out of the printer's box was the very beginning of the printing."

an Albion: "My beginnings were with a tiny 'Ruthven' press—on which I printed several little books—the 'Garland of Rachel' among them."[1] Though he was confused about the name of the press, Madan in his bibliography actually supplied a precise description of the Ruthven, showing how it was different from the Albion and many other hand-presses: ". . . the mechanism for applying the requisite pressure ran on wheels to a position over the paper and type; and not vice versa, i.e. not as in most hand-presses, where the screw is the fixture, and the forme is run to a position under the screw" (*Memorials*, pp. 60–61).

The youthful printing in Frome gradually diminished as Henry was sent off to various schools. He studied briefly at Grosvenor College in Bath, followed by King's College School in London, and finally at Worcester College, Oxford, where he took a first class degree in *literae humaniores* in 1859. After a brief stint as a lecturer at King's College, London, he was elected to a fellowship at Worcester in 1863 and remained there the rest of his life. Though the other members of the Daniel family had continued using the Ruthven press intermittently in Frome, in 1874 it was sent up to Oxford, because Henry wanted to do some more printing, this time in his rooms at Worcester. His first publication there was longer and more ambitious than anything he had done in Frome: *Notes from a Catalogue of Pamphlets in Worcester College Library*, an annotated list of 147 early pamphlets in his college library, issued in blue paper covers. ". . . the printing is not of a high standard, as if the printer had temporarily lost his cunning," Madan remarked rather crisply (*Memorials*, p. 82).

It was an inauspicious beginning for the Oxford phase of the Daniel Press, and only twenty-five copies of the *Notes* were distributed to the printer's friends. Two years later, however, Daniel produced another booklet, *A New Sermon of the Newest Fashion*, a

---

1. Henry Daniel to C. H. St. John Hornby, 3 November 1895 (Bridwell Library, Southern Methodist University). It should be noted that David Chambers, almost alone among modern printing historians, was unconvinced by Madan's assertion and recognized that the second Daniel press must have been a Ruthven: see Chambers and Ould, *The Daniel Press in Frome*, pp. 29–31.

> This chapter, Ladies, makes you a prefer
> Remedies, that will fortifie your Faces agair
> per, and in ſpite of all the maladies that be
> too, make them matchleſs: the only inconv
> fear from them is, that ſome of ye, when y‹
> glaſſes, may fall in love with your own ſh:
> linger away Martyrs to your ſelves.
>
> Twining curls are now much the mode, an‹
> paragons for Beauty, ſave thoſe whoſe grac
> reach the breaſts, and make ſpectators thir
> globes of Venus are upheld by the friendly aic
> twirls. If any affect the faſhion they may ſer

7 *A modern specimen of the Small Pica size of the Fell type—here much enlarged—used in the* GARLAND *and most other Daniel Press books.*

reprint of one of those early pamphlets in the Worcester College Library, that can be seen as the real launch of Henry Daniel's private press. "It is, I consider, my greatest curiosity," Daniel commented in 1884: "printed in college rooms, when I am ashamed to say, I was examining in Greats."[1] There are two noteworthy aspects to this little book. First, its text reminds us of how strongly Henry Daniel was drawn to seventeenth-century Anglo-Catholicism, as evidenced by some of the later Daniel Press titles. And second, *A New Sermon* is set in a very old but distinguished type that he had discovered at the Oxford University Press, just up Walton Street from Worcester College.

A great deal has been written about the revival of Bishop Fell's types [*Fig. 7*] in the nineteenth century, but there is surprisingly little authoritative evidence for how it actually came about.[2] What

---

1. Letter quoted in Dulau catalogue, November 1927, no. 188 (clipping in JJC 4).
2. The best account can be found in Martyn Ould and Martyn Thomas, *The Fell Revival* (Hinton Charterhouse: Old School Press, 2000).

is perfectly clear, however, is that Henry Daniel was a man of well-developed typographical tastes and that he must have been on the lookout during the 1870s for an archaic font that would harmonize with the antiquarian texts he wanted to print. Fell's types, which had been acquired by the University Press in the seventeenth century but had long since fallen into disuse, were exactly appropriate for his needs. Certainly the occasional direct comments about the matter by Daniel and his wife imply an active, personal search on his part for suitable types that eventually led him into the storerooms of the University Press. "The type I use is Fell's 17th [century] type, of which I hunted up the matrices at the Clarendon Press," he commented to St. John Hornby years later.[1] Emily Daniel was even more emphatic in emphasizing her husband's role in the rediscovery: "I do think credit is due to him for the unearthing & revival of the Fell type."[2]

Much to his regret, Henry Daniel was never able to afford a proprietary type, but he now had access to a distinguished font that would have been previously unknown to nearly all English readers, and it became the mainstay of the Daniel Press books. (Daniel nearly always preferred the small pica—equivalent to our modern 11-point size—but later also made use of a Fell black-letter and a larger italic.) Since, as Emily often observed, he didn't like to talk directly about his private press, it is difficult to know how he regarded his own work in relation to that of other, more celebrated presses. He certainly was aware of the typographical achievements of William Pickering and the Chiswick Press earlier in the century, and in later years the Daniels observed the triumphs of the Kelmscott Press and the Ashendene Press with mingled admiration and astonishment. Unfortunately Falconer Madan, after Daniel's death, made an extravagant claim that cannot really be sustained: "Dates appear to show that the Daniel Press was the first attempt to raise the standard of English Victorian printing—a work which was carried on with higher artistic and professional ideals and better opportunities on the establishment of the Kelmscott Press in

---

1. Daniel to C. H. St. John Hornby, 3 November 1895 (Bridwell Library).
2. Emily Daniel to Falconer Madan, 22 November 1911 (JJC 5).

8 [LEFT] *The Worcester College Chapel as refurbished by William Burges in the 1860s.*

9 [BELOW] *Worcester House, in which the Daniels lived from the time of their marriage until Henry's election as Provost in 1903.*

1891. The use of the Fell type in 1877 and the production of the *Garland of Rachel* in 1881 may fairly be regarded as the first genuine signs of the Revival of Printing in this country" (*Memorials*, pp. 46–47). Madan's implication that the Daniel Press somehow directly influenced the Kelmscott Press [*Fig. 10*] would have amused Henry Daniel, who understood that his own small, charming ventures in printing could not compete in the same league as the major private presses. "I was acquainted with Wm Morris, but don't think he even knew I was myself a Printer," he remarked wryly.[1] Emily Daniel, who was much more openly ambitious than her husband, realized the limitations imposed on their domestic-scale printing by scarcity of time and money. The Ashendene Press in particular, because the Daniels were on friendly terms with its proprietor, inspired feelings of rivalry and despair: "I don't think I am an envious person, but whenever I see anything from your press I always feel inclined to throw all our type into the Worcester pond & give up the whole thing!" she wrote to Hornby in 1899.[2]

Oxford, like Frome, was not at all the serene, tranquil place in Henry Daniel's time that it may seem to us today from the perspective of a more frenetic century. In 1859, as an undergraduate, he had served as librarian of the Oxford Union when Morris, Rossetti, and some other young artists were painting scenes from the *Morte d'Arthur* in the Union's debating hall; thus Daniel, the quiet adolescent from a provincial, clerical home, suddenly found himself at the center of one of the most turbulent episodes in the history

---

1. Henry Daniel to H. C. Marillier, 14 June 1903 (Mark Samuels Lasner Collection). There are indeed no references to Daniel in Morris's correspondence, but Sydney Cockerell, the secretary of the Kelmscott Press, saw the modest Daniel operation when he visited Oxford in September 1898—after Morris's death—and recorded in his diary that he and his host had "a nice talk about printing," though in a later letter Cockerell described Henry Daniel as "a very poor printer" (Arthur L. Schwarz, *Dear Mr. Cockerell, Dear Mr. Peirce: An Annotated Description of the Correspondence of Sydney C. Cockerell and Harold Peirce in the Grolier Club Archive* [High Wycombe: Rivendale Press, 2006], p. 94).

2. Emily Daniel to C. H. St. John Hornby, 1 December 1899 (Bridwell Library).

of the Pre-Raphaelite Brotherhood. That he was intensely sympathetic to the new cultural and aesthetic movements of his day there can be no doubt. In the 1860s, as a young don, he became a strong supporter of William Burges, who had been commissioned, primarily at Daniel's suggestion, to redecorate the chapel of Worcester College [*Fig. 8*]. Burges, a friend of the Pre-Raphaelites, created an astonishing center of worship for the college—wildly eclectic in style though vaguely medieval, with immense wall-paintings of saints and scriptural figures—that simply obliterated the old neoclassical interior. (There was a rumor that Henry Daniel was represented as his namesake, the Old Testament prophet, directly above the altar.) In a painful echo of the controversies that had earlier swirled around the Frome rectory, the Rev. Charles Browne, a Fellow of Worcester, in 1865 lodged an official complaint about these images, which Browne saw as papist and idolatrous, and for a full decade the debate raged on within the college. It should come as no surprise that Daniel, with his usual self-deprecating humor, in later years chose to represent himself in his printer's device as that other Daniel trapped in the lion's den.

10 *"I was acquainted with Wm Morris, but I don't think he even knew I was myself a printer,"* said *Henry Daniel.*

Henry Daniel was a man of peaceful temperament, but he was not at all the blundering, otherworldly figure described by Compton Mackenzie.[1] He held a succession of important positions at

---

1. Mackenzie's view of the Daniel family was strongly colored by the breakup of his engagement to Ruth Daniel. He had much to say (most of it vaguely unflattering) about the Daniels in the third volume of his immense autobiography, *My Life and Times* (London: Chatto & Windus, 1963–71), and, more obliquely, in his novel *Guy and Pauline* (London:

11 *The printing room of the Daniel Press as it looked on the day (in October 1919) when it was being dismantled for removal to the Bodleian Library.*

Worcester College, most notably that of Bursar, not a task usually assigned to the hopelessly fuzzy-minded. Mackenzie, however, was probably not the only contemporary who seriously underestimated this genial, unassuming Worcester don.

In August 1878 Henry Daniel married Emily Crabb Olive, a cousin with Somerset roots similar to his own, and they moved into a charming, rambling, college-owned house on Walton Street, close to the entrance of Worcester [*Fig. 9*]. The Daniels settled comfortably into their new home, known as Worcester House, soon filling it with Morris wallpapers and fabrics and Henry's substantial collection of old books, some of which overflowed onto the floor of his study. A door in the drawing-room led directly into the study, and through the drawing-room window they had a view

---

Martin Secker, 1929), where Henry Daniel appears, thinly disguised, as a comically eccentric country parson.

of an odd-looking, ramshackle cottage at the end of the garden. This two-storey building, which had earlier been occupied by a gardener, served a double function for the Daniels. On its ground floor Henry labored over his accounts (he had been appointed Junior Bursar of the college in 1870), while the upper floor, a dim, cluttered room, was crammed with printing equipment [*Fig. 11*]. Thereafter all the publications of the Daniel Press were produced in this cramped space, and from the beginning Emily was very actively involved in the typesetting and printing. "Some of the happiest hours of my life were spent in our little untidy printing room," she recalled many years later.[1] Emily soon had a child who died in infancy,[2] and in 1880 Rachel was born, followed by a second daughter, Ruth, in 1883; from an early age Rachel and Ruth trotted after their mother into the garden cottage, where they learned how to set type and to pull the lever of the press. Rachel in time even made decorative endpapers for some of the Daniel Press booklets.[3]

It is worth emphasizing how thoroughly a family affair the Daniel Press was, because Emily's role in particular has never been fully recognized. Her correspondence with contemporaries, especially St. John Hornby [*Fig. 12*],[4] shows her to be the undisputed power

---

1. Emily Daniel to C. H. St. John Hornby, 10 July 1915 (Bridwell Library).

2. Emily Daniel, in a letter to Falconer Madan, [6 May 1921], corrected an assertion in the proofs of Madan's bibliography that Rachel was her first child: "Rachel was my *first surviving* child, *not* first child" (JJC 2).

3. There was one other person, outside the family, who occasionally helped in printing the Daniel Press books: Arthur Henry Harvey, manager of the Machine Room at Oxford University Press. Emily Daniel, in a letter to Madan, 1 June 1921, offered a rather disparaging account of his services: "The man who helped us from the Press was not at all skilled— he was blind in one eye, the loss of his eye lost him his place at the Press, & Henry gave him some work as he was the son of his father's old organist at Frome—he was engaged on finally to wash the type—" (JJC 2). Harvey can be seen in the background of several photographs of the printing of the *Memorials* [*Fig. 15*], where he appears to be inspecting the finished sheets (JJC 3).

4. See William S. Peterson, "Hornby and the Daniels: Their Correspondence," *Matrix* 33 (Spring, 2015): 85–95.

behind the throne at the Press. While Henry's approach laid stress on the pleasure to be found in the printing itself, he lost interest in their publications—as Emily often complained—once they were completed. Emily, on the other hand, behaved like a real publisher: she was responsible for the choice of many of the texts, she kept in touch with authors, customers, and booksellers, and she was keenly interested in how to improve the distribution of their titles. It is also clear that by the latter half of the 1890s, Henry Daniel, increasingly burdened with college responsibilities, was losing his enthusiasm for printing, and during that period it was only Emily's energy and determination that kept the Daniel Press alive.

12 C. H. St. John Hornby.

Worcester College, located well out of the center of Oxford, had an almost rural atmosphere in the nineteenth century, and the Daniel home there became the center of quiet artistic activities and a serene domestic life. Verily Anderson Bruce, who knew the family well, described Emily Daniel as "an ardent church worker and amateur impresario and craft worker" and "an extremely good water-colourist and expert bookbinder" (though the bookbinding in fact came somewhat later).[1] John Masefield, in a tribute published in *The Times* after her death, similarly spoke of Emily as "a woman who brought a delicate distinction of beauty wherever she dwelt. She was one of the few survivors of the unsullied quiet Oxford of the time of Ruskin and of Pater. There was a greatness and fineness of accomplishment in all that she did in embroidering, painting, bookbinding, and penmanship."[2] The two exceptionally lively daughters (who naturally caught the eye of Lewis Carroll) of

---

1. Verily Anderson Bruce, *The Last of the Eccentrics: A Life of Rosslyn Bruce* (London: Hodder and Stoughton, 1972), pp. 62, 73.
2. "Mrs. Henry Daniel," *The Times*, 21 April 1933, p. 17.

course added a great deal to the charm of the Daniel household. As for Henry himself, Margaret Woods, a close friend of the Daniels, recalled him as an immensely charismatic aesthete in the guise of an Oxford don, adored by his wife and children.[1] During summer vacations the family often camped on a small houseboat in the Thames near the Oxfordshire village of Buscot, close to William Morris's country house at Kelmscott, and on at least one occasion the Daniel girls joined Jane Morris for tea at Kelmscott Manor.

The earliest Oxford publications of the Daniel Press were produced in this world of genteel amateurism, but in 1881 the appearance of *The Garland of Rachel* forced the Daniels to rethink the question of what they were trying to achieve through their printing press. Several of the contributors to the *Garland* were writers with growing reputations, the book was mentioned in various newspapers, and even in America, at least a few years later, collectors were competing fiercely to find almost-nonexistent copies of it. Clearly the Daniels' old system of quietly sending booklets to a few Oxford friends and selling them at little church bazaars, often in the garden of Worcester House, was no longer adequate. Though the Daniel Press remained agreeably modest in scale to the end, by the 1880s it had obviously become necessary to find a new system of distribution. The *Garland* was offered for sale, somewhat hesitantly, through two Oxford bookshops, Blackwell's and Gee's, and in about 1884 Henry printed a list of nine books (including the *Garland*), entitled *These are as yet the productions of the private press of Henry Daniel, Fellow of Worcester College, Oxford,* though a faintly discouraging note at the end explained that "a limited number of each of these works with the exception of the Prometheus [by Robert Bridges] may be obtained of Mr. Gee, Bookseller, the High Street, Oxford."

But in 1889 the Daniels took the more drastic step of authorizing the Bodley Head, a London bookshop and publishing house operated by Elkin Mathews and John Lane, to serve as a distribu-

---

1. See her recollections of the Daniels' home life in *Memorials*, pp. 22–31.

tor for the Daniel Press [*Fig. 13*].[1] It was an unexpected choice, because the Bodley Head was best known for its *avant-garde* literary and artistic tastes (it was the publisher of Beardsley and the *Yellow Book*), hardly the atmosphere one associates with the mostly very traditional Daniel Press. The Daniels were of course extremely idealistic, but it should not be assumed that they were naive; they were certainly aware that their new London agent moved in a world that they found uncongenial. (Emily Daniel, describing the various books she had received as Christmas gifts, including Stevenson's *A Child's Garden of Verses*, remarked crisply, "What a contrast to the Yellow Book!"[2]) But the Bodley Head offered the advantage of being a small, intensely personal operation; many friendly letters passed between the Daniels and its proprietors, and on at least a few occasions Henry sought their advice on the appropriate price and pressrun of a forthcoming Daniel Press publication. Characteristically, the initial approach to the Bodley Head seems to have been made by Henry Daniel, but thereafter the relationship was sustained primarily by a steady stream of correspondence between Lane and Emily.

On the whole, the Daniel Press–Bodley Head business connection seems to have been genial enough, though from the beginning the Daniels were uneasy about the substantial markups in prices by their London agent. A more serious source of potential friction came to the surface when Robert Bridges, in the autumn of 1893, discovered that one of his Daniel Press books, *The Growth of Love*, was being described in Lane's advertisements as a Bodley Head publication. Bridges saw this as a possible pretext for an unauthorized American edition by Lane, and for the next two years he fired

---

1. The relationship has been treated at some length by James G. Nelson in his article "The Bodley Head and the Daniel Press," *Papers of the Bibliographical Society of America* 77 (1982): 35–44, and his book *Elkin Mathews: Publisher to Yeats, Joyce, Pound* (Madison: University of Wisconsin Press, 1989), Appendix A. Nelson drew upon the Elkin Mathews correspondence in the Reading University Library, but there are also some letters between Lane and the Daniels in the Madan archive at the Bodleian Library (JJC 2).

2. Emily Daniel to Rosslyn Bruce, 27 December [1896?] (Worcester).

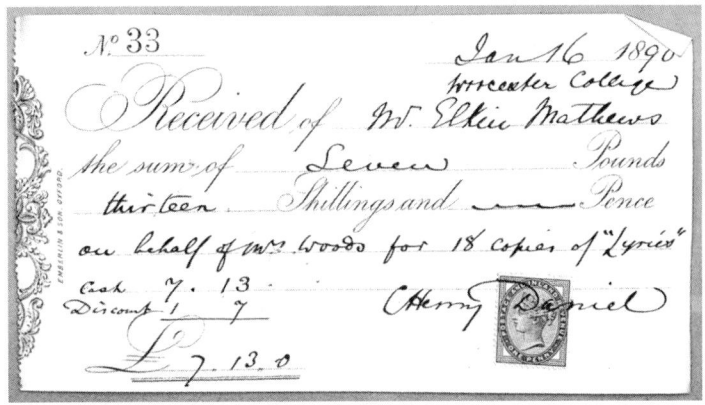

13 *Tangible evidence that the Daniel Press did bring in at least some modest income: an acknowledgement by Henry Daniel of £7 13s. from Elkin Mathews for eighteen copies of* LYRICS *by Margaret L. Woods (1888).*

off indignant letters to Henry Daniel about the matter. "I think it quite sufficient to prevent your sending any work of mine to him," he finally announced in 1895.[1] Since Bridges was by far the best-selling author of the Daniel Press, this was a serious threat. It is not clear exactly when the agreement with the Bodley Head came to a formal end, but it gradually fizzled out, no doubt primarily because of Bridges' grievance, and Lane's catalogues do not list any Daniel Press publications after 1896.

The appearance of Bridges' name on many of the Daniel Press title-pages gradually brought it a certain amount of national recognition. In 1890 eight of its books were on display at the third exhibition of the Arts and Crafts Exhibition Society in the New Gallery, London (where Morris, despite his characteristic silence on the subject, must surely have seen them), and Henry Daniel received frequent invitations from London book-lovers and bibliophilic organizations, though he seems to have been, on the whole, more comfortable in the familiar world of Oxford. There is no evidence that he ever visited the Kelmscott Press, but during the

---

1. Bridges to Henry Daniel, 2 December 1895 (Worcester).

1880s T. J. Cobden-Sanderson and St. John Hornby both climbed the stairs of the Daniels' garden cottage to see Oxford's celebrated private press in action. There they would have encountered a large Albion press [*Fig. 15*], acquired in 1882, that made it possible for Henry Daniel to undertake more ambitious books. *The Garland of Rachel* had been the last publication printed on the old Ruthven press. Now at last the Daniel family had access to a substantial printing machine, nearly as tall as Henry himself; no longer were they dependent upon a modest device that called up memories of mid-Victorian parlor printing.

Throughout the 1880s and early 1890s small books issued from the Daniel Press in a steady stream. The best-selling titles were usually by Bridges, but they were interspersed with books of more modest pretensions by other friends and contemporaries such as Margaret Woods, F. W. Bourdillon, T. H. Warren, and Walter Pater—and then of course there were always the reprints of older English writers (e.g. Keats, Milton, Anthony Wood). One of the most ambitious (and engaging) undertakings during these years was a series of short Oxford memoirs by various authors entitled *Our Memories: Shadows of Old Oxford*, issued in twenty parts between 1889 and 1893.

But toward the end of the century there was a discernible flagging of energy in the printing activities at Worcester House. Emily was understandably preoccupied with the responsibilities of raising two clever and attractive daughters, and there are some hints in her correspondence that by the turn of the century she was beginning to suffer from poor health. Henry, on the other hand, was increasingly absorbed in college affairs. As early as 1880 he had nearly been made Provost (i.e. the head) of Worcester College; slightly more than two decades later, in July 1903, he at last secured that position, and the history of the Daniel Press then effectively came to an end. Although the Daniels moved into a much grander home (the Provost's Lodge), the Albion press was to remain in the cottage behind Worcester House until Henry's death. The sole publication of the Daniel Press after Henry's election was a small collection of Latin prayers for use at the Worcester College Gaudy in June 1906. Thereafter the Albion gathered dust. "Yes, our poor

THE DANIELS AND THEIR PRESS

little press is quite dead I am sorry to say & am afraid there is no chance of its ever coming to life again," Emily lamented in 1915.[1]

Yet there was an odd little anticlimactic episode in the history of the Daniel Press. The toy press once used by Henry Daniel at Frome later fell into the hands of his nephew Henry Martin Daniel [*Fig. 14*], a naval officer, who printed a miniature book entitled *His Majesty's Valiants* (1928) in which the colophon announced, "THE PRINTER humbly presents this volume pleading for lenience towards his first book. The Press is the same as that on which his uncle and father collaborated at Frome, and on which in 1887 [*sic*] the former, Dr. Henry Daniel of Oxford, printed 'The Garland of Rachel.'" In private correspondence he described the book, then still in progress, as "the first production of the new Daniel Press."[2] When Falconer Madan discussed the matter with Emily Daniel, she was predictably distressed: "I do not want, in fact we none of us do, to have this press connected in any way with the 'Daniel Press'[—] the Daniel Press is sacred & is in the Bodleian— I have never seen any production of this press of Commander Daniel which was the toy press that C.H.O Daniel had as a little boy!"[3] However, in 1928 Henry Martin Daniel was court-martialed for disrespectful behavior toward an admiral; he abandoned his naval career, moved to South Africa, and nothing more was heard of the reborn Daniel Press.

14 *Henry Martin Daniel.*

The authentic heritage of the Daniel Press was, as Emily Daniel hinted, to be found in Oxford itself. Shortly after Henry's death in 1919, Emily and Ruth arranged for the Albion press and the

---

1. Emily Daniel to C. H. St. John Hornby, 10 July 1915 (Bridwell Library).
2. Henry Martin Daniel to Mr. Edwardes, 26 August 1924 (Stanford University Libraries).
3. Emily Daniel to Madan, 22 April 1928 (JJC 2).

15 *Two printers from the University Press—Albert Saxton and Thomas Price, with Arthur H. Harvey in the background—at work on* The Daniel Press: Memorials of C. H. O. Daniel *(1921) in the Bodleian Library, using Henry Daniel's Albion Press.*

other pressroom equipment and supplies to be transferred to the Bodleian. The press was set up in what is now the Upper Reading Room (then a picture gallery). "His dear press has found an honoured home in the Bodleian Library," Emily wrote to a friend that autumn, "just as he left it, with some Latin hymns set up in type, & with a case of his books by the side—it is all beautifully arranged, is indeed a fitting memorial of him."[1] At the Bodleian the Albion was soon used to print the *Memorials* [*Fig. 15*], the great final tribute to Henry Daniel and his private press, and for the extended Daniel family, including those from Somerset, the library was now transformed into a sacred shrine. They all came to see it. Very soon after the press was installed in its new home, Emily visited the Bodleian and found it "ideal[,] the very best memorial of him one could have." It gave her joy, she said, on a day of sadness when she was leaving behind the Provost's Lodge at Worcester.[2] Even Rachel, now married and living some distance away in Surrey, found the attraction of the old Albion press irresistible: "I should so very much like to see Fathers Press being worked in the Bodleian if I might?" she wrote to Madan in October 1921. "I do so hope I am not too late. Will the work still be going on next Wednesday if I went to Oxford that day.... I hope this is not an unreasonable request, but Mother & Ruth so loved seeing the dear old Press at work for the last time & I feel I must see it too."[3]

Just as the Daniel Press had begun in a Frome vicarage, it now ended, decades later in Oxford, as an affectionate, warmhearted family affair.

---

1. Emily Daniel to Rosslyn Bruce, 24 October 1919 (Mark Samuels Lasner Collection). The Daniel hand-press is still in the Bodleian Library: it is installed in the Bodleian Bibliography Room and is used for instructional purposes.
2. Emily Daniel to Madan, 11 October 1919 (JJC 2).
3. Rachel Daniel Lee to Madan, 25 October 1921 (JJC 2).

REFERENCES: [ALFRED DANIEL] Cockey, Edward. *A Sermon Preached in Trinity Church, Frome, on March 14th, 1875, on the Occasion of the Death of the Rev. Alfred Daniel*. Frome and London: Butler & Tanner, [1875]. ¶ [BENNETT] Bennett, Frederick. *The Story of W. J. E. Bennett, Founder of S. Barnabas', Pimlico, and Vicar of Froome [sic]-Selwood, and of His Part in the Oxford Church Movement of the Nineteenth Century*. London: Longmans, Green, 1909. — Bennett, William James E. *A Pastoral Letter to the Parishioners of Frome*. London: Joseph Masters, 1852. ¶ [DANIEL PRESS] Batey, Charles. "Horace Hart and the University Press, Oxford 1883-1915." *Signature* NS 18 (1954): 5–22. — Chambers, David, and Martyn Ould. *The Daniel Press in Frome*. Hinton Charterhouse: Old School Press, 2011. — "The Daniel Press: A Reminiscence." *Clarendonian* 31 (Autumn, 1977): 28–29. — *The Daniel Press: Memorials of C. H. O. Daniel with a Bibliography* [by Falconer Madan] *of the Press, 1845–1919*. Oxford: Printed on the Daniel Press in the Bodleian Library, 1921. (Addenda and corrigenda by Madan, 1922.) — *The Daniel Press: Pulls from Formes in the Clarendon Press, 1923*. [Oxford: Clarendon Press, 1923.] — Franklin, Colin. *Poets of the Daniel Press*. Cambridge: Rampant Lions Press, 1988. — Franklin, Colin. *The Private Presses*. Chester Springs, Penn.: Dufour Editions, 1969. — G[ibson], S[trickland]. "The Daniel Press." *Bodleian Quarterly Record* 3 (January 1921): 172–73. — Jacobi, Charles T. "The Work of the Private Presses. IV. The Daniel Press, 1845–1919." *Penrose Annual* 27 (1925): 31–36. — [Madan, Falconer.] "The Daniel Press at Frome and Oxford." *The Library* 4th ser., 1 (September 1920): 65–68. — [Madan, Falconer.] "The Daniel Press." *TLS*, 20 February 1903, pp. 55–56. (Reprinted in *The Daniel Press* [Wausau, Wis.: The Philosopher Press, Van Vechten & Ellis, 1904].) — *Memorials*. — Nelson, James G. "The Bodley Head and the Daniel Press." *PBSA* 77 (1982): 35–44. — Nelson, James G. *Elkin Mathews: Publisher to Yeats, Joyce, Pound*. Madison: University of Wisconsin Press, 1989. (See Appendix A.) — Newdigate, Bernard H. "Book-Production Notes: The Daniel Press." *London Mercury* 5 (March 1922): 524–25. — Ould, Martyn. *Printing at the Daniel Press*. Hinton Charterhouse: Old School Press, 2011. — Ould, Martyn, and Martyn Thomas. *The Fell Revival, Describing the Casting of the Fell Types at the University Press, Oxford, and Their Use by the Press and Others since 1864*. Hinton Charterhouse: Old School Press, 2000. — Parker, Joanna. *The Daniel Press: Extract from a Talk to the Wynkyn de Worde Society*. Presented as a keepsake for the Society, 1996. — Parker, Joanna. "Henry Daniel and His Private Press." *Worcester College Record* (1977): 48–51. — Peterson, William S. "Hornby and the Daniels: Their Correspondence." *Matrix* 33 (Spring, 2015): 85–95. — Peterson, William S. "The Daniel Press in America." *Journal of the Printing Historical Society* NS

20 (Spring, 2014): 39–45. — Plomer, Henry R. "Some Private Presses of the Nineteenth Century." *The Library* NS 1 (September 1900): 407–28. — Pollard, A. W. "Private Presses and Their Influence on the Art of Printing," *Ars Typographica* 1 (Autumn, 1934): 36–42. — Reedy, W. Curran. "The Daniel Press." *British Printer* 32 (August–September 1919): 101. — Rose, Jonathan, and Patricia Anderson, eds. *British Literary Publishing Houses, 1820–1880*. Detroit: Gale Research, 1991. (See Jennifer B. Lee, "Daniel Press," pp. 123–26.) — Turner, John. "The Daniel Press at Oxford." *Antiquarian Book Monthly Review* 10 (1983): 258–63. — Ephemera, manuscripts, proofs, etc. (Getty; Hilary Martin Daniel; John Johnson Collection, Bodleian Library [Falconer Madan's archive for his bibliography of the Daniel Press]); Oxford University Press archives; Tuerk). ¶ [FROME] Belham, Peter. *The Making of Frome*. Frome: Frome Society for Local Study, 1973. — McGarvie, Michael. *Around Frome*. (Images of England.) Stroud: Chalford, 1997. ¶ [HENRY DANIEL] *Alumni Oxonienses*. — *Catalogue of the Library of the Late Dr. Daniel, Provost of Worcester College, Oxford, and Founder of the Daniel Press*. Oxford: Leslie Chaundy, Bookseller, catalogue no. 39, 1920. — *Chronicle of... Cruttwell*. (See pp. 145—48.) — Daniel, C. Henry, and W. R. Barker. *Worcester College*. London: F. E. Robinson & Co., 1900. — "Isis Idols. No. CCLXIV. Rev. Charles Henry Olive Daniel, M.A. Provost of Worcester College." *Isis*, 19 March 1904, p. 249. — *Memorials*. — Parker, Joanna. "Henry Daniel and His Private Press." *Worcester College Record* (1977): 48–51. — W[arren], H[erbert]. "Obituary: Charles Henry Olive Daniel." *Oxford Magazine*, 17 October 1919, p. 6. — [Warren, Herbert] "The Provost of Worcester: Treasures of the Daniel Press." *The Times*, 8 September 1919, p. 14. (Obituary.) — Wilkinson, C. H., and John D. Haigh. "Daniel, (Charles) Henry Olive," in *ODNB*. — *WWW*. — Papers (Getty, Tuerk, Worcester). ¶ [HENRY MARTIN DANIEL] Gardner, Leslie. *The Royal Oak Courts Martial*. Edinburgh: Blackwood, 1965. — Glenton, Robert. *The Royal Oak Affair: The Saga of Admiral Collard and Bandmaster Barnacle*. London: L. Cooper, 1991.

2. THE GARLAND & ITS CONTRIBUTORS

RACHEL DANIEL was born on 27 September 1880, and it is clear that her father, who was always searching for ideas for small books that he could produce on his Ruthven press, decided very soon thereafter to publish a series of poems in tribute to his infant daughter. The specific precedent that he had in mind—suggested to him by Humphry Ward—was a seventeenth-century French manuscript, *La Guirlande de Julie*, an elaborately ornamented celebration of Julie d'Angennes, a beautiful young aristocrat. The collection consisted of poems by seventeen contemporaries, each supplying a madrigal in which a particular flower offered praise of her charms.

Henry Daniel's initial plan seems to have been to solicit contributions only from Oxford friends, but they in turn knew or recommended others who might be willing to write poems about his daughter, and eventually *The Garland of Rachel* included tributes by many poets of the day, some with only tenuous Oxford connections. The first writer that Daniel approached was C. L. Dodgson (22 November 1880 [**4.1**]), though that odd, shy figure (at Christ Church) initially submitted a wildly inappropriate piece of doggerel and did not offer a suitable poem until the following March. Daniel also hoped that he might be able to persuade another Oxford writer of national reputation, Walter Pater (at Brasenose College), but Pater, a brilliant prose stylist, was unprepared to write a poem or even a preface. At this early stage two persons were especially active in recommending or recruiting contributors: Daniel's old friend P. F. Willert (at Exeter College), who approached Frederick Locker and W. J. Courthope; and Andrew Lang (formerly at Merton College), who suggested the names of Edmund Gosse and Mary Robinson and served as an intermediary between Daniel and W. E. Henley. Nevertheless, despite the widening circle of contributors, the *Garland* retained a distinctly Oxford ambience.

In fact, when T. B. Mosher bought an unbound set of proofs and sheets of the book in 1902, Emily Daniel agreed to create in its margins a series of miniature paintings of the particular Oxford colleges associated with the individual poets [3.29].

A number of the poems were in Henry Daniel's hands by late 1880, and in March of the following year he began to send out proofs, though the typesetting and presswork went very slowly, partly because he was much distracted by his college duties and partly because Rachel, the subject of the book, suffered from a prolonged illness in 1881. The scheme he had in mind was to produce a copy (with an individualized title-page) for each of the eighteen contributors and then to print a further eighteen copies (with a generic title-page) for sale to the public. Though Daniel's books always display good taste in typography, the design of the *Garland* has a distinctly improvisational quality about it; that of course is part of its charm. The attractiveness of the book is much enhanced by the Fell type, Emily Daniel's miniation (i.e. her hand-drawn initial letters), the headpieces and printer's device designed by Alfred Parsons, and the white vellum binding by Morley & Sons. Henry Daniel was tempted to include an excerpt from Bishop John Earle's *Microcosmographie* (1628) but decided in the end to produce it as a separate leaflet, dated 18 October 1881, which was sent to all the contributors. The book itself was apparently also completed and distributed in October, shortly after Rachel's first birthday.

Clearly a number of the eighteen additional copies were given to friends and relatives, because in 1896 Daniel estimated that only six of them had been sold, though he added that "if a copy came into the market [now], the price would probably range from £7 to £10" [4.49]. The extreme rarity of the *Garland*—and of course the contribution by Dodgson—has made it one of the most sought-after of nineteenth-century English books. Henry Daniel, a deeply idealistic man, had obviously not been aware that he was creating a book destined to be pursued so energetically by bibliophiles in the future, though even at the time of publication Humphry Ward predicted to him that the *Garland* would someday realize "fabulous prices" [4.29], and Austin Dobson suggested, in an American magazine, that "the book is so great a typographical curiosity that if

THE GARLAND & ITS CONTRIBUTORS

any of the thirty-six copies ever get into the market they will probably 'exercise' the cupidity of bibliomaniacs."[1] Quite apart from its unusually high market value, the *Garland* continues to attract modern readers who are drawn to its visual charm, its atmosphere reminiscent of late Victorian Oxford, and the memorable picture it indirectly offers of the engaging domestic life of the Daniel family.

What follows is a series of brief sketches of the contributors to the *Garland*:

2.1 ❧ FRANCIS WILLIAM BOURDILLON (1852–1921)

The son of an Anglican clergyman, Bourdillon was educated at Haileybury and Worcester College and made a name for himself as a scholar and bibliographer of early French romances. He was best known during his lifetime for an edition and translation of *Aucassin et Nicolette* (1887), but he also issued a number of volumes of his own poetry, including *Among the Flowers and Other Poems* (1878), *A Lost God* (1891), *Sursum Corda* (1893), *Preludes and Romances* (1903), and *Christmas Roses* (1914), as well as a novel and a play. For some years he served as a private tutor to students near his home in Sussex and to the sons of Prince and Princess Christian of Schleswig-Holstein. During the summers he was an enthusiastic mountain-climber.

Bourdillon had a close friendship with Henry Daniel, which no doubt sprang from his undergraduate years, and visited him for the last time a few months before the Provost's death. His tribute to Daniel, a poem entitled "The Poets' Friend," portrays the Provost as someone who achieved fame inadvertently—a man "who but

---

1. [Dobson], "Bric-a-brac: The Garland of Rachel," *Century Illustrated Monthly Magazine* 23 (February 1882): 640.

claimed | *To love his fellow men*, and found | His name with unsought radiance crowned."[1] The poem, as Madan remarked, must have been one of the last that Bourdillon wrote. Earlier the Daniel Press had published two series of poems (in English) by Bourdillon, *Ailes d'Alouette* (1890 and 1902) [Madan nos. 19, 53].

C. J. Cruttwell, who confessed to a "predilection for sonnets," found Bourdillon's contribution to the *Garland* "exquisite" [4.38]. The manuscript of Bourdillon's poem (Tuerk) is dated December 1880.

Bourdillon's copy is unlocated.

REFERENCES: Bourdillon, F. W. "The Poet's Friend," in *Memorials*, p. [36]. — de Ricci. (See p. 192.) — "F. W. Bourdillon: Poet, Scholar, and Editor of Old French Romances." *The Times*, 14 January 1921, p. 13. (Obituary.) — Franklin [2]. (See pp. 88–91.) — W., W. A. "F. W. Bourdillon., 1852–1921." *Alpine Journal* 33 (March 1921): 409–11. (Obituary.) — *WWW*. — Correspondence (NYU, Tuerk, Worcester). — His collection of early French books and manuscripts is in the National Library of Wales.

2.2 ❧ ROBERT BRIDGES (1844–1930)

"Robert Bridges was, since the death of Hardy, the grandest surviving figure of the Victorian Age," the *Manchester Guardian* declared in 1930. Bridges was a celebrated literary personality in his day—Poet Laureate, no less—and his career was connected for many years with the fortunes of the Daniel Press. At Eton and Corpus Christi, Oxford, he displayed strongly high Anglican impulses but, somewhat unexpectedly, decided upon a medical career. At just about the time that he became a contributor to the *Garland*, however, he was in the midst of retiring as a physician and beginning to devote all his energies to writing.

What brought Bridges and Henry Daniel together was a set of

---

1. *Memorials*, p. [36].

shared typographical preoccupations. In the spring of 1880, thanks to their mutual friend James Thursfield, they entered into correspondence about the possibility of Daniel publishing a collection of poems by Bridges, who, nevertheless, decided almost immediately that he did not find the Daniel Press style of printing suitable for his own poems. ". . . though I admire your type and printing as much I hope as you would wish,—and certainly it is admirably suited to your reprints,—yet it happens not to be at all the kind of type I am looking for," Bridges wrote. "What I want is merely an evenly and clear cut small pica. . . . Anything old fashioned would not suit me. . . ."[1] After participating in the *Garland* project a year later, Bridges seems to have had a change of heart, and in 1883 the Daniel Press published his *Prometheus the Firegiver*, the first of numerous volumes by Bridges issued under that imprint. In fact, Bridges's conversion to the "old fashioned" types was so complete that in 1890 he allowed Daniel to reprint his *The Growth of Love* (1889) entirely in the Fell black letter. When it appeared, he wrote to describe his "ecstasy over your 'black letter'," and a few years later he announced to Daniel that "black letter is coming into fashion," adding that "I suppose Morris has assisted in this fad."[2]

Bridges' growing reputation prompted some critics and readers to wonder why he continued to have his books produced by the small, obscure Daniel Press. "Why did I print with Daniel?" Bridges responded. "Critics copied each other in asserting that I withheld my poems from the public. Here are some facts—Daniel wished for something to print: so I gave him my Prometheus. He printed 100 copies and sold them at ten shillings, giving me an immediate return of £15, altho' some of the 'subscribers' never paid up." He contrasted that with his treatment by commercial publishers, who promised him large royalties that never materialized.[3] For

---

1. Bridges to Daniel, 17 April 1880 (Worcester).

2. Bridges to Daniel, 27 September 1890 and 2 December 1893 (Worcester).

3. We are quoting from a fairly lengthy undated document—apparently a typescript copy—by Bridges about his relationship with the Daniel Press (Worcester). We know nothing about the circumstances under which it was written.

several years Bridges corresponded with Daniel about the possibility of publishing the poems of his friend Gerard Manley Hopkins; when that volume was finally issued by Oxford University Press in 1918, under Bridges' editorship, it caused a great stir, and one can only speculate what a Hopkins volume might have done for the reputation of the Daniel Press.

Bridges was a frequent visitor at Worcester House—always cheerful and lively—and became a close friend of Emily and her daughters; in 1919 he composed a piece of occasional verse about his memories of the Daniel family and their home. He recalled that often on winter evenings he was pushed out of the Bodleian by its closing bell and then retreated to Henry Daniel's study for bookish talk; in the summer he and the Daniels would sit in wicker chairs in their garden, the entrance to which was guarded by a gigantic sculpted bust from the Clarendon Building. *Verses Written for Mrs. Daniel* is a wry, amusing little poem that conveys nicely the warmth of the Daniels' domestic life and the happy relationship between Bridges and the family.

Because of Bridges' close ties with the Daniels, it is certainly possible that, unlike most of the other contributors to the *Garland*, he had actually laid eyes on the infant Rachel before he wrote his poem. When Henry Daniel asked him for some verse in November 1880, Bridges at first declined to make a commitment, but by the following March he had sent him a poem [*Pl. 1*] with characteristically self-deprecating remarks. The *Garland* came into his hands in October 1881, and he wrote to Daniel that "I think the book is very pretty indeed, and does great credit to your household press: and I wish that my verses were more worthy of the trouble and care that has been spent on them" [**4.25**]. But Andrew Lang and Humphry Ward both praised Bridges' poem as one of the best in the volume.

For Bridges' copy, see **3.2**.

REFERENCES: Barker, Nicolas. *The Printer and the Poet: An Account of the Printing of 'The Tapestry' Based upon Correspondence between Stanley Morison and Robert Bridges.* Cambridge: privately printed, 1970. — Bridges, Robert. *The Selected Letters of Robert Bridges, with the Correspondence of Robert Bridges and Lionel Muirhead.* Ed. Donald E. Stanford. 2 vols. Newark: University of Delaware Press, 1983–84. — Bridges, Robert.

THE GARLAND & ITS CONTRIBUTORS

Verses Written for Mrs. Daniel. Oxford: Clarendon Press, 1932. — "Death of the Poet Laureate." *Manchester Guardian*, 22 April 1930, p. 9. — Franklin [2]. (See pp. 23–45.) — H., C. H. "The Late Poet Laureate." *Manchester Guardian*, 25 April 1930, p. 7. (Tribute.) — Hamilton, Lee Templin. *Robert Bridges: An Annotated Bibliography, 1873–1988*. Newark: University of Delaware Press, 1971. (See p. 72.) — Jackson, Holbrook. "Robert Bridges, George Moore, Bernard Shaw, and Printing." *Fleuron* 4 (1925): 43–53. — McKay, George L. *A Bibliography of Robert Bridges*. New York: Columbia University Press, 1933. (Based on Frederick Coykendall's collection; see p. 161 for the *Garland*.) — "Mr. Robert Bridges, O.M. The Poet Laureate." *The Times*, 22 April 1930, p. 17. (Obituary.) — Nowell-Smith, Simon. "Mosher and Bridges." *Book Collector* 11 (Winter, 1962): 482–83. — Phillips, Catherine. "Bridges, Robert Seymour," in *ODNB*. — Phillips, Catherine. *Robert Bridges: A Biography*. Oxford and New York: Oxford University Press, 1992. — "The Poet Laureate: Death of Dr. Robert Bridges." *Manchester Guardian*, 22 April 1930, p. 12. — Thomas, Martyn. "Why Did Robert Bridges, Poet Laureate, Choose to Publish Many of His Poems with the Daniel Press?" *Journal of the Printing Historical Society* NS 20 (Spring, 2014): 47–51. — *WWW*. — Correspondence (Bodleian, Getty, Huntington, Tuerk, Worcester).

2.3 ❧ WILLIAM JOHN COURTHOPE (1842–1917)

W. J. Courthope, civil servant and poet (as well as literary scholar), won the Newdigate prize at Oxford and took a double first in 1866. He had a long and distinguished career, eventually becoming the First Civil Service Commissioner in 1892. He also published several volumes of verse, founded and co-edited the *National Review*, edited Pope and wrote a biography of him, and between 1895 and 1901 was Professor of Poetry at Oxford.

The surviving correspondence suggests that Courthope did not know Henry Daniel and had apparently been approached by P. F. Willert about a contribution to the *Garland*. "If you are not going to press in a great hurry I think we are sure to get something from Courthope," Willert wrote Daniel on 13 December 1880 [**4.9**]. After the book was published, Courthope confessed to Daniel, "For my own part I am only sorry I did not know the 'child' about whom I was asked to write was your little girl—I would then have made a more auspicious contribution to the 'garland'.

"I was only told that the subject was a child, and the birth of a little niece in winter suggested lines which I fear are rather too melancholy for the occasion [4.43]. The manuscript of his poem is dated January 1881 (Tuerk).

Several of Daniel's friends commented on the dark political tone of Courthope's poem. Willert described his contribution as "pessimist & reactionary (with a flavor of jingoism)" [4.21]; Humphry Ward remarked that Courthope's lines were "good but o! how gloomily Tory" [4.29]; John Addington Symonds described him as youthful in mind and spirit but a "rigid Tory";[1] and Andrew Lang summed up the case by complaining that "Courthope could not forget the General Election" [4.24].

On another occasion, Symonds offered this reading of Courthope's personality: "He has an excellent and sober judgment, strong prejudices, and an inexhaustible fund of humour. He is a most refreshing companion, never tiring you with fretful activity or the heaviness of his intellect, but flowing at an even level in a good full stream. You will find that he has ways of his own of looking at things, that he is perfectly spontaneous, that he rhymes with singular felicity and that there is a good, unquarried mass of raw material in him" (Symonds, *Letters and Papers*, p. 23).

Courthope's copy is unlocated.

REFERENCES: Courthope, W. J. *The Country Town and Other Poems.* London: Humphry Milford, Oxford University Press, 1920. (See A. O. Prickard, "Memoir.") — "Death of Mr. Courthope." *The Times,* 12 April 1917, p. 9. — Mackail, J. W. "W. J. Courthope, 1842–1917." *Proceedings of the British Academy* 9 (1917–18): 581–90. — Prickard, A. O., and Katherine Mullen. "Courthope, William John," in *ODNB.* — Symonds, John Addington. *Letters and Papers of John Addington Symonds.* Ed. Horatio F. Brown. London: John Murray, 1923. — *WWW.* — Correspondence (Getty, Tuerk).

---

1. *The Letters of John Addington Symonds*, ed. Herbert Schueller and Robert L. Peters, 3 vols. (Detroit: Wayne State University Press, 1967–69), 2:701.

THE GARLAND & ITS CONTRIBUTORS

2.4 ❦ CHARLES JAMES CRUTTWELL (1812–1892)

Cruttwell, a London solicitor, was an uncle of Henry Daniel (Daniel's mother was a Cruttwell) with a flair for occasional verse: two early poems, *The Tomb of Bonaparte* and *Lines on the Christening of His Royal Highness the Prince of Wales,* were issued under Pickering's imprint in 1842, and later Skeffington published a collection entitled *Margaret and Other Poems* (1871). Nevertheless, Cruttwell did little writing for publication during the rest of his life, and Daniel's decision to include his poem in the *Garland* was clearly an act of family loyalty.

When Cruttwell sent a copy of *The Tomb of Bonaparte* to his nephew in 1885, he described it as his favorite: "As I think 'Bonaparte' the only poem worth the name I ever wrote, & as I sent it to print, the ink yet wet, it is almost of course that its faults are many. During 34 years various corrections have occurred to me, & I think in presenting it to one so practised a critic as you it ought to appear with the best face; but, not to spoil Whittingham's type, the emendations accompany separately.... I confess to all an author's vanity & to more than most authors' fussiness."[1]

Cruttwell's letters to Daniel are cheerful, affectionate, and full of family gossip; unlike many of the other contributors to the *Garland*, he actually knew the infant Rachel ("the darling little child") but was unacquainted with most of his fellow-poets in the volume. He submitted his poem on 20 December 1880 and sent Daniel a revision of the final two lines on the last day of the year [**4.11** and **4.12**].

Cruttwell's copy is unlocated.

REFERENCES: *Chronicle of... Cruttwell.* (See pp. 109–10.) — Foster, Joseph. *Men-at-the-Bar.* London: Reeves & Turner, 1885. (See p. 109.) — National Probate Calendar (1892). — Web sources. — Correspondence (Tuerk, Worcester).

---

1. Cruttwell to Henry Daniel, 9 December 1885 (Worcester).

2.5 ɞ CHARLES HENRY OLIVE DANIEL (1836–1919)

For HENRY DANIEL, see Chapter 1; for Daniel's copy, see **3.5**.

2.6 ɞ AUSTIN DOBSON (1840–1921)

Son of a civil engineer of French descent, Dobson was educated at Coventry and the Gymnase, Strassburg, and later worked at the Board of Trade most of his adult life. There he met Edmund Gosse, who was also connected with the commercial department of the Board of Trade as a translator, and they became lifelong friends. His first two volumes of poetry, *Vignettes in Rhyme* (1873) and *Proverbs in Porcelain* (1877), constituted his best work, but he continued to write the rest of his life, including a substantial number of literary biographies and memoirs.

Dobson did not belong to the Daniels' circle of Oxford friends, and it seems reasonable to assume that his name was first mentioned as a possible contributor by Gosse. Recalling the episode in 1919, Dobson wrote that "when, about 1880, I was one of the now sadly thinned list of contributors to *The Garland of Rachel*, I became so (I think) on the invitation of a third party, and there, as far as I was concerned, the matter ended. I never, to the best of my belief, had the privilege of meeting the late Provost, and have no knowledge of the other issues of the Daniel press save the *Six Idillia* of Theocritus which was given to me by Mr. Alfred Parsons."[1]

After the *Garland* was published, several of the other contributors praised Dobson's poem: Andrew Lang, for example, decided that the poems by "Bridges and Dobson are best" [**4.24**], and Humphry Ward described Dobson's contribution as "charming" [**4.29**]. Harington spoke of it as one of "the nicest" [**4.30**].

Dobson has the distinction of being the first contributor to the

---

1. Dobson to C. H. Wilkinson, 10 November 1919 (Berol Collection, NYU).

Garland to reprint his poem. In February 1882 he sent a manuscript copy to Jeanette L. Gilder, editor of *The Critic* (New York), who published it the following month. He also provided the first account in America of the book—in the *Century Illustrated Monthly Magazine*—at about the same time.[1] The latter, published anonymously, has occasionally been attributed to Gosse, but the manuscript, now in the Brown University Library, is definitely in Dobson's handwriting, though there are hints in the correspondence that Gosse was, as usual, pulling strings in the background to arrange for its publication.

For Dobson's copy of the *Garland*, see 3.6. Of this book, his son later wrote, ". . . my father's copy was sold at his book sale, and I shall never cease to regret the fact that I failed to secure it against a bidder the depth of whose purse appeared fathomless" (Alban Dobson, *Austin Dobson: Some Notes*, p. 232).

REFERENCES: [Child, Harold Hannyngton.] "Austin Dobson." *TLS*, 8 September 1921, p. 577. (Obituary.) — "Death of Austin Dobson. Exquisite Literary Art." *The Times*, 3 September 1921, p. 11. — Dobson, Alban. *Austin Dobson: Some Notes*. London: Humphry Milford, Oxford University Press, 1928. (See p. 232.) — Dobson, Alban. *A Bibliography of the First Editions of Austin Dobson*. London: First Edition Club, 1925. — [Dobson, Austin.] "Bric-a-brac: The Garland of Rachel." *Century Illustrated Monthly Magazine* 23 (February 1882): 639–40. (The manuscript is in the Harry Lyman Koopman Collection, Brown University Library.) — Gwynn, S. L., and Nilanjana Banerji. "Dobson, (Henry) Austin," in *ODNB*. — "Mr. Austin Dobson." *Manchester Guardian*, 3 September 1921, p. 8. (Obituary.) — Murray, Francis Edward. *A Bibliography of Austin Dobson*. Derby: Francis Murray, 1900. (See p. 75.) — *WWW*. — Correspondence (Getty, Newberry, NYU).

2.7 ❧ CHARLES L. DODGSON ("LEWIS CARROLL")

Dodgson wrote the celebrated *Alice* stories under the pseudonym of Lewis Carroll, but he also led another life as a shy, reclusive don at Christ Church, Oxford, and it was no doubt in this latter role

---

1. [Austin Dobson], "Bric-a-brac: The Garland of Rachel," *Century Illustrated Monthly Magazine* 23 (February 1882): 639–40.

that he became acquainted with the Daniels. Henry Daniel had sent him one of the fifty copies of *A New Sermon of the Newest Fashion*, the second publication of the Daniel Press, in 1877;[1] hence there must have been some kind of friendship by that date, though his later correspondence with the Daniels suggests that Dodgson's primary point of connection with the family was through Emily rather than Henry Daniel. By the 1880s he began to appear occasionally at Worcester House for tea with Emily and her two young daughters.

Walter Pater suggested to Henry Daniel that Dodgson might be a suitable contributor to the *Garland* [4.3], but by then Daniel, responding to pressure from his wife, had already approached Dodgson, who unfortunately submitted an extremely flippant poem beginning "Oh pudgy podgy pup! | Why *did* they wake you up?", and added that "I hate babies" [4.2]. This odd piece of verse was never accepted by Daniel, though someone (Emily?) set it in type, because a proof of it has survived [*Pl. 2*], and by the following March a penitent Dodgson was promising to write something more suitable [4.16]. At this point he seems to have become increasingly enthusiastic about the project and persuaded his friend Sir Richard Harington to submit a Latin translation of Dodgson's second poem. When he received his copy of the *Garland* in the autumn of 1881, Dodgson recorded in his diary that "it is bound in vellum, and is quite a work of art" (*Diaries*, 2:401). Near the end of his life, Dodgson approached Daniel for permission to reprint the poem [4.48], but it apparently did not appear in print again until after his death.[2]

---

1. Dodgson's copy bears an inscription from Henry Daniel, 26 February 1877: see Dulau catalogue no. 195 (March 1932), *A Catalogue for Typophiles*, item 106.

2. The one possible exception to this generalization is a clipping—probably from a magazine rather than a newspaper—tipped in Thomas Hutchinson's copy of *Alice's Adventures in Wonderland* (New York: Macmillan, 1887) at the Princeton University Library—which begins, "My readers will thank me for inserting here the contribution of Lewis Car-

Meanwhile, Dodgson remained on friendly terms with the Daniel household. In 1883 he drew a pencil portrait of Rachel, though he was unsatisfied with it (*Letters*, 2:418), and when in 1892 Daniel sent him another Daniel Press book, Dodgson jokingly referred to Rachel and Ruth as "the two wild creatures (a Lioness and a Tigress, as I guess) who devastate your house, and make it a terror to timid callers" (*Letters*, 2:882). In January 1894 Emily Daniel offered him a Daniel Press book (probably Blake's *Songs of Innocence*) and a photograph of her daughters.[1] But his relationship with the Daniels reached an apogee of sorts in the summer term of that year when Rachel and Ruth appeared (the former as Alice) in a production of *Alice in Wonderland* and *Through the Looking-glass* in the Worcester House garden.[2] There was a persistent rumor in Oxford that the elderly Dodgson watched the rehearsals from a distance. Though Dodgson's first poem for the *Garland* certainly reflected great bewilderment about the purpose of the book, he was nevertheless one of two contributors—the other being Bridges—who, in the end, established a close friendship with Rachel Daniel.

For Dodgson's copy, see **3.7**.

REFERENCES: Ayres, Harry Morgan. "Lewis Carroll and The Garland of Rachel." *Huntington Library Quarterly* 5 (October 1941): 141–45. — Carlson, David, and Jeffrey Eger. *Dodgson at Auction*. Somerville, N.J.: D & D Galleries, 1999. — Dodgson, C. L. *The Diaries of Lewis Carroll*. Ed. Roger Lancelyn Green. 2 vols. New York: Oxford University Press, 1954. — Dodgson, C. L. *The Letters of Lewis Carroll*. Ed. Morton N. Cohen. 2 vols. New York: Oxford University Press, 1979. — Lovett, Charlie. *Lewis Carroll among His Books: A Descriptive Catalogue of the Private Library of Charles L. Dodgson*. Jefferson, N.C.: McFarland, 2005. (See no. 524.) — "Memorial Notices: The Rev. C. L. Dodgson." *Manchester Guardian*, 15 January 1898, p. 8. — Stern, Jeffrey. *Lewis Carroll, Bibliophile*. Luton: White Stone Publishing, 1995. (See p. 20.) — Stern, Jeffrey, ed.

---

roll to this, the supreme 'birthday book' of the nineteenth century." The poem is then quoted in its entirety. The clipping is undated and its source not indicated, but the typography suggests a late nineteenth- or early twentieth-century origin.

1. Dodgson to Emily Daniel, 27 January 1894 (Getty).

2. A letter from Dodgson to Emily Daniel, 11 March 1895 (sold by Christie's, 22 April 1994), reveals that she organized the performance.

Lewis Carroll's Library: A Facsimile Edition of the Catalogue of the Auction Sale following C. L. Dodgson's Death in 1898, with Facsimiles of Three Subsequent Bookseller's Catalogues Offering Books from Dodgson's Library. Silver Spring, Md.: Lewis Carroll Society of North America, 1981. — Williams, Sidney H., Falconer Madan, and Roger Lancelyn Green. *The Lewis Carroll Handbook.* Rev. ed. Folkstone: Dawson, 1979. — Correspondence (Getty, Huntington, Princeton, Tuerk).

2.8 ⁊ SIR EDMUND W. GOSSE (1849–1928)

Gosse came from a most unlikely background: his parents were members of the Plymouth Brethren, and even before his birth they assumed that he would someday devote his life to a religious cause. Gosse's father, a biologist of considerable reputation, made himself an object of ridicule in 1857 when he published a book entitled *Omphalos,* in which he argued that since God must have created Adam with a navel (even though he had not come out of a womb), it followed therefore that the Garden of Eden was filled with artifacts—such as tree rings and dinosaur bones—falsely suggesting a very ancient history for our planet. Edmund Gosse later wrote a stirring memoir, *Father and Son* (1907), about his father's heroic struggle to reconcile the claims of science and faith.

From this cramped atmosphere, Gosse emerged into a larger world and managed to transform himself into perhaps the most eminent man of letters in late Victorian and Edwardian England. As his obituary in *The Times* declared, "No man of his time had a larger acquaintance with the world of literature, or a quicker sympathy for fresh adventures in poetry and criticism." Though he nominally worked as an assistant librarian at the British Museum and subsequently as a translator at the Board of Trade, Gosse's energies were devoted mainly to writing at a furious pace and moving in the London literary world. He had a talent for knowing everybody: he traveled in Scandinavia, he became acquainted with Browning and the Pre-Raphaelites, and throughout his life he maintained close ties with French thinkers and authors. The one major setback in his brilliant career was a public attack by John Churton Collins on his scholarship; Gosse lamented in a letter to Henry Daniel that "for the first two days I was absolutely felled by it. But on the least examination it all fades into a mist of pedantry."[1]

There is scattered evidence suggesting that Gosse may not have met Daniel before he was asked to contribute to the *Garland* (though they undoubtedly had many mutual acquaintances), but once Gosse had been introduced into the Daniel circle, he became, characteristically, a most enthusiastic collector and promoter of what he called their "delicate & slow-moving press."[2] Gosse expressed excitement about the *Garland* and announced to Henry Daniel that "no such beautiful book . . . has been produced in England for many years."[3]

In the same letter he disclosed his plans for the first article about the *Garland*, written by his friend Austin Dobson, that would appear in an American periodical, the *Century Illustrated Monthly Magazine*. After Daniel's death, Gosse himself contributed a long, appreciative review of the *Memorials* to the *Sunday Times* in 1922 (reprinted in his *More Books on the Table* the following year). In it Gosse made a strong claim for the literary significance of the *Garland*: "The young lady to be celebrated was beautiful, with a translucent pallor of complexion and hair that was like spun gold. Nevertheless, it is a delicate and a perilous thing to celebrate the charms of a belle who has not yet reached her first birthday. Several of the chosen bards had not sufficient courage to accept the task, but, surprisingly, no fewer than seventeen faced the music that they made.

"Conjoint efforts of this kind were something of a novelty forty years ago, and *The Garland of Rachel* was very widely discussed. It was composed entirely by those of the new generation who were prominent at that date: it was almost a manifesto."

1. Gosse to Daniel, 22 October 1886 (Bodleian MS. Eng. Lett. e.48, fol. 120).

2. Gosse to Daniel, 1 December 1893 (Bodleian MS. Eng. Lett. e.48, fol. 130).

3. Gosse to Daniel, 6 November 1881 (private collection of Hilary Daniel).

For Gosse's copy, see 3.8.

REFERENCES: *A Catalogue of the Gosse Correspondence in the Brotherton Collection, Consisting Mainly of Letters Written to Sir Edmund Gosse in the Period from 1867 to 1928*. Leeds: Brotherton Library, 1950. — Charteris, Sir Evan. *The Life and Letters of Sir Edmund Gosse*. London: Heinemann, 1931. — Cox, E. H. M. *The Library of Edmund Gosse*. London: Dulau & Co., 1924. (See p. 83.) — "Death of Sir Edmund Gosse. The Great Literary Celebrity." *Western Daily Express*, 17 May 1928, p. 4. — Gosse, Edmund. *More Books on the Table*. London: Heinemann, 1923. (Chapter on Daniel Press reprinted from *Sunday Times*, 1 January 1922, p. 5.) — Gosse, Edmund. "The Daniel Press" (letter). *TLS*, 27 February 1903, p. 59. — Lister, R. J. *A Catalogue of a Portion of the Library of Edmund Gosse, Hon. M.A. of Trinity College, Cambridge*. London: Privately printed at the Ballantyne Press, 1903. (See p. 34.) — "Our London Correspondent. Sir Edmund Gosse." *Manchester Guardian*, 17 May 1928, p. 10. (Obituary.) — "Sir Edmund Gosse. Poet and Critic." *The Times*, 17 May 1928, p. 18. (Obituary.) — Thwaite, Ann. *Edmund Gosse: A Literary Landscape*. London: Secker & Warburg, 1984. — Thwaite, Ann. "Gosse, Sir Edmund William," in *ODNB*. — Woolf, James D. "Sir Edmund Gosse: An Annotated Bibliography of Writings about Him." *English Literature in Transition* 11, no. 3 (1968): 126–72. — *WWW*. — Correspondence (Bodleian Library; Brotherton Collection, Leeds University).

2.9 ❧ SIR RICHARD HARINGTON (1835–1911)

Sir Richard Harington, 11th Baronet, of Whitbourne Court, near Worcester, was educated at Eton and Christ Church, Oxford, and was called to the bar in 1858. He had a long career as a Justice of the Peace and a county court judge and wrote occasional pamphlets on legal questions. He appears not to have known Henry Daniel before 1881, and there are indications in his correspondence that Harington's contribution to the *Garland* was probably suggested by Dodgson, his old tutor. At about this time Harington seems to have been an occasional visitor at Christ Church, where his eldest son was an undergraduate, and while there he usually called on Dodgson.

His letters to Daniel and others reveal two intense preoccupa-

THE GARLAND & ITS CONTRIBUTORS

tions: his repeated attempts to revise some lines in his Latin translation of Dodgson's poem, and his interest in the craft of printing. He submitted his poem for the *Garland* on 30 March 1881, and almost immediately, on the following day, he sent in corrections, which, to his distress, were not incorporated in the published text [see **4.20**]. Afterwards he complained that his second letter had gone astray or perhaps had been ignored by the printer. Despite this misunderstanding, he remained on friendly terms with Daniel and apparently visited Worcester House in the summer of 1881 in order to see the Daniel press in operation. He confessed that he was "sadly ignorant in technical terms," but he was an enthusiastic amateur printer with a cobbled-together parlor press, which he used for printing, among other things, a prologue to "some private theatricals" at Whitbourne Court.[1]

For Harington's copy, see **3.9**.

REFERENCES: "Memorial Notices." *Manchester Guardian*, 7 February 1911, p. 7. — "Sir Richard Harington." *Newcastle Journal*, 7 February 1911, p. 10. (Obituary.) — *WWW*. — Correspondence (Getty, Tuerk, Worcester).

2.10 ❧ WILLIAM ERNEST HENLEY (1849–1903)

Henley, a London poet and literary journalist who had been educated at the Crypt Grammar School in Gloucester, suffered from poverty and tuberculosis throughout much of his life; part of his left leg was also amputated in the late 1860s. Despite his poor health, he was a tall, strong-looking man with unkempt red hair and beard and was celebrated for his lively, forceful conversation. That same vitality comes through in his celebrated sequence of poems *In Hospital*, which describes his prolonged confinement in the Royal Infirmary in Edinburgh during the 1870s, and particularly in

---

1. Harington to Henry Daniel, 13 June 1881 and 26 June 1890 (Worcester).

"Invictus" (1875), the one poem of his that is still occasionally quoted today ("I am the master of my fate: | I am the captain of my soul").

While in hospital he met Robert Louis Stevenson, with whom he developed a remarkably intense friendship. For more than a decade they carried on a cheerful, amusing correspondence, and Stevenson even based the character of his Long John Silver upon Henley's intimidating physical presence and his loud, ferocious talk. They also co-authored four plays. But in 1888 the close relationship deteriorated into a quarrel, and after Stevenson's death in 1894 the irritable Henley carried on a vendetta against his old friend. Henley's bad temper was no doubt exacerbated by increasingly fragile health in the final years of his life.

It appears that Andrew Lang had arranged for Henley to contribute to the *Garland*, since Lang sent the manuscript on to Henry Daniel in December 1880 [4.5]. Henley was extremely self-deprecating about his poem: "For my part, I could wish that I had been content to speak plain English, & had left French to my betters," he remarked in a letter to Henry Daniel [4.31], and to C. M. Falconer he described it as "a rather poverty-stricken tour-de-force."[1] Characteristically, the proof of Henley's poem (Getty) is heavily revised and discolored by a streak of unidentified liquid (beer? wine?).

Nevertheless, Mary Robinson thought it was one of the three best contributions to the volume [4.44], and Humphry Ward, more ambivalently, described it as "fearfully & wonderfully idiomatic" [4.29].

Henley's copy is unlocated.

REFERENCES: Connell, John (*pseud.* of John Henry Robertson). *W. E. Henley*. London: Constable, 1949. — Henley, W. E. *The Selected Letters of W. E. Henley*. Ed. Damian Atkinson. Aldershot and Burlington, Vt.: Ashgate, 2000. — Mehew, Ernest. "Henley, William Ernest," in *ODNB*. — "Mr. W. E. Henley." *The Times*, 13 July 1903, p. 6. (Obituary.) — [Quiller-Couch, Sir Arthur.] "William Ernest Henley." *TLS*, 17 July 1903, p. 221. (Obituary.) — "William Ernest Henley." *Manchester Guardian*, 13 July 1903, p. 5. (Obituary.) — *WWW*.

---

1. This comment appears in a transcription by Constance Astley of Henley's letter to Falconer, 26 January 1897 (JJC 2).

2.11 ❧ ANDREW LANG (1844–1912)

Lang, a Scot, studied briefly at St. Andrews University and the University of Glasgow but in 1865 enrolled at Balliol College, Oxford, where he took a first in *literae humaniores* and then was offered a fellowship at Merton College. In 1875 he married and moved to London, launching a career as a professional writer. Though he had a somewhat world-weary manner (Margaret Woods called him "Mr. Languid"), Lang proved to be an energetic and prolific author. He became, in rapid succession, a poet, translator (from French), reviewer, journalist, anthropologist, and folklorist. The invitation to contribute to the *Garland* came to him just as he was working on his most ambitious poem, *Helen of Troy* (1882).

Lang's correspondence with Henry Daniel reveals an unquestionably cordial relationship, but in a letter to his American friend Irving Way, written in November 1882, he disclosed his true opinion of the *Garland*: "It must be hard to get books when catalogues have to come from so far. Fortunately, as you are interested in the Garland of Miss Daniel, I can send you a copy, which, I hope, will reach you safely. You will find no merit in it, but rarity..." [**4.45**]. Lang thus has the double distinction of being the first contributor to dispose of the *Garland* and of sending the first copy of the book to the United States. To our knowledge, no other *Garland* contributor sold or gave away the volume during his or her lifetime.

For Lang's copy, see **3.11**.

REFERENCES: Demoor, Maryasa, ed. *Friends over the Ocean: Andrew Lang's American Correspondence, 1881–1912*. Gent: Rijksuniversiteit Gent, Faculteit van de Letteren en Wijsbegeerte, 1989. — Donaldson, William. "Lang, Andrew," in *ODNB*. — Falconer, C. M. *The Writings of Andrew Lang, M.A., LL.D., Arranged in the Form of a Bibliography, with Notes by C. M. Falconer*. Dundee: Privately printed, 1894. — Green, Roger Lancelyn. *Andrew Lang: A Critical Biography*. Leicester: E. Ward, 1946.— Lang, Andrew. *Dear Stevenson: The Letters of Andrew Lang to Robert Louis Stevenson*. Ed. Marysa Demoor. Leuven: Peeters, 1990. — "Mr. Andrew Lang."

The Times, 22 July 1912, p. 11. (Obituary.) — WWW. — Correspondence (Getty, University of Minnesota, Samuels Lasner, Tuerk, Worcester).

2.12 ❧ FREDERICK LOCKER[-LAMPSON] (1821–1895)

Locker (afterwards Locker-Lampson) was a passionate bibliophile and a writer of light verse. As a young man he held a minor post in the Admiralty, but eventually he withdrew to the countryside. He lived in a beautiful house in the village of Rowfant, Sussex, inherited from the father of his second wife, and there he devoted much of his time to building his Rowfant Library, as he called it, which focused on the masterpieces of English literature from Chaucer to Swinburne, always in first editions. Near the end of his life, however, he turned his attention to foreign authors as well.

It appears that it was Willert who approached Locker about contributing to the *Garland*, because he reported to Henry Daniel on 13 December 1880 that Locker had sent him "an impassioned address to Mrs. Langtry!! wh[ich] I sent back at once explaining that however great her innocence she could scarcely be considered a child" [4.9]. A note—presumably to Willert—at the head of the manuscript of the published poem reads: "Yesterday when I sent you those verses about Mrs. L. I forgot that Mr. D. required they shd. be about a *child*. Will you return them & substitute the following" (Tuerk). Locker complained repeatedly that he found it difficult to write about an infant whom he had never met, and after publication, he remarked, "If I had *seen* the Collection before I sent you my verses I think I could have sent you something much more appropriate" [4.33]. However, the following year he sent a valentine to Rachel [4.42].

C. J. Cruttwell, in a letter to his nephew Henry, 21 December 1881, offered this unenthusiastic appraisal of Locker's poem: "Mr Locker I cannot unriddle. I am afraid some frail fair damsel has played him a practical joke in his college garden. Are you in his secret?" [4.38].

For Locker's copy, see 3.12.

REFERENCES: Baker, William, and Kenneth Womack, eds. *Nineteenth-Century British Book-Collectors and Bibliographers*. Dictionary of Literary Biography, 184. Detroit: Gale Research, 1997. (See Barbara Quinn Schmidt, "Frederick Locker-Lampson," pp. 258–64.) — Bates, Madison C. *That Delightful Man: A Study of Frederick Locker.* Cleveland: Rowfant Club, 1960. — Birrell, Augustine. *Frederick Locker-Lampson: A Character Sketch.* London: Constable, 1920. — Locker-Lampson, Frederick. *My Confidences: An Autobiographical Sketch Addressed to My Descendants.* London: Smith, Elder, 1896. — [Locker-Lampson, Frederick.] *The Rowfant Library: A Catalogue of the Printed Books, Manuscripts, Autograph Letters, Drawings and Pictures Collected by Frederick Locker-Lampson.* London: Bernard Quaritch, 1886. (An Appendix was published in 1900.) — L[ocker] L[ampson], O[liver]. *Recollections of Frederick Locker Lampson by His Son.* Peterborough: privately printed by the Peterborough Press, n.d. — "Mr. Frederick Locker-Lampson." *The Times,* 29 May 1895, p. 11. (Obituary.) — Correspondence (Columbia University, Getty, Huntington Library).

2.13 ❧ ERNEST JAMES MYERS (1844–1921)

Myers, translator and poet, was raised in the Lake District, son of a clergyman and brother of F. W. H. Myers, founder of the Society for Psychical Research. He took a first class in Classical Moderations at Balliol College and subsequently became a Fellow of Wadham.

Ernest Myers built a solid reputation as a writer and scholar. Though he became a barrister in 1874, he never practiced law but instead devoted his energies mainly to the translation of classical texts and to the writing of verse. He published three volumes of poetry—*Poems* (1877), *The Defence of Rome* (1880), and *The Judgement of Prometheus* (1886)—most of which was later reprinted in *Gathered Poems* (1904). He also had political ambitions, never realized, and was active in several educational and scholarly organizations.

Myers was extremely modest about his contribution to the *Gar-*

land: he afterwards spoke of it as "meagre," and when he submitted the poem to Henry Daniel, he remarked wryly that "if you take my advice you won't add it."[1]

Myers's copy is unlocated.

REFERENCES: Bell, A. C., and Megan A. Stephan. "Myers, Ernest James," in *ODNB*. — "Death of Mr. Ernest Myers. Scholar and Poet." *The Times*, 28 November 1921, p. 12. — Correspondence (Getty, Tuerk, Worcester).

2.14 ❧ A. MARY F. ROBINSON (1857–1944)

Mary Robinson was raised in a literary household in London and studied at University College there; her first book, *A Handful of Honeysuckle* (1878), was a collection of poems, though most of her later work was historical and biographical. In 1888 she married James Darmesteter, a French Orientalist, and spent the rest of her life in France. After Darmester's early death in 1894, she married Emile Duclaux, the director of the Pasteur Institute in Paris. She was fully bilingual and became a well-known contributor to both English and French journals.

There is no indication that Robinson was within the Daniels' circle of friends. The initial suggestion that she might contribute to the *Garland* came from Andrew Lang [4.5], and Humphry Ward, who knew her very well, seems to have made the arrangements for her participation. When her poem arrived in December 1880, Ward sent it on to Henry Daniel with the comment that "the charming Miss Robinson writes—'Here is a lullaby which I have written *to* Baby Rachel & not *at* or *of* Baby Rachel—so you must measure it by her standard of appreciation & not by yours'. The verses are not her best, but I think they will do!" [4.8].

There were delays in getting Robinson's copy of the book to her, because she traveled so frequently on the Continent, but finally, in

---

1. See **4.32** and **4.7**.

March 1882, it came into her hands, and she predicted that someday Rachel would be "proud of the book as an artistic production. The little frontispiece [i.e. the preface] is, in its way, a perfect thing, to my mind. The poems are all very pretty & charming & full of delicate humour. I like Mr. Dobson's & Mr. Symonds's, & Mr. Henley's the best" [4.44].

Robinson's copy is unlocated.

REFERENCES: Franklin [1]. (See pp. 483–84, 489.) — Halévy, Daniel, ed. *Mary Duclaux et Maurice Barrè: Lettres Échangée*. Paris: Bernard Grasset, 1960. — Holmes, Ruth Van Zuyle. "Mary Duclaux, 1856–1944: Primary and Secondary Checklists." *English Literature in Transition* 10, no. 1 (1967): 27–46. — "Mme. Duclaux. English and French Literature." *The Times*, 14 April 1944, p. 8. (Obituary.) — [Morgan, Charles L.] "Menander's Mirror: Mary Duclaux." *TLS*, 22 April 1944, p. 195. (Tribute.) — "Obituary: Mme. Duclaux." *Manchester Guardian*, 15 April 1944, p. 7. — Correspondence (Getty, Tuerk).

2.15 ❧ JOHN ADDINGTON SYMONDS (1840–1893)

Symonds, the son of a prominent physician near Bristol, developed a strong interest in classical art and culture while still very young, but on the whole he had a troubled childhood and adolescence, mainly because of anxiety about his sexual identity. He was educated at Harrow and Balliol College and became briefly a Fellow of Magdalen College, where he experienced a physical and emotional collapse in 1863. His doctor recommended marriage as a cure for homosexuality, and Symonds followed his advice the following year; but in search of greater sexual freedom and also in response to a diagnosis of tuberculosis in his left lung, he began to spend much of his time in Italy and Switzerland, often in the company of a series of male lovers. By the 1880s his main residence was Davos, Switzerland, which Andrew Lang described as "a kind of glacial Cannes apparently"[1]

---

1. *The Letters of Andrew Lang to Robert Louis Stevenson*, ed. Marysa Demoor (Leuven: Peeters, 1990), p. 49.

DANIEL PRESS & GARLAND OF RACHEL

Thanks to an inheritance, Symonds lived there in considerable material comfort, but for the rest of his life he wrestled awkwardly with sexual questions, mainly by writing lengthy studies about the homoerotic overtones of Greek and Italian art and literature in earlier centuries. He composed poetry only occasionally and did not feel entirely at home in that medium. In fact, he admitted to Henry Daniel that his poem for the *Garland* had actually been written before he had even heard of Rachel's existence [4.18].

For Symonds's copy, see 3.15; see also the copy of the *Garland* given by the Daniel family to Symonds's nephew [3.31].

REFERENCES: Babington, Percy L. *A Bibliography of the Writings of John Addington Symonds*. London: John Castle, 1925. (See pp. 73–74.) — Brown, Horatio F. *John Addington Symonds*. 2 vols. New York: Scribner's, 1895. — Furse, Katharine. *Hearts and Pomegranates: The Story of Forty-five Years, 1875 to 1920*. London: Peter Davies, 1940. — Grosskurth, Phyllis. *John Addington Symonds: A Biography*. London: Longmans, 1964. — Markgraf, Carl. "John Addington Symonds: An Annotated Bibliography of Writings about Him." *English Literature in Transition* 18 (1975): 79–138. — Markgraf, Carl. "John Addington Symonds: Update of a Bibliography of Writings about Him." *English Literature in Transition* 28, no. 1 (1985): 59–78. — Norton, Rictor. "Symonds, John Addington," in *ODNB*. — Symonds, John Addington. *Letters and Papers of John Addington Symonds*. Ed. Horatio F. Brown. London: John Murray, 1923. — Symonds, John Addington. *The Letters of John Addington Symonds*. Ed. Herbert Schueller and Robert L. Peters. 3 vols. Detroit: Wayne State University Press, 1967–69. — Symonds, John Addington. *On the English Family of Symonds*. Oxford: privately printed, 1894. — Symonds, Margaret. *Out of the Past*. London: John Murray, 1925. — Correspondence (NYU, Tuerk).

2.16 ৯ THOMAS HUMPHRY WARD (1845–1926)

Humphry Ward, son of a Hull clergyman, earned a first class degree from Brasenose College, Oxford, and became a Fellow of Brasenose in 1869 and a tutor in 1870; he remained in Oxford until 1881, when he moved to London, assuming the position of chief art critic of *The Times*. He was the author and editor of several books, including *The English Poets* (1880) and *Men of the Reign* (1885).

In 1872 he married Mary Arnold, niece of Matthew Arnold, and

THE GARLAND & ITS CONTRIBUTORS

their home in North Oxford became a well-known center of social life for their university friends, including Walter Pater, who lived just a few doors away. It was Humphry Ward who originally suggested the idea of *The Garland of Rachel*, and it seems clear from contemporary correspondence that the Wards and Daniels were on very friendly terms. In fact, Mary Ward— whose literary fame eclipsed that of her husband after the publication of her novel *Robert Elsmere* (1888)—also discovered a unique copy of *Sixe Jdillia* by Theocritus in the Bodleian Library and soon persuaded Henry Daniel to reprint it in 1883.[1] The Wards, in other words, were ultimately responsible for two of the Daniel Press titles.

When he finally got his first glimpse of *The Garland of Rachel*, Humphry Ward declared that the book "is a masterpiece within & without" and predicted that in the future "it will be collected with strange passion," because "some Rothschild or Bodleian will give fabulous prices to complete the collection of the 17 different title-pages" [**4.29**].

For Ward's copy, see **3.16**.

REFERENCES: "Mr. Humphry Ward. Art Critic and Writer." *The Times*, 19 May 1926, p. 21. (Obituary.) — Peterson, William S. *Victorian Heretic: Mrs Humphry Ward's Robert Elsmere*. Leicester: Leicester University Press, 1976. — Sutherland, John. *Mrs. Humphry Ward: Eminent Victorian, Pre-eminent Edwardian*. Oxford: Clarendon Press, 1990. — Trevelyan, Janet Penrose. *The Life of Mrs. Humphry Ward*. London: Constable, 1923. — Ward, Mary A. *A Writer's Recollections*. 2 vols. New York and London: Harper & Brothers, 1918. — Ward, T. Humphry. "Reminiscences: Brasenose, 1864–1872." *Brasenose Quatercentenary Monographs* 2, part 2, no. 14 (1910): 69–78. — Woods, Margaret L. "Mrs Humphry Ward: A Sketch from Memory." *Quarterly Review* 234 (July 1920): 147–60. — *WWW*. — Correspondence (Getty, Tuerk, Worcester). — Diaries (University College, London).

---

1. Edmund Gosse, "The Daniel Press" (letter), *TLS*, 27 February 1903, p. 59.

2.17 ❧ ALBERT WATSON (1828–1904)

Albert Watson has the distinction of being perhaps the most socially awkward and reclusive of the contributors to the *Garland*, even more so than Dodgson. Humphry Ward, a longtime acquaintance, described Watson as "dear, shy, shrinking, genial, learned" (Ward, p. 76). He spent his entire lengthy academic career at Brasenose College, Oxford, and was briefly its Principal; he was known among his contemporaries as a kind and enormously erudite man, but he published little except for an edition of Cicero's letters, and for the most part he retreated from the world in his college rooms. His death was characteristic. On a Sunday morning he attended a service at St. Mary the Virgin, the university church, then later in the day learned, to his distress, of the loss of an old friend, the President of Corpus Christi, and the following morning was found dead in his bed.

Watson, as one might expect, was diffident about his *Garland* poem ("my poor little offering" he called it), which was published almost anonymously (with just the letter "W"), and in 1897 he vigorously declined to sign a copy of it in Falconer's facsimile. Henry Daniel described this reluctance to admit his authorship "pure bashfulness."[1]

For Watson's copy, see **3.17**.

REFERENCES: H[eberden], C[harles] B[uller]. *An Address Given in Brasenose College on Sunday Evening, Nov. 27, 1904, in Memory of the Rev. Albert Watson, Fellow and Formerly Principal of the College*. Oxford: Privately printed, 1904. — "Memorial Notices: Rev. Albert Watson." *Manchester Guardian*, 22 November, 1904, p. 12. — "Memorial Notices: The Rev. Albert Watson." *Manchester Guardian*, 23 November 1904, p. 12. (Tribute.) — "The Rev. Albert Watson." *The Times*, 22 November 1904, p. 4. (Obituary.) — Ward, T. Humphry. "Reminiscences: Brasenose, 1864–1872." *Brasenose Quatercentenary Monographs* 2, part 2, no. 14 (1910): 69–78. — Correspondence (Getty, Tuerk, Worcester).

---

1. See **4.28** and **4.63**.

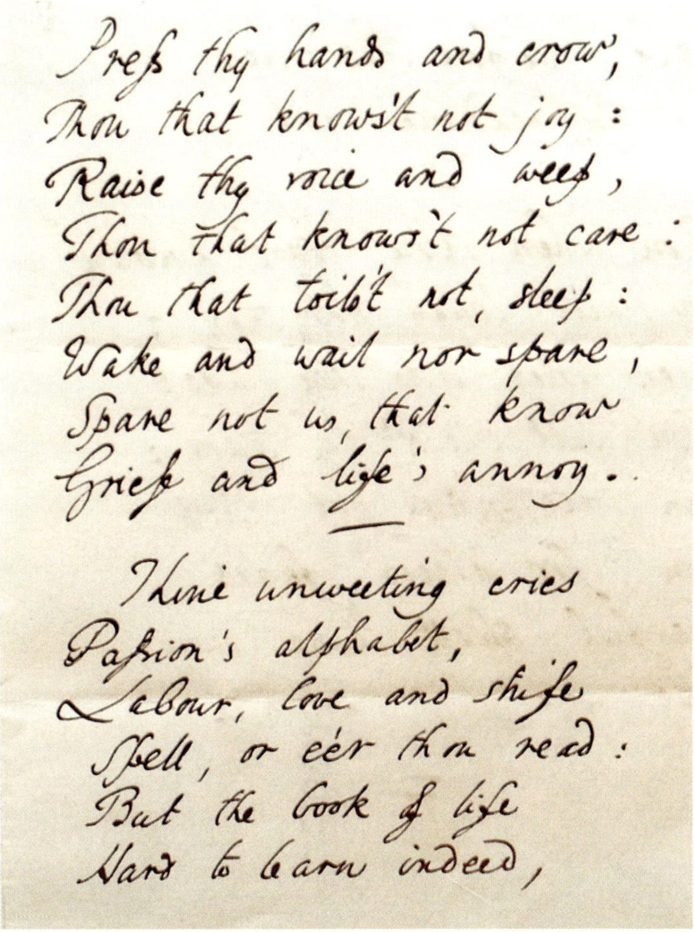

> Press thy hands and crow,
> Thou that know'st not joy:
> Raise thy voice and weep,
> Thou that know'st not care:
> Thou that toil'st not, sleep:
> Wake and wail nor spare,
> Spare not us, that know
> Grief and life's annoy..
>
> ———
>
> Thine unweeting cries
> Passion's alphabet,
> Labour, love and shife
> Spell, or e'er thou read:
> But the book of life
> Hard to learn indeed,

Plate 1 "Press thy hands and crow, | Thou that know'st not joy. . . ." The first page of Robert Bridges' contribution to the *Garland*. "If you are not better pleased with them than I was on seeing them again," he remarked to Henry Daniel on 1 March 1881, "pray do not print them."

OH pudgy podgy pup!
Why *did* they wake you up?
Those crude nocturnal yells
Are *not* like silver bells:
Nor never would recall
Sweet Music's ' dying fall.'
They rather bring to mind
The bitter winter wind
Through keyholes shrieking shrilly
When nights are dark and chilly:
Or like some dire duett,
Or quarrelsome quartette,
Of cats who chant their joys
With execrable noise,
And murder Time and Tune
To vex the patient Moon!

Lewis Carroll.

Plate 2 Lewis Carroll's initial contribution to *The Garland of Rachel* was not at all satisfactory, but it was in fact set up in type, complete with miniation by Emily Daniel. Falconer Madan claimed that this proof was not created by Henry Daniel, so presumably it was produced by Emily—who had a close friendship with Carroll—for her own amusement.

Mar. 10/81

What hand may wreathe thy natal crown,
  O tiny tender Spirit-blossom,
That out of Heaven hast fluttered down
      Into this Earth's cold bosom?

And how shall mortal bard aspire —
  All sin-begrimed & sorrow-laden —
To welcome, with the seraph-choir,
      A pure & perfect Maiden?

Are not God's minstrels ever near,
  Flooding with joy the woodland mazes?
Which shall we summon, Baby dear,
      To carol forth thy praises?

With sweet sad song, the Nightingale
  May soothe the broken hearts that languish
Where graves are green — the orphans' wail,
      The widow's lonely anguish:

The Turtle-dove with amorous coo
  May greet the Maid that fondly lingers
To twine her bridal wreath anew
      With soft caressing fingers:

But human loves and human woes
  Would dim the radiance of thy glory —
Only the Lark such music knows
      As fits thy stainless story.

The world may listen as it will —
  She recks not, to the skies upspringing:
Beyond our ken she singeth still
      For very joy of singing.
                    Lewis Carroll.

Plate 3 Finally, several months later, Carroll agreed to produce a more suitable poem. "I am penitent now," he said on 7 March 1881, "and ready to do what I can."

A NURSERY RHYME

Lullaby, Baby, and dream of a rose,
The reddest and sweetest that Eden knows.
There flowers in Eden a rose without thorn
For every baby that ever is born.

How shall I sing you, Child, for whom
So many lyres are strung;
Or how the only tone assume
That fits a Maid so young?

Plates 4–5 For Thomas Bird Mosher's copy, Emily Daniel supplied a series of miniature paintings of Oxford scenes. These two examples accompany the poems by Mary F. Robinson and Austin Dobson. (The headpieces are by Alfred Parsons.)

BALLADE RACHEL

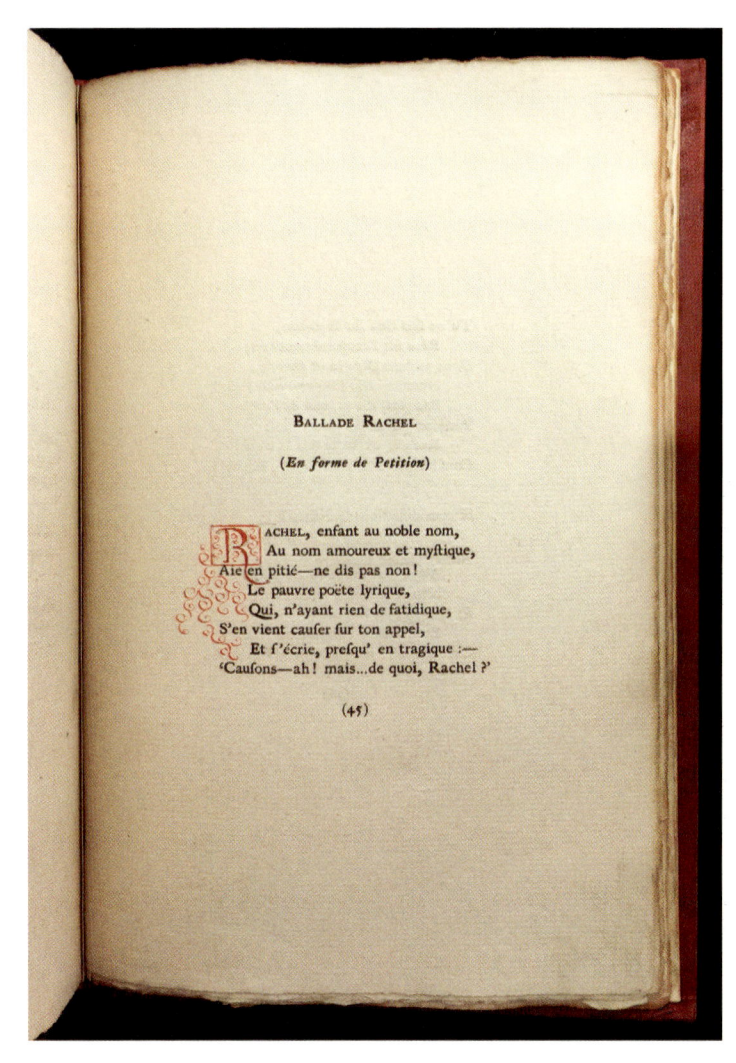

(*En forme de Petition*)

R ACHEL, enfant au noble nom,
　　Au nom amoureux et myſtique,
　Aie en pitié—ne dis pas non !
　　Le pauvre poëte lyrique,
　　Qui, n'ayant rien de fatidique,
　S'en vient cauſer ſur ton appel,
　　Et ſ'écrie, preſqu' en tragique :—
　'Cauſons—ah ! mais...de quoi, Rachel ?'

(45)

Plate 6 The opening of W. E. Henley's poem in *The Garland of Rachel* (Huntington Library copy). It is the only one in French, though two other contributions to the volume are in Latin.

Plate 7 Morley's blue levant morocco binding of the *Garland* (Wormsley Library).

Plate 8 Leonard Mounteney's goatskin binding of the *Garland* (Newberry Library).

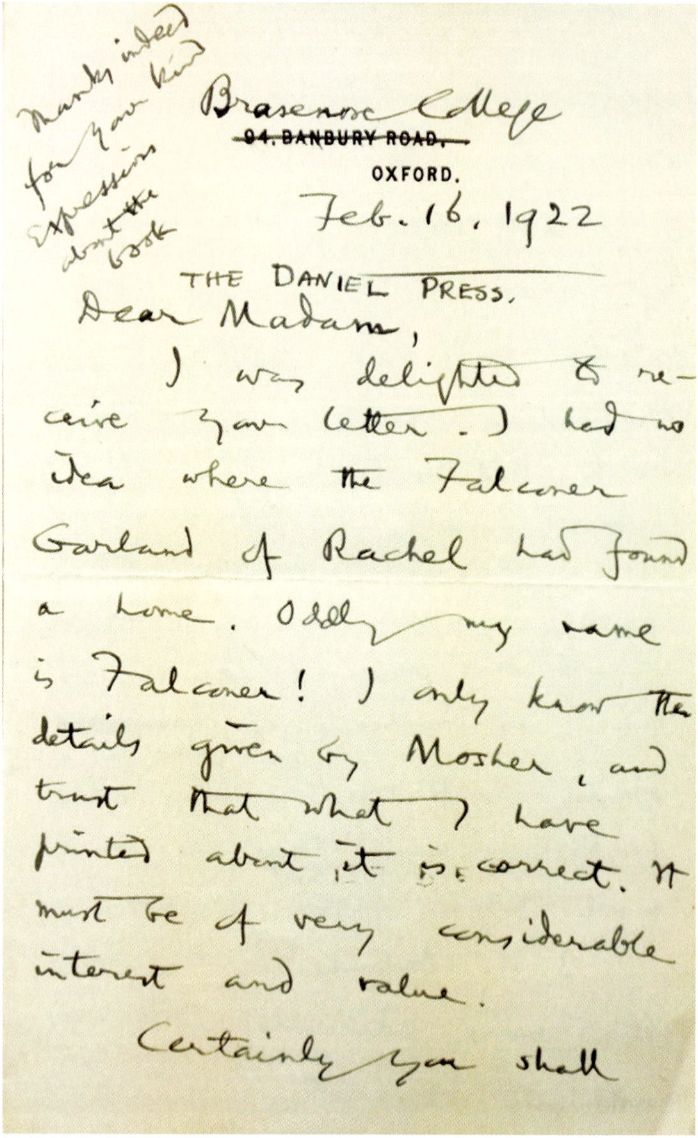

Many thanks indeed for your kind expressions about the book

Brasenose College
~~94, Banbury Road,~~
OXFORD.
Feb. 16, 1922

THE DANIEL PRESS.

Dear Madam,

I was delighted to receive your letter. I had no idea where the Falconer Garland of Rachel had found a home. Oddly my name is Falconer! I only know the details given by Mosher, and trust that what I have printed about it is correct. It must be of very considerable interest and value.

Certainly you shall

Plate 9 Madan was aware of the existence of C. M. Falconer's facsimile of the *Garland*, but he was startled and pleased to discover in 1922 that it was in the hands of Constance Astley.

THE GARLAND & ITS CONTRIBUTORS

2.18 ❧ MARGARET L. WOODS (1855–1945)

Margaret Louisa ("Daisy") Bradley, whose father later became Dean of Westminster, was educated mainly at home but in a household filled with literary interests and aspirations. (In fact, all of her siblings became writers.) In 1879 she married the Rev. Henry G. Woods, then a Fellow and subsequently the President of Trinity College, Oxford. She seems to have found Oxford intellectually stimulating but slightly claustrophobic, yet her essay on "Henry Daniel and His Home" in the *Memorials* volume skillfully captured the tone of the Daniels' domestic life; Madan and others thought it perhaps the most distinguished contribution to the book. After Henry Woods' death, she described Henry Daniel as one of her husband's two "oldest & dearest friends."[1]

Some years earlier she had escaped to the more congenial world of London when her husband was made Master of the Temple in 1904. Meanwhile, she had launched a literary career of some consequence. Margaret Woods' poem in the *Garland* was her first piece of writing to attract attention, and her novel *A Village Tragedy* (1887) brought her an even wider audience. For the rest of her life she continued to produce a stream of surprisingly varied works, including novels, poems, verse drama, memoirs, literary criticism, and travel books. The Daniel Press published two of her later books, *Lyrics* (1888) and *Songs* (1896).

In the *Garland* she indulges in the fiction that her poem is written by her young son Gilbert. When the published book reached her, she wrote to Henry Daniel that "we [i.e. she and her husband] shall both always value the book much, & tell Gilbert about it when he is older" [4.23].

For Woods' copy, see **3.18**.

REFERENCES: Franklin [2]. (See pp. 77–79.) — G., V. "Mrs. Woods: An Appreciation." *The Times*, 4 December 1945, p. 6. — Hopkins, Clare.

---

1. Margaret Woods to Henry Daniel, 4 August [1915] (Worcester).

Trinity: 450 Years of an Oxford College Community. Oxford: Oxford University Press, 2005. (See pp. 296–97.) — "Mrs. Woods: Poet and Novelist." *The Times*, 3 December 1945, p. 7. (Obituary.) — Thesing, William B., ed. *Late Nineteenth and Early Twentieth Century British Women Poets.* Detroit: Gale Group, 2001. (See Martha S. Vogeler, "Margaret L. Woods," pp. 352–60.) — Vogeler, Martha S. "Woods [*née* Bradley], Margaret Louisa Woods," in *ODNB*. — Woods, Margaret L. "Mrs Humphry Ward: A Sketch from Memory." *Quarterly Review* 234 (July 1920): 147–60. — Woods, Margaret L. "Oxford in the 'Seventies.'" *Fortnightly* 156 (September 1941): 276–80. — *WWW*. — Correspondence (NYU, Worcester).

3. A CENSUS

IN this chapter we have attempted to record the physical characteristics and histories of all the known copies of *The Garland of Rachel*. The Daniel family, in both their public and private comments, claimed that thirty-six copies were printed, but in fact the size of the edition is a rather more complicated issue. The copy that Emily Daniel sold to T. B. Mosher in 1902, for example, was then a set of unbound sheets and proofs [**3.29**], and the *Garland* now in the Huntington Library is obviously a collection of proofs, some of which are smudged with ink stains [**3.38**]: it seems unlikely that these two copies were ever envisioned as a part of the edition of thirty-six.[1]

The Garland of Rachel is an octavo printed on watermarked Van Gelder paper, with a page size of 8.6 × 5.5 inches (22 × 13.5 centimeters),[2] untrimmed but top edge gilt. The most common binding is white vellum with gilt tooling and marbled endpapers; the title appears on the front cover but not the spine [*Fig. 21*]. Henry Daniel's printer's device is used twice, and two headpieces by Alfred Parsons are repeated throughout the book. The *Garland* is printed in black only with the Fell small pica type; the ornamental initial at the beginning of each poem is drawn ("miniated") by Emily Daniel.[3]

We have tried to describe the individual books as concisely as possible. We have indicated the presence of silk ribbons (book-

---

1. A small technical distinction: we are listing the Mosher copy (Newberry Library) as part of the main census, because it consists at least in part of sheets and is heavily ornamented by Emily Daniel, whereas the Huntington volume is unquestionably a set of proofs that happen to have been bound.
2. In other words, the page size of this book.
3. For a more detailed bibliographical description of the book by Falconer Madan, see *Memorials*, p. 86.

marks) sewn into the headbands, but we have remained silent about protective tissues, since they are ephemeral and often fall out of a book with the passing of time. We have, however, always indicated whether or not a copy of the *Garland* is accompanied by Henry Daniel's separately printed preface, and we have of course also recorded the wording of the title-page (which was different for each contributor).

The symbol † indicates that we have personally examined the book in question. In other cases we have depended upon information supplied to us by collectors, librarians, booksellers, and published sources.

Conttributors' copies

3.1 F. W. BOURDILLON COPY

Location unknown.
For BOURDILLON, see 2.1.

3.2 ROBERT BRIDGES COPY

Mark Getty (private collection, Wormsley Library), England.† ¶ Bridges–Andreini–Houghton–Getty copy.

Vellum binding. With preface sewn in. Title-page: "By Robert Bridges and Divers Kindly Hands." Signature of Robert Bridges on preliminary blank leaf. Bookplates of John Manuel Andreini and Arthur A. Houghton, Jr.

PROVENANCE: Robert Bridges. — John Manuel Andreini. — Samuel Marx (New York), 19 October 1932 [*Fine library of Joseph Manuel Andreini*], lot 512 (sold for $135). — Arthur A. Houghton, Jr. — Christie (London), 13 June 1979, lot 152 [*Library of Arthur A. Houghton, Jnr.*] (sold for £2,200 to Colin Franklin). — Colin Franklin — J. Paul Getty (purchased from Franklin). — Mark Getty (by inheritance).

A CENSUS

For ROBERT BRIDGES, see 2.2.

JOHN MANUEL ANDREINI (1850–1932), a senior member of the Wall Street banking firm of Lawrence Turnure & Co., was an ardent bibliophile, a member of both the Grolier[1] and Rowfant clubs, and one of the leading collectors of the Daniel Press in America. His correspondence makes it clear that he had a friendly relationship with Emily Daniel and purchased most of the Daniel Press ephemera directly from her, though he was distressed when he was not notified of the first sale of Henry Daniel's books by Chaundy in 1920.

It was Emily Daniel who alerted Andreini that Falconer Madan had published (anonymously) a checklist of the Daniel Press in the *Times Literary Supplement* in February 1903. Andreini wrote to Madan later that year: "I would like very much to have your very scientific list of this Press reprinted here (for collectors) from the Times, with credit. My idea would be to have a limited issue of fifty copies nicely printed. Would you like to have your own authorship acknowledged in it or would you prefer to remain anonymous? Your name is not known here in connection with the list, in fact the list was unknown here, even by Mr. Mosher, and I think it would add considerably to the good fame of the Press to have your name appear in this reprint."[2] Andreini did in fact secure Madan's permission to reprint it and arranged for its publication by a small private press in Wisconsin, the Philosopher Press, in 1904.

Andreini was also a collector of bookplates, many of them later donated to the New York Public Library, and complained that "it is a branch of collecting which does not seem to appeal to many book lovers—in fact some of them look with great disfavour upon it, forgetting that we cannot all have the same collecting tastes and showing therefore a lack of broad views on the subject of hobbies."[3]

---

1. Andreini donated six Daniel Press titles to the Grolier Club in 1911, but they have since been deaccessioned.
2. Andreini to Madan, 19 November 1903 (JJC 5).
3. Andreini to T. B. Mosher, 14 November 1912 (Houghton Library,

DANIEL PRESS & GARLAND OF RACHEL

ARTHUR A. HOUGHTON, Jr. (1907–1990), grandson of the founder of Corning Glass Works, was made president of a subsidiary company, Steuben Glass, in 1933 and devoted much time and energy to raising the quality of its products. As an undergraduate at Harvard, he had become interested in English literature and rare books, and he subsequently donated his Keats collection—the finest in the world—to Harvard's rare book library, the Houghton Library, which he endowed and which was named after him. He also displayed a prolonged interest in Lewis Carroll. Houghton owned the Bridges copy of the *Garland*, a set of proofs of the book [3.37], and Falconer's manuscript transcription [3.40], all of which were acquired by Colin Franklin at the 1979 Christie sale (see PROVENANCE above) and then resold to Getty.[1] Houghton, as a patron of the arts, served on countless boards and committees and in the early 1940s was briefly curator of rare books at the Library of Congress. At one point he intended to give his Carroll collection to the Morgan Library, but instead it was dispersed at the Christie auction in 1979.

J. PAUL GETTY (1932–2003), son of the richest man in the world, had an exceptionally turbulent youth and middle age, but in his later years he turned to philanthropy on a grand scale (including a donation of £50 million to the National Gallery in London), created a replica of the Oval cricket ground at his country estate in the Chilterns, and erected a picturesque library—just up the road from the cricket pitch—to house his impressive collection of books and manuscripts. Getty bought only the finest examples of European books, and he was especially drawn to outstanding bindings. His exten-

Harvard University, MS Am 1096).
  1. One of Franklin's articles—"Garlands of Rachel," *Book Collector* 30 (Winter, 1981): 479–490—is based on these three items.

A CENSUS

sive Daniel Press collection seems to have come entirely from Colin Franklin.

MARK GETTY (b. 1960) inherited the bulk of his father's fortune, including the library. Unlike his father, he has led a relatively undramatic life and is chairman of Getty Images, Inc. In recent years he has allowed the Garsington Opera to shift its summer performances to the Wormsley estate.

REFERENCES: [ANDREINI] "Joseph M. Andreini. Formerly Was Senior Member of Lawrence Turnure & Co." *New York Times*, 27 June 1932, p. 17. (Obituary.) — Madan, Falconer. *The Daniel Press*. Wausau, Wis.: The Philosopher Press, Van Vechten & Ellis, 1904. — S., K. G. "New Prints at the Library." *New York Times*, 10 April 1932, p. N5. — Correspondence (Worcester, Harvard, JJC). ¶ [GETTY] Cunningham, John, and Matthew Engel. "Sir Paul Getty." *Guardian*, 18 April 2003, p. 31. (Obituary.) — Fletcher, George, ed. *The Wormsley Library: A Personal Selection by Sir Paul Getty, K.B.E.* London: published for the Wormsley Library by Maggs Bros. Ltd. with the Morgan Library, 1999. (Exhibition catalogue.) — Maggs, Bryan. "Birth of the Wormsley Library." *Matrix* 31 (Winter, 2012): 9–14. — Pearson, John. *Painfully Rich: The Outrageous Fortune and Misfortunes of the Heirs of J. Paul Getty*. New York: St. Martin's Press, 1995. — "Sir Paul Getty." *The Times*, 18 April 2003, p. 35. (Obituary.) — "Sir Paul Getty: Heir to an Oil Fortune Who Emerged from Personal Tragedy to Become a Philanthropist on a Grand Scale." *Daily Telegraph*, 18 April 2003, p. 29. (Obituary.)— *Who's Who*. (For Mark Getty.) ¶ [HOUGHTON] Bond, W. H. "Arthur A. Houghton, Jr.," in *Grolier 2000*. (See pp. 160–62.) — Houghton, Arthur A., Jr. *Remembrances*. Queenstown, Md.: privately printed, 1986. (See "Lewis Carroll," pp. 125–31.) — James, George. "Arthur Houghton Jr., 83, Dies; Led Steuben Glass." *New York Times*, 4 April 1990, p. B8.

3.3 ❧ W. J. COURTHOPE COPY

Location unknown.

For COURTHOPE, see **2.3**.

3.4 ❧ C. J. CRUTTWELL COPY

Location unknown.

For CRUTTWELL, see **2.4**.

DANIEL PRESS & GARLAND OF RACHEL

3.5 ❧ HENRY DANIEL COPY

Location unknown. ¶ Henry Daniel–Bemis–Spoor–Hersholt–Doheny copy.

Vellum binding (probably by Morley), variant with single-leaf all over pattern. Title-page: "By H. D. and Divers Kindly Hands." With preface (tipped in). Bookplates of John A. Spoor and F. B. Bemis. Note on flyleaf: "exceedingly rare, only 6 [sic] copies printed."

PROVENANCE: Charles Henry Olive Daniel. — Frank Brewer Bemis. — John A. Spoor. — Parke-Bernet (New York), 26 April 1939, lot 238 [*Renowned library of the late John A. Spoor*, part 1] (sold for $155). — Goodspeed's Book Shop catalogue 383 (1945), no. 47. — Jean Hersholt. — Sotheby Parke-Bernet (New York), 23 March 1954, lot 340 [*English and American first editions . . . collected by Jean Hersholt, Beverly Hills, California*] ($250; with the Mosher reprint). — Estelle Doheny. — Doheny Memorial Library. — Christie (New York), 19 May 1989, lot 2239 [*Estelle Doheny collection*] (sold for $6,000).

For CHARLES HENRY OLIVE DANIEL, see Chapter 1.

FRANK BREWER BEMIS (1861–1935) was associated with Estabrook & Company, a Boston banking firm, for forty-five years, and in later life he served on the committees of the Harvard University Library and the Harvard University Press. He had a considerable reputation as a collector of books, Chinese porcelain, and Georgian silver and was a member of the Grolier Club from 1924 until his death. He was also an officer of the Club of Odd Volumes near the end of his life.

Charles Goodspeed, the Boston bookseller, described Bemis as "the most modest of men concerning his possessions and . . . no one whom I have known has shown such reluctance to allow the nature and extent of his library to be known." Goodspeed added that it was a relatively small but impressive library, "the best private collection of first editions of English literature in America."

JOHN A. SPOOR (1851–1926), a wealthy Chicago businessman, listed his occupation in *Who's Who in America* as simply "capitalist." The *Chicago Tribune* offered this summary of his busy career: "Mr. Spoor, who was chairman of the board of directors

A CENSUS

of the Union Stockyards and Transit company at the time of his death, had been active until two years ago in more than a dozen business enterprises." He was also a trustee of the Newberry Library as well as president of the Caxton Club and a member of the Grolier Club (1903–1926). His literary interests centered around English writers of the nineteenth century, and his collection was especially strong in such figures as Keats, Shelley, Wordsworth, and Tennyson. Unfortunately his heirs decided not to sell his library until 1939, on the eve of the Second World War, and the prices realized were disappointing.

JEAN HERSHOLT (1886–1956), a Danish actor who had a long, successful career in Hollywood, was much admired for his numerous charitable and humanitarian activities. His books were sold a year before his death by Sotheby Parke-Bernet (see PROVENANCE above), and in a foreword to the catalogue he described how his collecting interests had begun in childhood with the stories of Hans Christian Andersen but soon extended to other writers. Part of his library, however, was dispersed before the auction to the Hans Christian Andersen Museum (Odense, Denmark), the University of California at Los Angeles, and the Library of Congress.

CARRIE ESTELLE DOHENY (*née* Betzold) (1875–1958), wife of a California oil millionaire, became interested in book-collecting during the 1920s and fell under the influence of the dealer Alice P. Millard. Initially she acquired fore-edge paintings and American literature but later turned her attention to western Americana, English literature, and fine printing, now with A. Edward Newton as her mentor.

A convert to Roman Catholicism, she left

[61]

her splendid library to St. John's Seminary in Camarillo, Calif., but some years after her death, the Archbishop of Los Angeles decided to dispose of her 15,000 books and manuscripts, claiming that they were not heavily used and were too expensive to insure. The collection was sold by Christie's in a series of eight sessions in New York, London, and Los Angeles between 1987 and 1989.

REFERENCES: [BEMIS] Buhler, Kathryn C. "The Frank Brewer Bemis Collection of Silver." *Bulletin of the Museum of Fine Arts* (Boston) 34 (October 1936): 78–83. — "Frank B. Bemis." *New York Times*, 11 March 1935, p. 17. (Obituary.) — Goodspeed, Charles. *Yankee Bookseller.* Boston: Houghton Mifflin, 1937. (See pp. 146–50.) — "In Memoriam." *Bulletin of the Business Historical Society* 9 (March 1935): 30–31. — Richmond, Carleton R. "Frank Brewer Bemis," in *Grolier 75.* (See pp. 105–06.) ¶ [DOHENY] *The Book as a Work of Art: An Exhibition of Books and Manuscripts from the Library of Mrs. Edward Laurence Doheny.* Los Angeles: Printed by Ward Ritchie, 1935. — *Catalogue of Books and Manuscripts in the Estelle Doheny Collection.* 3 vols. Los Angeles: Ward Ritchie Press, 1940–55. — "Doheny Library Opened." *New York Times*, 13 September 1932, p. 19. — "The Estelle Doheny Collection in the Edward Doheny Memorial Library." *Quarterly News-letter of the Book Club of California* 22 (Spring, 1957): 35–43. — "Mrs. E. L. Doheny Dies: Widow of Oil Millionaire Was Coast Philanthropist." *New York Times*, 31 October 1958, p. 29. — Reif, Rita. "Auctions: A Collection of Rare Books." *New York Times*, 13 March 1987, p. C33. — Rosenblum, Joseph, ed. *American Book Collectors and Bibliographers.* 1st ser. Dictionary of American Literary Biography, 140. Detroit: Gale Research, 1994. (See Francis J. Weber and Josephine Arlyn Bruccoli, "Carrie Estelle Doheny," pp. 64–69.) — Schad, Robert O. "The Estelle Doheny Collection." *New Colophon* 3 (1950): 229–42. — Shaffer, Ellen. "Reminiscences of a California Collector: Mrs. Edward Doheny, 1875–1958." *Book Collector* 14 (Spring, 1965): 49–59. — Weber, Francis J. *Southern California's First Family: The Dohenys of Los Angeles.* Fullerton, Calif.: Lorson's Books and Prints, 1993. ¶ [HERSHOLT] "Jean Hersholt, 69, Is Dead on Coast." *New York Times*, 3 June 1956, p. 86. — "Notes on Sales." *TLS*, 7 May 1954, p. 304. — *WWW in America.* ¶ [SPOOR] Dickinson, pp. 293–94. — "John A. Spoor, City Leader, Is Dead at 76." *Chicago Daily Tribune*, 16 October 1926, p. 1. — "John A. Spoor Dead." *New York Times*, 16 October 1926, p. 17. — "Notes on Sales: The John A. Spoor Library." *TLS*, 27 May 1939, p. 320. — Piehl, pp. 173–74. — "Spoor's Estate $1,400,000, Says Official List." *Chicago Daily Tribune*, 8 November 1927, p. 21. — *WWW in America.*

A CENSUS

3.6 ~ AUSTIN DOBSON COPY

Beinecke Library, Yale University. [1979 794] ¶ Dobson–Whitall–Simmons–Saks–Boegner copy.

Vellum binding. With preface (tipped in). Title-page: "By Austin Dobson and Divers Kindly Hands."

Bookplates of Austin Dobson, W. Van Whitall, Park E. Simmons, and John Saks.

PROVENANCE: Austin Dobson. — Sotheby, 13 March 1922, lot 38 [*Property of the late Austin Dobson*] (sold to Maggs for £26). — Maggs. — W. Van Whitall. — American Art Association, 14–16 February 1927, lot 369 [*Notable library of Major W. Van R. Whitall, of Pelham, New York*] (sold for $135). — American Art Association, 17–18 November 1937, lot 113 [*Splendid library of the late Parke E. Simmons*] (sold for $190). — John Saks. — Margaret Phipps Boegner. — Christie (New York), 20 April 1979, lot 226 [*Property of Mrs. Etienne Boegner*] (sold for $3,400). —Beinecke Library.

For AUSTIN DOBSON, see **2.6**.

WILLIAM VAN RENSSELAER WHITALL (1869–1945), son of Brigadier-General Samuel R. Whitall, had a brief military career of his own and then went on to marry Ellen Stevens and founded W. Van R. Whitall, Inc. (New York and Philadelphia), a manufacturing company that specialized in road-building equipment. In the American Art Association auction catalogue of his library (1927) there is a strong hint of financial distress: "Unforeseen business contingencies which cannot be denied will necessitate the residence of the present owner and collector of this splendid library, for a considerable period, in England and France. It is therefore chance, rather than inclination to stop collecting or lagging literary interest on the part of Major Whitall, which has led to his decision to disperse the collection." He then left his home in Pelham, N.Y., and by the time of his death he had lived for so long in Monte Carlo that there was a legal dispute about where his will should be probated.

He had begun collecting seriously only in middle age. His library displayed a particular interest in nineteenth-century writers, including George Borrow, Blake, Lamb, Coleridge, FitzGerald, Keats, and Shelley, as well as the books of Bruce Rogers. He contributed an early bibliography of Edwin Arlington Robinson to a critical study by Lloyd R. Morris (1923). His wife Ellen Stevens Whitall was a frequent benefactor of various cultural institutions and seems to have been also a collector: when a *New Yorker* contributor visited her in Pelham in 1934, she was pleased to display the manuscript of *Anthony Adverse*, part of which had been written in their home.

PARKE EDMUND SIMMONS (1858–1936), a wealthy and socially prominent Evanston, Ill., lawyer who collected both art and books, was president of the Caxton Club and a member of the Grolier Club (1919–34). His interests lay mainly in modern books, including those designed by Bruce Rogers, but he also owned a leaf from the Gutenberg Bible. Many of his books and manuscripts had come from the John Quinn sale.

Simmons' first wife died in 1915, and in 1931 he married Mary de Diemar Wright, a widow, twenty years younger than himself. When they divorced a year later, the Chicago newspapers were filled for weeks with lurid headlines about their mutual accusations (he claimed she had tricked him into marriage by pretending to be pregnant, and she wept in court as she described how he had persuaded her against her will to marry him); in the end she won a settlement of $40,000 but no alimony.

JOHN SAKS (1913–1983), of the department store family, began collecting in 1936 when he purchased heavily at the Marsden Perry sale. He was drawn especially to books printed on vellum and to titles issued by the major British and American private presses: he owned, for example, complete sets of the Kelmscott, Doves, and Ashendene books—nearly all on vellum—and he also had a strong interest in fine bindings. Saks was a Fellow of the Pierpont Morgan Library and an active member of the Grolier Club.

MARGARET BOEGNER (1906–2006), *née* Phipps, was the granddaughter of Andrew Carnegie's partner at the United States Steel Corporation and the daughter of the founder of the Grace Shipping Line. She devoted most of her energies to the maintenance of a large garden on her parents' estate in Nassau County, New York, which after their deaths she opened to the public. She served as chair of the Old Westbury Gardens, a nonprofit organization. It is not clear what kinds of books she collected.

REFERENCES: [BOEGNER] Boegner, Peggie Phipps, and Richard Gachot. *Halcyon Days: An American Family through Three Generations.* New York: Old Westbury Gardens and Harry N. Abrams, 1986. — "Deaths." *New York Times*, 18 September 2006, p. A25. — Gachot, Richard. "Halcyon Memories." *Old Westbury Garden News* 29, no. 3 (Fall/Holiday, 2006): 1, 3–5. (Available online.) — Hevesi, Dennis. "Margaret Phipps Boegner, 99; Founded Old Westbury Gardens." *New York Times*, 19 September 2006, p. B8. (Obituary.) ¶ [SAKS] "Deaths." *New York Times*, 1 June 1983, p. B5. — Dickinson. (See pp. 278–79.) — Massey, Stephen C. "John Saks," in *Grolier 2000*. — Papers (Grolier Club Library). ¶ [SIMMONS] Brooks, Philip. "Notes on Rare Books." *New York Times*, 14 November 1937, p. 137. — "French Antiques on Sale This Week... Library of Late Evanston, Ill., Lawyer to Be Dispersed." *New York Times*, 14 November 1937, p. 91. — "Park Simmons Leaves Estate to His 3 Sisters." *Chicago Daily Tribune*, 17 October 1936, p. 27. — "Rare Books Bring $20,017. Simmons Library Auction Ends—$510 Paid for Limited Editions." *New York Times*, 19 November 1937, p. 21. — "Recent American Auctions." *TLS*, 22 January 1938, p. 64. ¶ [WHITALL] Allen, Hervey. "An Appreciation," in *The Notable Library of Major W. Van R. Whitall of Pelham, New York.* New York: American Art Association, 17–18 November 1937. — Morris, Lloyd R. *The Poetry of Edwin Arlington Robinson: An Essay in Appreciation.* New York: George H. Doran Company, 1923. (With a bibliography by W. Van R. Whitall.) — "Notes on Rare Books." *New York Times*, 6 February 1927, p. BR25. — "Penny 'Rubaiyat' Is Sold for $3,200: First Edition of FitzGerald's Translation Is Auctioned with Whitall Collection." *New York Times*, 16 February 1927, p. 18. — "Rare old Books to Be Sold. Whitall Library Contains Many Valuable First Editions." *New York Times*, 13 February 1927, p. E11. — "Shelley's 'Adonais' Is Sold for $8,400... Total for All Books Reaches $120,840." *New York Times*, 17 February 1927, p. 8. — "The Talk of the Town." *New Yorker* 10 (27 October 1934): 15. — Ancestry.com. — Web sources.

DANIEL PRESS & GARLAND OF RACHEL

3.7 ↠ C. L. DODGSON COPY

Fales Library, New York University.† [Berol Non-circulating PR-1223 .G25 1881 copy 2] ¶ Dodgson–Moss–Berol copy.

Vellum binding. With preface. Title-page: "By Lewis Carroll and Divers Kindly Hands." In a red box also containing two letters, some clippings relating to the 1898 Dodgson sale, and the preface (each accompanied by typed notes or transcriptions by Moss).

Stamped notice on front flyleaf: "PRINTED IN ENGLAND". On a rear flyleaf Dodgson has penciled an emended version of two lines in the fifth stanza of Harington's poem: "Dat voces turtur, Veneri devota moratur | Quâ nova nupta diu,".

RELATED MATERIAL: Henry Daniel to C. L. Dodgson, 11 May 1887 [4.46]; Henry Daniel to W. E. Moss, 31 May [1898] [4.64]; leaves of the title-page and p. 22 of the 1898 sale of Dodgson's books, with the auctioneer's bill of sale to W. E. Moss.

PROVENANCE: C. L. Dodgson. — Edmund J. Brooks (Oxford), 11 May 1898, no. 413 [*Property of the late Revd. C. L. Dodgson*] (sold for £12 10*s*. to William E. Moss).[1] — William E. Moss. — Sotheby, 2 March 1937, lot 537 [*Property of Lt.-Col. W. E. Moss of the manor house, Sonning-on-Thames, Berks.*] (sold as part of lots 533–82— a set of the Daniel Press publications—for £170 to Maggs). — Maggs. — Alfred C. Berol. — New York University (gift from his widow, Mrs. Madeleine Rossin Berol, and son, Kenneth R. Berol, December 1974).

For C. L. DODGSON, see **2.7**.

Lt.-Col. WILLIAM E. MOSS (1875–1953) caused a considerable stir when he bought in 1898 the first *Garland* sold at auction—

---

1. Typed note by Moss on his copy of the relevant page of the catalogue: "The underbidder was the late Mr James Tregaskis, who was sitting beside the present owner" (NYU). The catalogue is reprinted in Jeffrey Stern, ed., *Lewis Carroll's Library: A Facsimile Edition of the Catalogue of the Auction Sale following C. L. Dodgson's Death in 1898, with Facsimiles of Three Subsequent Bookseller's Catalogues Offering Books from Dodgson's Library* (Silver Spring, Md.: Lewis Carroll Society of North America, 1981); and Stern, *Lewis Carroll, Bibliophile* (Luton: White Stone Publishing and the Lewis Carroll Society, 1997).

A CENSUS

Lewis Carroll's copy—for what many regarded as the exceptionally high price of £12 10s. After the sale, Henry Daniel wrote to thank Moss for "the compliment you paid my book in expending so many shekels on its purchase" and sent him a copy of the preface, which Carroll had evidently mislaid [4.7]. Moss, who lived in Sonning-on-Thames, Berkshire, had collected books all his adult life, with particular emphasis on William Blake and English sixteenth-century bindings, and part of his library was donated to the Bodleian Library by Moss himself and later by his widow; the greater part of the collection, however, was sold at Sotheby's in 1937 (see PROVENANCE above).

Moss also did some private printing in his home, and after his death an Albion press—much smaller than Henry Daniel's—and various kinds of type and equipment that he had used came to the Bodleian Library through the intervention of John Johnson.[1]

ALFRED CHARLES BEROL (1892–1974), whose surname was originally Berolzheimer, was the grandson of the founder of what became the Eagle Pencil Company, New York, over which he later presided. His collecting interests lay primarily in Americana and nineteenth-century English literature, and many of his books went to Columbia University Library (of which he was a trustee). But his great passion was Lewis Carroll (he owned nearly 500 letters from Dodgson and seventy-five photographs by him), and it was this preoccupation that led him to *The Garland of Rachel*, and that book in turn aroused a more general interest in the Daniel Press. He bought heavily at the sale of C. H. Wilkinson's collection, and in the fashion that characterized all of his bibliophilic activities, he frequently sought multiple copies of a single title for the sake of minor variants. He owned, for example, no less than three copies of the *Garland*, all of which were given by his family to NYU as a part of Berol's Carroll collection (one of the

---

1. Herbert Davis to Ruth Daniel, 10 March 1953 (Worcester).

largest and best in the world). He also donated twenty-one Daniel Press books (not including the *Garland*) to Harvard.

REFERENCES: [BEROL] "Alfred Berol, 81, of Eagle Pencils." *New York Times*, 16 June 1974, p. 47. (Obituary.) — Dickinson. (See p. 40.) — Ellenbogen, Rudolph. "Alfred C. Berol," in *Grolier 2000*. (See pp. 35-37.) — "English Literature and Americana from the Collection of Alfred C. Berol." *Grolier Club Gazette* NS 9 (February 1969): 25-30. (See p. 27.) — Lohf, Kenneth A. "Alfred C. Berol 1892-1974. In Memoriam." *Columbia Library Columns* 24 November 1974): 43-45. — McGuire, Patrick. "An Ardent Carroll Collector." *American Book Collector* 6 (January-February 1985): 19-26. — *WWW in America*. — Berol's handlist of his Lewis Carroll collection and notes on the collection are at New York University. ¶ [MOSS] [Hanson, L. W. "Lieut.-Col. W. E. Moss." *The Times*, 26 February 1953, p. 10. (Tribute.) — "The Moss Library." *TLS*, 13 March 1937, p. 192. — Web sources.

3.8 ❧ EDMUND W. GOSSE COPY

British Library, London.† [Ashley 3277] ¶ Gosse–Wise copy.

Vellum binding. With preface (laid in). Title-page: "By Edmund Gosse and Divers Kindly Hands." Bookplates of Edmund William Gosse (by E. A. Abbey) and Thomas James Wise; three ownership stamps of the British Library.

PROVENANCE: Edmund W. Gosse. — Thomas J. Wise. — British Museum (as part of Wise's Ashley Library, purchased from Wise's widow, 1937). — British Library.

For EDMUND W. GOSSE, see 2.8.

THOMAS J. WISE (1859-1937) was known during much of his lifetime as one of the most distinguished English book collectors of the modern era. He was primarily interested in English literature of the nineteenth and early twentieth centuries—in fact, he was to a large degree responsible for the new fashion of collecting Romantic and Victorian writers—and he had assembled a personal library that was beyond parallel. But during the 1880s, as a leading figure in the Browning and Shelley societies in London,

A CENSUS

he had created a number of facsimile reprints for their members, and this experience evidently persuaded him that it was possible to produce plausible imitations of older books. With the collaboration of Harry Buxton Forman, he began to produce a series of forgeries—usually of editions of books or pamphlets hitherto unknown, since they were more difficult to discredit—that fooled collectors and experts until John Carter and Graham Pollard's *An Enquiry into the Nature of Certain Nineteenth Century Pamphlets* (1934) exposed their fraudulence. Wise spent his final years unconvincingly protesting his innocence.

It is not known how or when Wise acquired Gosse's copy of the *Garland*, but it should be noted that they were close friends.

REFERENCES: [WISE] Barker, Nicolas, and John Collins. *A Sequel to an Enquiry into the Nature of Certain Nineteenth Century Pamphlets*. London and Berkeley: Scolar Press, 1983. — Bell, Alan. "Wise, Thomas J.," in *ODNB*. — Carter, John, and Graham Pollard. *An Enquiry into the Nature of Certain Nineteenth Century Pamphlets*. Ed. Nicolas Barker and John Collins. 2nd ed. London and Berkeley: Scolar Press, 1983. — Collins, John. *The Two Forgers: A Biography of Harry Buxton Forman and Thomas James Wise*. New Castle, Del.: Oak Knoll Books, 1992. — Marsden, W. A. "The Ashley Library." *British Museum Quarterly* 12 (January 1938): 20–21. — "Mr. T. J. Wise: Bibliographer, Editor, and Collector." *The Times*, 14 May 1937, p. 17. (Obituary.) — Partington, Wilfred. *Forging Ahead: The True Story of the Upward Progress of Thomas James Wise, Prince of Book Collectors, Bibliographer Extraordinary and Otherwise*. New York: G. P. Putnam's Sons, 1939. — Todd, William B., ed. *Thomas J. Wise Centenary Studies*. Austin: University of Texas Press, 1959. — [Wise, Thomas J.] *The Ashley Library: A Catalogue of Printed Books, Manuscripts and Autograph Letters Collected by Thomas James Wise*. 11 vols. London: privately printed, 1922–36. (See 10:118, with *Garland* title-page reproduced on facing page.) — Wise, Thomas J. *Letters of Thomas J. Wise to John Henry Wrenn: A Further Inquiry into the Guilt of Certain Nineteenth-Century Forgers*. Ed. Fannie E. Ratchford. New York: Knopf, 1944. — WWW.

3.9 ❧ SIR RICHARD HARINGTON COPY

Location unknown. ¶ Harington–Poor–Quinn copy.

Vellum binding. With preface (laid in). In a crushed green levant morocco solander case. Bookplate of Henry W. Poor.

DANIEL PRESS & GARLAND OF RACHEL

PROVENANCE: Sir Richard Harington. — Henry W. Poor (acquired before 1901). — Anderson Galleries, 23–25 February 1909, lot 136 [*Library of Henry W. Poor*, part 4] (sold for $51). — John Quinn. — Anderson Galleries (New York), 10 December 1923, lot 2302 [*Library of John Quinn*] (sold for $175 to Drake). — Drake (dealer). — Colin and Charlotte Franklin (Culham, Oxfordshire), catalogue 5 [*Privately printed*], Autumn, 1972, no. 55 (£560).

For Sir RICHARD HARINGTON, see **2.9**.

HENRY W. POOR (1844–1915), a New York banker, was known to his contemporaries primarily as the publisher of *Poor's Railway Manual*. The report of his death in the *New York Times* summed up his varied career with this headline: "Henry W. Poor Dies; Railway Publisher. Head of Poor's Manual and Banker Expires Suddenly at His Home, at 71. Made and Lost a Fortune. . . . An Art and Book Collector." When he was still enjoying prosperity in the first decade of the twentieth century, he bought Daniel Press books and ephemera directly from Emily Daniel, with whom he had a friendly relationship.[1] At the time he was regarded as the foremost collector of Daniel Press books in America, and Mosher's reprint of the *Garland* (1902) included, as an appendix, a checklist of the Daniel Press titles owned by Poor. The list shows that he owned the *Garland* by that date; in fact, his correspondence with Emily Daniel indicates that he had the *Garland* at least a year earlier. He also owned a second (generic) copy of the *Garland* [**3.19**].

Poor collected English literature, private press books, fine bindings, and illuminated manuscripts on a large scale, but in 1908 his business ventures collapsed, and his immense Lexington Avenue mansion was seized by creditors and his library was auctioned. Nearly a third of his books and manuscripts were bought by Henry

---

1. Poor to Emily Daniel, 5 July 1901 (Worcester); Emily Daniel to Poor, 6 May 1903 (NYU). There were also numerous letters from Emily Daniel laid in the Daniel Press books sold in the Anderson Galleries auction.

E. Huntington, then starting to form his own library in California. Poor died a few years later.

JOHN QUINN (1870–1924), son of Irish immigrant parents in Ohio, became the foremost collector and patron in the early twentieth century of literary and artistic modernism. His usual style was to purchase directly from writers and artists (many of whom he knew personally), and he came to own, among many other things, the typescript of Eliot's *The Waste Land* and the manuscript of Joyce's *Ulysses*. Quinn's splendid library, which was sold near the end of his life, was especially rich in Anglo-Irish material. He had an excellent collection of Daniel Press titles, nearly all of which came from the Poor sale.

One interesting piece of information that has emerged in recent years is that he had a prolonged romantic relationship with William Morris's daughter May.

REFERENCES: [POOR] "$1,450 for a Book. Caxton Edition of the Polychronycon Fetches It at H. W. Poor Sale." *New York Times*, 13 January 1909, p. 3. — Dickinson. (See p. 262.) — "Henry W. Poor Dies; Railway Publisher." *New York Times*, 14 April 1915, p. 13. — "Sale of Mrs. Poor's Library." *New York Times*, 2 May 1909, p. 4. — Smith, Geoffrey D. "Great Auctions of the Past: The Henry W. Poor Auction." *Fellowship of American Bibliophilic Societies* 13 (Winter, 2009): 7–9; (Fall, 2009): 7–9. — Correspondence (Worcester). ¶ [QUINN] Londraville, Janis. "The Private Voice of May Morris." *Journal of Pre-Raphaelite Studies* 2, no. 2 (1993): 28–37. (Excerpts from letters to Quinn.) — Londraville, Janis, ed. *On Poetry, Painting, and Politics: The Letters of May Morris and John Quinn*. Selinsgrove, Pa.: Susquehanna University Press, 1997. — Mattson, Francis O. "The John Quinn Memorial Collection: An Inventory and Index." *Bulletin of the New York Public Library* 78, no. 2 (Winter, 1975): 145–230. — "Mr. John Quinn." *The Times*, 29 July 1924, p. 14. (Obituary.) — Pound, Ezra. *Selected Letters of Ezra Pound to John Quinn, 1915–1924*. Ed. Timothy Materer. Durham, N.C.: Duke University Press, 1991. — Quinn, John. *The Letters of John Quinn to William Butler Yeats*. Ed. Alan Himber. Ann Arbor, Mich.: UMI Research Press, 1983. — Reid, B. L. *The Man from New York: John Quinn and His Friends*. New York: Oxford University Press, 1968. — Rosenblum, Joseph, ed. *American Book-Collectors and Bibliographers.* 2nd ser. (Dictionary of Literary Biography, 140.) Detroit: Gale Research, 1997. (See Rosenblum, "John Quinn," pp. 233–46. — Walsh, James L. "John Quinn: Lover, Book-Lover, Art Amateur." *Catholic World* 120 (November 1924): 176–84. — Zilczer, Judith. "The Dispersal of the John Quinn Collection." *Archives of American Art Journal* 19, no. 3 (1979): 15–21; 30, no. 1/4 (1990): 35–40. — Zilczer, Judith. *The Noble Buyer: John Quinn, Patron of the Avant-Garde.* Washington, D.C.: Hirshhorn Museum, 1978.

3.10 ⁕ W. E. HENLEY COPY

Location unknown.
For HENLEY, see 2.10.

3.11 ⁕ ANDREW LANG COPY

Rare Books, T. C. Wilson Library, University of Minnesota, Minneapolis. [820.1 G18a] ¶ Lang–Way copy.
Vellum binding. In a leather-covered solander case. No preface. Title-page: "By Andrew Lang and Divers Kindly Hands." University of Minnesota bookplate. Penciled note on front flyleaf: "See the account of Hookes's *Amanda* in *The Philobiblion* vol. 2, pp. 87 and 105."[1]
RELATED MATERIAL: [*Tipped in*]: [*front endpaper*] list, 4 pp., printed by Henry Daniel of Daniel Press publications from 1875 to 1884 (begins "These are as yet the productions of the private press of Henry Daniel, Fellow of Worcester College, Oxford"); [*rear flyleaf*] clipping from the *Dundee Advertiser*, 23 May 1898, about the Falconer facsimile. ¶ [*Laid in*] typed list of contributors to the *Garland*; description of the volume, probably by a bookseller, indicating that this copy is the one presented to Andrew Lang; brief typewritten description of book, ending with "Not for sale"; typed note discussing the prices of various copies of the book (a handwritten note at the bottom attributes this to Temple Scott in the *Dial*, 1 June 1898); catalogue listing, with the *Garland* for sale for

---

1. "Notes on Neglected English Poets: N. Hookes." *Philobiblion* 2 (April 1863): 87–91; (May 1863): 105–07.

A CENSUS

£165; Lang to W. I. Way, 26 November [1882] [**4.45**]; typescript copy of this letter; Austin Dobson's article about the *Garland* in the *Century*, February 1882; three additional exhibit labels for unrelated books, two with illustrations by Mrs. W. Irving Way; scrap of paper bearing letterhead of Way & Williams, Publishers, Importers and Booksellers, The Monadnock, Chicago; manuscript note listing the 18 contributors (with these notes in the margin: "Armour has one. Stedman has one I think. M.C.D. Borden, 25 E. 5th N.Y. had Foote copy").

PROVENANCE: Andrew Lang. — W. Irving Way (gift from Lang, December 1882). — James Laurie (dealer, Minneapolis). — University of Minnesota (purchased from Laurie, June 1979).

For ANDREW LANG, see **2.11**.

WASHINGTON IRVING WAY (1853–1931), Canadian by birth, moved south and first worked for two American railroad companies and later for a Philadelphia publisher. In 1895 he became the senior partner of Way & Williams, a small Chicago publishing firm dedicated to fine printing, and immediately traveled to England, where he persuaded William Morris to allow Way & Williams to co-publish the Kelmscott Press edition of Rossetti's *Hand and Soul* (the only Kelmscott book issued in America). On the same trip he met Andrew Lang for the first time, though for several years before this Lang and Way had been exchanging friendly letters and gifts, most notably Lang's copy of the *Garland*, which came into Way's hands in late 1882 [**4.45**]. In 1900 Way wrote a lengthy account of the Daniel Press for the *Inland Printer* (Chicago).

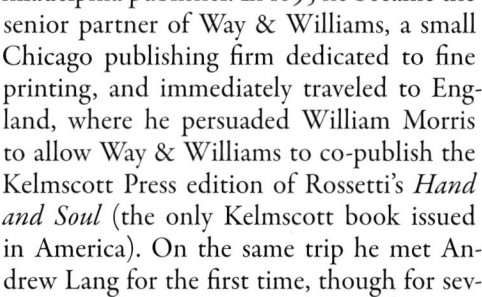

Way & Williams had a brief lifespan, primarily because Way was focused on producing outstanding typography, whereas Williams was increasingly dismayed by their poor commercial success; in 1904 Way moved to Los Angeles, where he remained the rest of his life, always heavily involved in bibliophilic activities. He was active in the Grolier Club and was one of the founders of the Caxton Club in Chicago and the Zamorano Club in Los Angeles. During his later years in California he supported himself, somewhat precariously, as a book scout and a salesman of subscription editions. He could only afford to live in hotel rooms, but to the end of his life he was full of amusing stories about the world of fine printing. In 1922 the *Los Angeles Times* described him as an "obscure celebrity."

There is no full account of Way's colorful life, but he did leave behind an autobiographical fragment that was first published in *Hoja Volante* in 1968 and later reprinted as a monograph in 1974.

REFERENCES: [WAY] Apostol, Jane. *Olive Percival: Los Angeles Author and Bibliophile*. Los Angeles: Department of Special Collections, University Research Library, University of California, Los Angeles, 1992. (See pp. 14–15.) — Bidwell, John, ed. *A Bibliophile's Los Angeles*. Los Angeles: William Andrews Clark Memorial Library, UCLA, 1985. (See Robert Rosenthal, "Los Angeles & Chicago: Two Cities, Two Bibliophiles," pp. 3–27.) — Clary, William W. *Fifty Years of Book Collecting*. Los Angeles: Zamorano Club, 1962. (See pp. 7–19.) — "Deep in Lethal Oblivion Bath: Los Angeles Has Famed Two Who Are 'Unknown.'" *Los Angeles Times*, 20 August 1922, p. III-28. — Earle, Homer P. "W. Irving Way: Rescued from the Archives." *Hoja Volante* 91 (February 1968): 5–7. — Way, W. Irving. *An Autobiographical Fragment*. [Los Angeles: Zamorano Club, 1974]. — Way, W. Irving. "The Daniel Press, Oxford." *Inland Printer* 25 (September 1900): 785–87. — Way, W. Irving. "A Visit to William Morris." *Modern Art* 4 (Summer, 1896): 78–79. — There is a collection of T. B. Mosher's letters to Way at the Huntington Library.

3.12 ❧ FREDERICK LOCKER COPY

Butler Rare Book and Manuscript Library, Columbia University, New York, N.Y.† [B825B76 G 1881] ¶ Locker–Coykendall copy.

Vellum binding. With preface (tipped in; inscribed "Worcester House | Oxford" by Henry Daniel at foot of first page). Title-page: "By Frederick Locker and Diverse Kindly Hands."

Bookplates: Frederick Locker; Columbia University gift plate ("Presented by Frederick Coykendall, '95)." Penciled note by Locker on flyleaf: "This Mr D. wrote & asked me to write some Verses for a book he was printing, & I said I wd do so, but I did not understand the character of the book, or I hope I might have done something a little more to the point. | F. L. L."

A CENSUS

RELATED MATERIAL [originally laid in but now kept separately]: corrected proof, single leaf, of Dodgson's contribution (reproduced in Eyres, p. 145); two letters from Daniel to Locker, 5 November 1881 and 15 February 1882 [**4.34** and **4.42**].

PROVENANCE: Frederick Locker. — Sotheby, 4 March 1920, lot 252 [*Property of a gentleman*] (sold to Thorp for £22 10*s*.). — Thorp. — Frederick Coykendall. — Columbia University (gift from Coykendall, December 1940).

For FREDERICK LOCKER, see **2.12**.

FREDERICK COYKENDALL (1872–1954), president of the Cornell Steamboat Company, which was owned by his family, was closely associated with Columbia University for many decades. In 1916 he was elected to the university's board of trustees, and at the end of his six-year term he was made a life trustee. For twenty years he served as chairman of the board. During his long tenure he focused particularly upon the reorganization and development of the Columbia University Press, of which he was the director.

He was also president of the Grolier Club from 1935 to 1939 and collected mainly nineteenth- and early twentieth-century writers. Coykendall was a frequent contributor to bibliographical journals and was the author of *A Note on The Monk* (1935) and *Arthur Rackham: A List of Books Illustrated by Him* (1922). His collection went to Columbia University Library at his death.

We know that Coykendall had acquired the *Garland* by 1933, because in that year it was listed in a bibliography based upon his Robert Bridges collection.[1]

REFERENCES: [COYKENDALL] "Coykendall Dies; Columbia Trustee." *New York Times*, 19 November 1954, p. 23. — "Coykendall to Head Columbia Trustees." *New York Times*, 13 January 1933, p. 12. — Dickinson. — *WWW in America*. — Papers (Columbia University Library).

---

1. George L. McKay, *A Bibliography of Robert Bridges* (New York: Columbia University Press, 1933), p. 161.

DANIEL PRESS & GARLAND OF RACHEL

3.13 ❧ ERNEST MYERS COPY

Location unknown.

The Getty copy of the *Garland* [3.24] has, laid in, proofs of the Myers title-page ("By Ernest Myers and Divers Kindly Hands") and Myers's poem, but there is no indication that the book itself, which has the generic title-page, belonged to Myers. Hence the Myers copy remains unlocated, though there is one early glimpse of it in the PROVENANCE below.

PROVENANCE: Ernest Myers. — Sotheby (London), 20 June 1904, lot 150 (sold for £10 10s. to Parker & Co.).[1] — Parker & Co.

For ERNEST MYERS, see 2.13.

3.14 ❧ MARY F. ROBINSON COPY

Location unknown.

For MARY F. ROBINSON, see 2.14.

3.15 ❧ JOHN ADDINGTON SYMONDS COPY

Fales Library, New York University, New York, N.Y.† [PR1223 .G25 1881 copy 3] ¶ Symonds–Thomas–Berol copy.

Vellum binding. No preface. Title-page: "By John Addington Symonds and Divers Kindly Hands." Armorial bookplate of John Addington Symonds.

In a crimson morocco slipcase containing the *Garland* and the letters listed below. In gilt lettering on the slipcase: "WITH AUTOGRAPH LETTERS | BY CONTRIBUTORS | INCLUDING | JOHN ADDINGTON SYMONDS | EDMUND GOSSE | LEWIS CARROLL | AUSTIN DOBSON | ANDREW LONG [*sic*] | ROBERT BRIDGES | W. E. HENLEY | FREDERICK LOCKER".

RELATED MATERIAL: C. L. Dodgson to Emily Daniel, 9 July 1883; Symonds to Miss Poynter, 1 July 1887; Frederick Locker to

---

1. There is some uncertainty about this copy. It is bound in olive morocco by Morley and is described in *Book Prices Current* as part of a sale of Myers's books, but there is no mention of Myers in the Sotheby catalogue.

Miss Courtney, 20 February 1880; Andrew Lang to "Dear Sir," 1 July 1887; Robert Bridges to Doyne [?], 27 December 1902; Edmund Gosse to [Jeanette L.] Gilder, 18 December 1889; Henry Daniel to Elkin Mathews, 27 June 1899; postcard, Frederic Myers to Rev. W. Rees, 28 February 1906; Francis W. Bourdillon to "Dear Sir," 19 November 1878; Margaret L. Woods to [C. H.] Wilkinson, n.d. [*c.* 1920] [**4.76**]; Austin Dobson to [Sydney] Pawling, 4 March 1895; W. E. Henley to Bernard Partridge, [3 August 1895]; Emily Daniel to Dame Katharine Furse, 3 January 1920 (with an annotated typed transcription) [**4.77**]. (The American Art Association catalogue [see below] makes it clear that these various letters had been assembled by an earlier collector, presumably Thomas rather than Berol.)[1]

PROVENANCE: John Addington Symonds. — Katharine Furse (by inheritance; until *c.* 1920). — Abel Cary Thomas. — American Art Association, 18–19 March 1936, lot 94 [*Library of Abel Cary Thomas, New York City*, part 2] (sold to Alfred F. Goldsmith for $310). — Alfred F. Goldsmith (dealer, New York). — Alfred C. Berol. — New York University (gift from his widow, Mrs. Madeleine Rossin Berol, and son, Kenneth R. Berol, December 1974).

For JOHN ADDINGTON SYMONDS, see **2.15**. For another copy with Symonds's name on the title-page (but not his copy), see **3.31**.

Dame KATHARINE FURSE (1875–1952), daughter of John Addington Symonds, spent most of her childhood in Switzerland. She trained as a hospital nurse in England and was responsible for creating the V.A.D. (Voluntary Aid Department), which cared for the sick and wounded during wartime. In 1900 she married Charles W. Furse, a painter, whose work included the well-known portrait of Henry Daniel reproduced as a frontispiece in the *Memorials* volume. Charles Furse died unexpectedly in the autumn of 1904, and his widow, left to raise two young boys, moved in with

---

1. We have printed only two of these letters, because the rest do not deal with *The Garland of Rachel* or the Daniel Press.

her mother.[1] Later she turned to Henry Daniel for advice about selling her father's copy of the *Garland*, but her letter arrived after Daniel's death in September 1919 [4.77].

ABEL CARY THOMAS (1883–1945), a New York lawyer, was a descendant of Miles Standish and Governor William Bradford (of the Plymouth colony). He served as secretary and general counsel of Warner Brothers Pictures, and in 1935 he was one of six executives of motion picture companies indicted for violating anti-trust laws. The case against Thomas, however, was later dismissed by a U.S. district court in St. Louis.

The catalogue of his library (see PROVENANCE above) indicates that he collected first editions, autograph letters, and manuscripts, mainly of English and American writers. He had a strong interest in Dodgson, which probably explains his ownership of the *Garland*.

For ALFRED C. BEROL, see Dodgson copy [3.7] above.

REFERENCES: [FURSE] Furse, Katharine. *Hearts and Pomegranates: The Story of Forty-five Years, 1875 to 1920*. London: Peter Davies, 1940. — Mathews, V. L. "Furse [née Symonds], Dame Katharine," in *ODNB*. ¶ [THOMAS] "Abel Cary Thomas, Warners' Ex-Counsel." *New York Times*, 23 February 1945, p. 17. (Obituary.) — Sargent, Murray, ed. *History of the Class of 1905, Yale College*. 2 vols. New Haven, Conn.: Yale University, 1908. (See 2:269.) — U.S. Indicts 9 Film Firms in Trust Quiz." *Washington Post*, 12 January 1935, p. 1.

3.16 ❧ T. H. WARD COPY

Private collection, U.K.

Vellum binding (slightly soiled). With preface (laid in). Title-page: "By Thomas Humphry Ward and Divers Kindly Hands."

PROVENANCE: Thomas Humphry Ward. — Bertram Rota Ltd. cat. 301 [Summer, 2005], no. 1430 (£12,000; sold to private collector, U.K., in 2006). — Present owner.

For THOMAS HUMPHRY WARD, see **2.16**.

---

1. Janet Catherine Symonds to T. B. Mosher, 23 June 1905 (Mosher papers, Houghton Library).

A CENSUS

3.17 ❦ ALBERT WATSON COPY

Rare Book Room, Gleeson Library, University of San Francisco, San Francisco, Calif. [PR1223 .G25 1881] ¶ Watson–Barlow copy.

Vellum binding. With preface (laid in). Title-page: "By A.W. and Divers Kindly Hands."

PROVENANCE: Albert Watson. — Chiswick Book Shop. — William P. Barlow (purchased from Chiswick Book Shop on 4 August 1971 for $1,255). — University of San Francisco (gift from Barlow, December 1982).

For ALBERT WATSON, see **2.17**.

WILLIAM P. BARLOW, Jr. (b. 1934), following in his father's footsteps, became a Certified Public Accountant and joined the family firm. In 1978 he set up his own accounting firm in San Francisco, Barlow & Hughan. He is a well-known collector of eighteenth-century printing and bibliographical material and has served as president of several bibliophilic organizations, including the Book Club of California, the Gleeson Library Associates, and the Bibliographical Society of America. Barlow received the Sir Thomas More Medal for Book Collecting (1989) and the Hubert Howe Bancroft Award (2004).

REFERENCES: Information from John Hawk (Gleeson Library). — [BARLOW] Web sources.

3.18 ❦ MARGARET L. WOODS COPY

Harry Ransom Center, University of Texas at Austin. [PR 1223 G25 1881 WEA] ¶ Woods–Weaver copy.

Vellum binding. With preface (laid in). Title-page: "By M. L. Woods and Divers Kindly Hands." HRC bookplate: "From the Lewis Carroll collection of Warren Weaver."

PROVENANCE: Margaret L. Woods. — Duschnes catalogue 150 (1960), no. 62 ($500). — Duschnes catalogue 152 (1962), no. 53 ($600) — Warren Weaver. — University of Texas (acquired as part of the Warren Weaver collection, November 1969).

For MARGARET L. WOODS, see **2.18**.

WARREN WEAVER (1894–1978) had an impressive career as

a mathematician, was the author of several books on communication and machine translation, and later became a director of the Rockefeller Foundation and a trustee of the Sloan Foundation. From early childhood he displayed a passion for accumulating books: he recalled later that his very first acquisition was a battered reprint of *Alice in Wonderland*, which he stamped "Warren Weaver, No. 1." As an adult, he put together a major Lewis Carroll collection (now at the University of Texas) and wrote a book entitled *Alice in Many Tongues: The Translations of Alice in Wonderland* (1964).

REFERENCES: [WEAVER] Lovett, Charlie. *Warren Weaver: Scientist, Humanitarian, Carrollian.* [Austin, Tex.]: Lewis Carroll Society of North America, 2000. — Taylor, Robert N., comp. *Lewis Carroll at Texas: The Warren Weaver Collection and Related Dodgson Materials at the Harry Ransom Humanities Research Center.* Carroll Studies, no. 8. Austin, Tex.: Harry Ransom Humanities Research Center, 1985. (See no. 421 and Weaver, "In Pursuit of Lewis Carroll," pp. 9–15, reprinted from *Library Chronicle of the University of Texas at Austin*, NS no. 2 [November 1970]: 38–45.) — Weaver, Warren. *Alice in Many Tongues: The Translations of Alice in Wonderland.* Madison: University of Wisconsin Press, 1964. — Web sources.

Other copies

3.19 ✥ BIRMINGHAM PUBLIC LIBRARIES

William Ridler Collection, Birmingham Public Library (on loan). ¶ Poor–Ridler copy.

Vellum binding. No preface. Title-page: "By Divers Kindly Hands." Bookplates of Henry W. Poor and William Ridler.

PROVENANCE: Henry W. Poor. — William Ridler. — Ann Ridler. — William Ridler Collection (on loan to the Birmingham Public Libraries).

For Poor, see 3.9. (Poor also owned another copy of the book.)

A CENSUS

WILLIAM RIDLER (1901–1980) spent his childhood in Kings Norton, near Birmingham, and later became an antiques dealer in Oxford. There he gradually assembled an impressive collection of modern British private press books—including a nearly full run of the Daniel Press imprints—and in 1971 published a useful checklist of titles that had been overlooked by earlier scholars of fine printing such as Will Ransom and G. S. Tomkinson. A revised edition of his checklist was issued in 1975. Dorothy Harrop recalled that when she first glimpsed Ridler's library at his Oxford home in 1971, she "was astonished at the riches it contained for there was not a press of any note from which there was no example. His other great love was illustrated books, and he possessed many fine examples in addition to the press books, works from the turn of the century being particularly prominent" (*Catalogue*, p. 2).

His widow Ann Ridler has placed the collection on loan at the Birmingham Public Libraries, with the understanding that it will be bequeathed to that institution at her death.

REFERENCES: [RIDLER] Harrop, Dorothy A., comp. *Catalogue of the William Ridler Collection of Fine Printing*. Birmingham: Birmingham Public Libraries, 1989. (See no. 610.) — Harrop, Dorothy A. "Will Ridler, 1901–1980: A Private Man and His Collection." *Matrix* 4 (1984): 122–28. — Ridler, William. *British Modern Press Books: A Descriptive Check List of Unrecord Items*. Rev. ed. Folkestone: Dawson, 1975.

3.20 ❧ BODLEIAN LIBRARY

Bodleian Library, Oxford University, Oxford, England.† [Arch. C d.42]

Vellum binding. With preface (tipped in). Title-page: "By Divers Kindly Hands."

Penciled note on verso of free front endpaper: "Gee, June, 1885." Library stamp on p. [v]: "BODLEIAN LIBRARY | OXFORD | 20 JUL 85."

PROVENANCE: Gee (Oxford dealer). — Bodleian Library (purchased from Gee, 20 July 1885).

The Bodleian also owns a second copy of the preface from the Broxbourne Library.

3.21 ⁊ CAMBRIDGE UNIVERSITY

Cambridge University Library. [Rare Books, Broxbourne.c.66.] ¶ Ehrman copy.

Vellum binding. With preface (tipped in). Title-page: "By Divers Kindly Hands." Armorial bookplate of Albert Ehrman; gift bookplate ("CAMBRIDGE UNIVERSITY LIBRARY | FROM THE BROXBOURNE LIBRARY | Presented through the Friends of the National Libraries | by John Ehrman, M.A., F.B.A. | July 1978").

Signature of Rachel Daniel on recto of first leaf of the preface. Note in Albert Ehrman's hand on preface: "Signed for me by Rachel Daniel | (at back) | Exceedingly scarce | AE." Note (in another hand?) on front endpaper: "*very* rare sold for £28—1905". Note on rear endpaper: "Collated & complete, B. Quaritch". With printed slip from a bookseller's catalogue giving details of the Margaret L. Woods copy, offered at $600 (presumably this is the entry in the Duschnes catalogue 152 [1962], no. 53—the copy now at the University of Texas [**3.18**]).

PROVENANCE: Quaritch. — Albert Ehrman. — John Ehrman (by inheritance). — Cambridge University Library (gift from John Ehrman through the Friends of the National Libraries, July 1978).

ALBERT EHRMAN (1890–1969), who worked in the family business of importing industrial diamonds, was described by Nicolas Barker as "one of the most distinguished of contemporary collectors and a notable benefactor of many of the national libraries." His library—named after the English village in which he had a home—consisted mainly of incunables, but he was also drawn to modern English fine presses and owned, for example, a substantial number of Kelmscott Press books. The collection was broad and deep, with special strengths in early printing, bindings, and type-specimens.

JOHN EHRMAN (1920–2011), an historian, lent his father's library to the Bodleian in 1970; a few years later, in 1978, it was divided between the Bodleian and Cambridge University Library.

REFERENCES: Information from Emily Dourish (Cambridge University Library). ¶ [EHRMAN] Barker, Nicolas. "Albert Ehrman: 6 February 1890–12 August 1969." *Book Collector* 19 (Winter, 1970): 455–64. — Bidwell, John. "Albert Ehrman," in *Grolier 2000*. (See pp. 84–87.) — "Broxbourne Library." *Bodleian Library Record* 8 (June 1971): 239–40. — "The Broxbourne Library." *Bodleian Library Record* 10 (December 1979): 78–80. — Ehrman, Albert. "The Broxbourne Library." *Book-Collector's Quarterly* 2 (March 1931): 45–56. — Fern, Alan M. "Typographical Specimen Books: A Check-list of the Broxbourne Collection." *Book Collector* 5 (Autumn, 1956): 256–72. — "Main Part of Library for Bodleian and Cambridge." *The Times*, 23 June 1978, p. 16. — [Muir, Percy.] "Private Libraries—xviii. The Broxbourne Library." *TLS*, 24 June 1939, p. 380. — Nixon, Howard M. *Broxbourne Library: Styles and Designs of Bookbindings from the Twelfth to the Twentieth Century*. With an introduction by Albert Ehrman. London: Maggs Brothers for the Broxbourne Library, 1956. — *WWW*. (See for John Ehrman.)

3.22 ❧ CLAREMONT COLLEGES

Honnold Library, Claremont Colleges [Z 232 D6 G18 1881 (Oxford Collection)]. ¶ Clary copy.

Green morocco binding with gilt rules and lettering by Morley (signed). No preface. Title-page: "By Divers Kindly Hands." No miniation. Bookplate of the Clary Oxford Collection.

Laid in are pages from two dealer catalogues describing other copies of the *Garland*: Walter M. Hill (Chicago), n.d., copy with Henry Daniel's signature, 1887 (now at NYU) [**3.28**]; and Philip C. Duschnes (New York), Catalogue 150, October 1961, Margaret Woods's copy (now at the University of Texas [**3.18**]).

PROVENANCE: Quaritch catalogue 823 (1961), no. 126 (offered as part of a group of seventy-two Daniel Press titles, £1,150/$3,229). — William. W. Clary (purchased *c*. 1961) — Claremont College (gift from Clary to the Honnold Library's Oxford Collection, *c*. 1961).

WILLIAM W. CLARY (1888–1971), a Los Angeles attorney, was a graduate of Pomona College and devoted much of his time and energy to a group of southern California colleges now known as the Claremont University Consortium. He was an enthusiastic book collector, mainly of English literature, and since he was a board member of several of those colleges, which claimed to be emulating the collegiate pattern of Oxford University, he began to ransack bookstores for anything connected with Oxford. For the most part, he donated these books to the Honnold Library at Claremont as soon as he acquired them; hence his copy of the *Garland* (which is a quintessentially Oxford book) probably came to the library in about 1961, when he purchased it.

EXHIBITIONS: "The Garland of Rachel: Poetry & Dr. Daniel's Press at Oxford, 1874 to 1906. An Exhibition of Poetry Printed at the Daniel Press," Special Collections, Honnold Mudd Library, 15 September–31 October 1990. The exhibition was advertised by means of a broadside printed by Susan M. Allen, which included the text of Dodgson's poem. These cases were on display: *The Garland of Rachel*; Lewis Carroll; Mrs. Margaret L. Woods and Francis W. Bourdillon; Robert Bridges; other poetry printed at the Daniel Press.[1] ¶ "Snarks, Jabberwocks, Crocodiles, & Mice Tails: Lewis Carroll, the Poet and the Parodist, Illuminated," UCLA Library Department of Special Collections, University of California, Los Angeles, 2 November 1998–31 January 1999. (Case 12 was devoted to the *Garland*.)

REFERENCES: [CLARY] Briggs, Grace M., ed. *The William W. Clary Oxford Collection: A Descriptive Catalogue*. Oxford: Printed by Oxford University Press for the Honnold Library, 1956. *Supplementary Catalogue*, ed. Catharine K. Firman, 1965. (*Garland* not listed in either volume.) — Clary, William. "Contemporary Collectors XLIV: An Oxford Collection." *Book Collector* 17 (Summer, 1968): 177–89. — Clary, William W. *Fifty Years of Book Collecting*. Los Angeles: Zamorano Club, 1962. — Dickinson. — "William Webb Clary—1888–1971." *Honnold Library Record* 12 (Fall, 1971): 1–2.

3.23 ꙮ HILARY MARTIN DANIEL (PRIVATE)

Hilary Martin Daniel (private collection), Frome, England.† ¶ George Alfred Daniel–Alfreda Daniel–Hilary Martin Daniel copy.

Vellum binding. With preface (laid in). Title-page: "By Divers Kindly Hands."

---

1. A copy of this broadside is in the Mark Samuels Lasner Collection.

A CENSUS

PROVENANCE: George Alfred Daniel. — Alfreda Daniel (by inheritance). — Hilary Martin Daniel (by inheritance).

GEORGE ALFRED DANIEL ((1839–1875), younger brother of Henry Daniel, was educated at King's College, London, became a solicitor, and in 1864 was made a partner in the law firm of Wilson Clement Cruttwell (his uncle) in Frome. (His mother recorded in her diary that a solicitor in London had said of her son, "I have had many steady, well conducted young men, but I have never had one like G. Daniel.") Like other members of the Daniel and Cruttwell families, he was a leading public figure in Frome for several decades. He married Jane Isabella Morrison in 1866, and there is a Burne-Jones window dedicated to his memory in Holy Trinity Church, Frome.

It seems reasonable to assume that his copy of the *Garland* was a gift from Henry Daniel at the time of publication.

ALFREDA GEORGIANA SUSAN DANIEL (1878–1955), daughter of George Alfred and Jane Daniel, remained in Frome and the nearby village of Nunney all her life and never married. Chambers and Ould suggest that she may have been involved in some of the later printing at Frome. In the 1911 census she was visiting a cottage hospital and was described as a "mission worker."

HILARY MARTIN DANIEL (b. 1931), a retired solicitor, lives near Frome and is the son of Alfred M. G. Daniel and the grandson of George Alfred Daniel. He inherited the *Garland* from his aunt Alfreda, and he says that he holds the book in trust for his family.

REFERENCES: [A. DANIEL] Chambers, David, and Martyn Ould. *The Daniel Press in Frome.* Hinton Charterhouse: Old School Press, 2011. (See pp. 28, 53.) — *Chronicle of... Cruttwell.* (See p. 151.) — Various genealogical records (Ancestry.com). — Correspondence (Worcester). ¶ [G. A. DANIEL] *Chronicle of... Cruttwell.* (See p. 49.) — Hilary Martin Daniel notebook. — [H. M. DANIEL] Moxon, John, ed. *Frome: A Special Town.* [Frome]: Rotary Club of Frome, [1996]. (See Hilary Martin Daniel, "Living Here," pp. 16–19.)

DANIEL PRESS & GARLAND OF RACHEL

3.24 ☙ MARK GETTY (PRIVATE)

Mark Getty, England (private collection, Wormsley Library).† ¶ Sligh–Getty copy.

Blue levant morocco binding [*Pl. 7*] with gilt tooling, signed by Morley of Oxford. With preface (laid in). Title-page: "By Divers Kindly Hands."

Bookplate of Nigel Sligh. Proofs of title ("By Ernest Myers and Divers Kindly Hands"), half-title, and Myers's poem laid in.

This copy is listed as Ernest Myers's in *Book Prices Current*, apparently because of the accompanying proofs, but the title-page of the book does not include his name, and we therefore assume that it was not his copy.

PROVENANCE: Thornton (Oxford) catalogue 276, November 1934, item 1308 (£45). — Nigel Sligh (purchased 1936). — Nigel Sligh's collection sold *en bloc* to Bayntun. — Bayntun (sold to Colin Franklin). — Colin Franklin (sold to J. Paul Getty, 1978). — J. Paul Getty. — Mark Getty (by inheritance).

NIGEL ARCHIBALD SLIGH (1905–1972), son of a publisher, matriculated at Worcester College in 1924 and, after reading Law, graduated in October 1927 with a Fourth Class degree. Though most of the Daniel Press books that Colin Franklin sold to Paul Getty came from Sligh's library, Franklin admitted that he knew nothing about him (and in fact misspelled his name) "except that he corresponded with Colonel Wilkinson of Worcester College who helped him in adding certain of the unobtainables." Beyond that, as Franklin said, the details are sketchy. Sligh took the bar exam in 1930 and later became a barrister; and in that year he also married Vivienne Burgoyne in London. He published several novels, mostly with African settings, between 1947 and 1955.

For J. PAUL GETTY and MARK GETTY, see Bridges copy [3.2].

REFERENCES: [SLIGH] "Forthcoming Marriages." *The Times*, 21 October 1930, p. 17. — Franklin, Colin. "Garlands of Rachel." *Book Collector* 30 (Winter, 1981): 479–490. — College information supplied by Joanna Parker. — Sligh's notes about his copy of the *Garland* are in the Getty collection.

A CENSUS

3.25 ❧ LIBRARY OF CONGRESS

Rare Book Division, Library of Congress, Washington, D.C.† [PR-1223 .G25 1881] ¶ Hartshorne copy.

Vellum binding. With preface (tipped in). Title-page: "By Divers Kindly Hands." Bookplates of EHC (or ECH?) and Robert Hartshorne.

RELATED MATERIAL: Small typed card laid in, with various typed notes: "Wormser"; "Parke-Bernet sale no. 701 113 | Bid $200 [*handwritten note:* 150] | DCM 10/18/45."

PROVENANCE: EHC (or ECH). — Robert Hartshorne. — Parke-Bernet (New York), 29 October 1945, no. 194 [*Press publications: Ashendene, Kelmscott, Daniel, Strawberry Hill and other famous presses; rare Americana, important maps, first editions. Selections from the library collected by the late Robert Hartshorne, of Highlands, New Jersey*] (sold for $150). — Richard S. Wormser (dealer, New York and Bethel, Conn.). — Library of Congress.

We have been unable to identify EHC/ECH.

ROBERT HARTSHORNE (1866–1927), who seems to have played a role similar to that of an English country squire of earlier centuries, was a descendant of an old family in Monmouth County, New Jersey. He was a graduate of Yale, belonged to the Grolier Club (1903–1927), and collected private press books—as well as western Americana and early voyages and travels. Madan described him in 1922 as one of the leading American collectors of the Daniel Press (*Addenda & Corrigenda*, p. 7).

REFERENCES: [HARTSHORNE] "Robert Hartshorne." *New York Times*, 15 January 1927, p. 15. (Death notice.) — Sheppard, John S. "The Late Robert Hartshorne" (letter). *New York Times*, 24 January 1927, p. 16. — Web sources.

3.26 ❧ JON A. LINDSETH (PRIVATE)

Jon A. Lindseth (private collection), Cleveland, Ohio.

Vellum binding. No preface. Title-page: "By Divers Kindly Hands." No marks of ownership.

DANIEL PRESS & GARLAND OF RACHEL

PROVENANCE: Maggs Brothers. — Jon A. Lindseth (purchased from Maggs, early 1990s).

JON A. LINDSETH (b. 1934), a graduate of Cornell and president of Kindt-Collins, a chemical and petrochemical company in Cleveland, collects mainly nineteenth-century books, with a strong emphasis on Lewis Carroll and fables. He is the editor of a study of *Alice in Wonderland* translations and is at work on a book-length account of his collection of Jewish fables. Lindseth is a member of the Grolier Club, which hosted an exhibition of his extensive Carroll collection in 1998. He was also co-curator of another Grolier exhibtion, "Alice in a World of Wonderlands: The Translations of Lewis Carroll's Masterpiece" (2015).

At one time he owned two copies of the *Garland*; he sold the other copy to the University of Melbourne (see below) through Sophie Schniedeman Rare Books in 2009.

REFERENCES: [LINDSETH] Lindseth, Jon, ed., with Alan Tannenbaum. *Alice in a World of Wonderlands: Translations of Lewis Carroll's Masterpiece*. 3 vols. New Castle, Del.: Oak Knoll Press, 2015. — *Yours Very Sincerely, C. L. Dodgson (Alias "Lewis Carroll"): An Exhibition from the Jon A. Lindseth Collection of C. L. Dodgson and Lewis Carroll, on View at the Grolier Club, April 1 through May 29, 1998*. New York: Grolier Club, 1998. — Web sources.

3.27 ℰ UNIVERSITY OF MELBOURNE

Special Collections, University Library, University of Melbourne. [UniM Bail SpC/PRIV] ¶ Lindseth copy.

Full russia binding (triple borders in gilt on both covers, spine in compartments, marbled endpapers); stamped "Bound by Morley. Oxford" inside the front cover. Title-page: "By Divers Kindly Hands."

PROVENANCE: Jon Lindseth. — Sophie Schniedeman Rare Books. — University of Melbourne (purchased from Schniedeman, February 2009).

For JON LINDSETH, see above.

REFERENCES: Information from Special Collections.

A CENSUS

3.28 ❧ NEW YORK UNIVERSITY

Fales Library, New York University, New York, N.Y.† [Berol Non-circulating PR1223 .G25 1881 copy 1] ¶ Henry Daniel–Armour–Berol copy.

Vellum binding (slight signs of wear). With preface (laid in). Title-page: "By Divers Kindly Hands." Signed "C. Henry Daniel | October 25. 1887." on front flyleaf.[1] Bookplate of George Allison Armour.

PROVENANCE: Henry Daniel. — George Allison Armour. — American Art Association, 22–23 April 1937, lot 235 [*Library of the late George Allison Armour*] (sold for $300). — Walter M. Hill (dealer, Chicago) catalogue 160, autumn, 1937, no. 20 ($450). — Walter M. Hill catalogue 168, 1940, no. 20 [*Catalogue of English literature of eighteenth and nineteenth century authors from the library of the late John A. Spoor and other recent purchases*] ($390). — Alfred C. Berol — New York University (gift from his widow, Mrs. Madeleine Rossin Berol, and son, Kenneth R. Berol, 1974).

For HENRY DANIEL, see Chapter 1.

GEORGE ALLISON ARMOUR (1855–1936), a wealthy Chicago philanthropist, moved in bookish circles. He was one of the founders of the Caxton Club and had broad collecting interests that included Shakespeare, the English romantics, and the Kelmscott and Doves presses. Through his friendship with Edmund Gosse, he became acquainted with Thomas J. Wise and bought some books from him (*Letters of Wise to Wrenn*, p. 11). He also carried on a correspondence with Henry Daniel, to whom he wrote on 17 January 1892 to thank him for the Daniel Press edition of Herrick (Madan no. 22): "When it is admired sufficiently—for the time—it will find a proper resting place in a case where fourteen other ex-

---

1. It is possible that this is an ownership signature by Henry Daniel, but it is more likely to be a signature by Daniel for Armour, who bought a number of books directly from the Daniel family.

amples of the 'Daniel Press' are gathered" (Worcester). Did those "fourteen other examples" then include *The Garland of Rachel*? If so, that would make Armour's copy the second one to reach America.

A few years later, on 27 February 1896, Armour wrote to Daniel, "My friend, Mr. [John Henry] Wrenn, of this town [Chicago], gives me much anxiety in imparting the information that there has been a new issue of the Daniel Press, a copy of which I have not got—a Keats. You know the joy it will give me to have one. I once relied on a Mr. Gee, in High Street—for these pleasures, but of late he has not been quite sure. Is it possible you have a copy left? and are you willing to part with it to me." He added that he was now living in Princeton, "the university town that comes nearest, in this country, to Oxford and where I hope to give you a welcome some day" (Worcester).

For ALFRED C. BEROL, see Dodgson copy, above [3.7].

REFERENCES: [ARMOUR] Dickinson. — "George Armour, Chicago Native, Dies in Jersey." *Chicago Daily Tribune*, 9 June 1936, p. 16. — Wise, Thomas J. *Letters of Thomas J. Wise to John Henry Wrenn: A Further Inquiry into the Guilt of Certain Nineteenth-Century Forgers*. Ed. Fannie E. Ratchford. New York: Knopf, 1944. — Correspondence (Worcester).

3.29 ⁊ NEWBERRY LIBRARY

Wing Collection, Newberry Library, Chicago, Ill.† [Wing ZP 845 .D212] ¶ Daniel family–Mosher–Sloan—Abel copy.

Red goatskin binding [*Pl. 8*] with elaborate gilt tooling by Leonard Mounteney (signed "MOUNTENEY, BINDER" on bottom edge of front turn-in). Blue silk endpapers. Extra leaves at end for tipped-in documents. No preface.[1] Title-page: "By Divers Kindly Hands." Marginal illuminations (of Oxford scenes) by Emily Daniel [*Pls. 4–5*].

---

1. As a letter from Williams & Norgate to Mosher, 10 May 1902, indicates, they supplied him separately with a proof of the preface, but it is no longer with Mosher's copy of the *Garland*. (The letter is in the Newberry Library, originally inserted in the Newberry copy of Mosher's reprint of the *Garland*.)

A CENSUS

A note, presumably by a bookseller (Hamill & Barker?), is written in pencil on the rear endpaper: "20(A) A3–37 | $350.00. | Daniel Press | One of 36 copies. | ALS with MS of Austin Dobson tipped in | Various other letters including several from Emily Daniel about the book and the illumination of the initials. | Thomas Mosher's copy."

This copy was used by Mosher for his reprint of the *Garland*. In a letter apparently to Mosher (see Sotheby Park-Bernet catalogue below, 10 May 1948), Emily Daniel wrote: "I am now at Messrs. Williams & Norgate's request sending a copy (the last we have) in sheets absolutely as it came from the press."

RELATED MATERIAL [*tipped in on a blank leaf following p. 16*]: Austin Dobson to Jeanette Gilder, 14 February 1881, with manuscript of Dobson's poem. ¶ [*tipped in on leaves following the printer's mark*, p. 68] Typescript poem entitled "To Rachel Taylor" by John P. Clark; Emily Daniel to T. B. Mosher, 28 December 1901 [**4.66**]; note by Emily Daniel, 20 February 1902 [**4.67**]; C. M. Falconer to Mosher, 1 March 1902 [**4.68**]; Emily Daniel to Mosher, 3 August 1902 [**4.71**]; Emily Daniel to Mosher, 30 November 1902 [**4.72**]; Rachel Daniel to Mosher, 30 November 1902 [**4.73**]; Williams & Norgate to Mosher, 30 December 1901; Emily Daniel to Mosher, 4 January 1903 [**4.74**]; Emily Daniel to Mosher, 21 February 1903 [**4.75**]; newspaper clipping from the *Dundee Advertiser*, 23 February 1898, about C. H. Falconer; Leonard Mounteney to Charles H. Sloan, 3 March 1949 [**4.81**]; Clement Shorter to Mosher, 9 April 1902 [**4.70**]; Jeanette L. Gilder to Mosher, 18 January 1902; Gilder to Mosher, 24 January 1902; Shorter to Mosher, 19 March 1902; Falconer to Mosher, 29 March 1902 [**4.69**].

PROVENANCE: Daniel family. — Williams & Norgate (dealer, Oxford). — Thomas B. Mosher (purchased in sheets from Williams & Norgate, March 1902). — Sotheby Parke-Bernet (New York), 10 May 1948, lot 80 [*Library of the late Thomas Bird Mosher, Portland, Maine*] (sold in sheets for $80).[1] — Charles H. Sloan.

---

1. Philip Bishop reports that in his three marked copies of the catalogue the word "order" appears next to this lot, suggesting that the book was purchased by phone bid or an advance order.

DANIEL PRESS & GARLAND OF RACHEL

— Allison Abel (by inheritance) — Hamill & Barker (dealer, Chicago). — Newberry Library (purchased from Hamill & Barker, November 1961).

THOMAS BIRD MOSHER (1852–1953), born into a seafaring family in Maine, established himself as a publisher in Portland, specializing in elegant, unauthorized reprints of English literary works. His editions were unquestionably pirated, issued without the consent of their authors, yet he often attempted to establish a friendly relationship with them and sent occasional voluntary royalties across the Atlantic. In the 1890s he developed a particular interest in the Daniel Press and began issuing reprints of several of its titles, including *The Garland of Rachel* (1902).

His *Garland* was a characteristic Mosher production: it was issued in an edition of 450 copies, printed on Van Gelder handmade paper and bound in Japan vellum boards, with silk ties and a slip case. In addition to the text of the Daniel Press edition, Mosher supplied a later poem by T. H. Warren entitled "Hesperides" (about Rachel and Ruth Daniel), Henry Daniel's preface, an excerpt from an article by Henry R. Plomer, and a checklist of Daniel Press publications based on the collection of Henry W. Poor. Mosher also contributed a lengthy preface in which he described, in occasionally amusing detail, the difficulties he experienced in trying to locate a copy of the *Garland* in order to reprint it. With the help of C. M. Falconer and Clement Shorter, he eventually learned that Emily Daniel still had one copy of the book in unbound sheets (some of them used by Henry Daniel as proofs), which she sold to him though the bookselling firm of Williams & Norgate.

Mosher did his best to maintain a cordial connection with the Daniel family. There is some evidence suggesting that he may have called upon the Daniels in Oxford in April 1901; he corresponded with Emily, Ruth, and Rachel over a number of years; and he sent large bundles of complimentary copies of his books to them. But the Daniels, like many of their contemporaries, were baffled by Mosher's behavior and alternated between elaborate courtesy and barely concealed hostility in their comments to and about him. When Falconer Madan sent Emily Daniel the proofs of his bibliography in 1921, she offered this sharp summary of the family's attitude toward Mosher: "I see you say referring to American Garland of Rachel on Page *32*. 'The book was printed with Mr Daniel's consent in the United States'. I don't think Henry could have given leave for its publication in America[—]the poems were written for his private printing— I am not certain of this, but I remember this—he was asked [by] the publishers to bring out an Edition of Our Memories, but he would not hear of it as he said they were for his private printing—& I should imagine referred also to the Garland of Rachel— I thought it worth while to mention this. The Pirated Edition [by Mosher] of Bridges Growth of Love was certainly not given leave for nor the 'Child in the House' [by Pater]— I believe you have my copy of Bridges' 'Growth of Love' (pirated copy) it has his name in it—but he [Bridges] gave me the copy as he was so annoyed at it being pirated."[1]

Madan himself was torn between contempt for Mosher's piracies and admiration for their fascinating introductions. As a bibliographer, he found the elaborate textual apparatus of Mosher's *Garland* irresistible; in a private letter he confessed that "I am not fond of old Moshwig and his odious ways, but he does make his editions *interesting*" (Madan, *C. H. O. Daniel vs. Thomas B. Mosher*).

CHARLES H. SLOAN (1865–1958), son of a Kentucky miner, dropped out of school after the eighth grade and spent most of his early years in Ironton, Ohio, where he worked in the wholesale and retail leather business and operated a bicycle shop. By the 1920s he had become a serious book-collector, especially of modern British and American private presses, and during that decade he moved to Columbus. His name appears occasionally in directories of American booksellers, but his business must have been very modest and was carried on in his home in Columbus. Nevertheless, he acquired a notable collection of books, many of which were rebound by Leonard Mounteney in Chicago. He was almost entirely unknown in the bibliophilic world, and his local reputation was that of an

---

1. Emily Daniel to Madan, 3 June 1921 (JJC 2).

eccentric old man who rode his bicycle through the streets of Columbus every day.

When Sloan died at the age of 93, he had no living relatives, and his sole legatee was his housemate, ALLISON A. ABEL (1893–1982), a retired junior high school teacher. As Sloan declared in his will, "All my property, real or personal or stocks, I give and bequeath to Allison A. Abel, who has been as a son to me, making my life as pleasant as possible for me, taking all responsibilities from me, so I want him to have all I leave, for his pleasure and profit." Abel therefore inherited Sloan's books and must have sold the *Garland* (perhaps to Hamill & Barker?) within a few years.

We strongly suspect that the poem by JOHN P. CLARK addressed to RACHEL TAYLOR (neither of whom we have been able to identify) is only tangentially connected with this copy of the *Garland*. The poem is a typescript carbon copy, with Clark's signature at the bottom in ink. The most likely explanation is that the book that Clark was presenting to this Rachel was Mosher's edition of the *Garland*; he probably sent the typescript poem to Rachel herself and a carbon copy to Mosher; and Mosher, admiring the sentimental gesture, may have kept the copy of the poem with his unbound sheets of the Daniel Press *Garland*. That at least is the most plausible theory we can offer about John Clark and Rachel Taylor; we have been unable to find any evidence that either of them owned the Daniel Press edition of the *Garland*.

REFERENCES: [ABEL] Census reports. — Social Security Death Index. ¶ [MOSHER] Bishop, Philip R. *Thomas Bird Mosher: Pirate Prince of Publishers*. New Castle, Del.: Oak Knoll Press; London: British Library, 1998. — *The Garland of Rachel*. Portland, Maine: T. B. Mosher, 1902. — Hatch, Benton L., ed. *A Check List of the Publications of Thomas Bird Mosher of Portland Maine* MDCCCXCI MDCCCCXXIII. Amherst, Mass.: Printed at the Gehenna Press for the University of Massachusetts Press, 1966. (See no. 225.) — Madan, Falconer. *C. H. O. Daniel vs. Thomas B. Mosher: A Letter from F. Madan to R. W. Rogers*. San Francisco: Roxburghe Club, 1983. — Nowell-Smith, Simon. "Mosher and Bridges." *Book Collector* 11 (Winter, 1962): 482–83. — Stevens, Edward F. *Thomas Bird Mosher of Portland, Maine*. Portland, Me.: Southworth-Anthoesen Press, 1941. — Strouse, Norman H. *The Passionate Pirate*. North Hills, Penn.: Bird & Bull Press, 1964. — Correspondence/papers (Harvard, Newberry, NYU,

A CENSUS

Worcester). — Information from Philip R. Bishop. ¶ [SLOAN] "Deaths and Funerals: Charles H. Sloan." *Ironton Tribune*, 8 April 1958, p. 12. — "Deaths and Funerals: Sloan." *Columbus Evening Dispatch*, 4 April 1958, p. 4A. — Census reports. — Will (supplied by Franklin County Probate Court, Columbus, Ohio).

3.30 ❧ PRINCETON UNIVERSITY

Parrish Collection, Princeton University Library, Princeton, N.J.†
[Dodgson 654] ¶ Bement–Parrish copy.

Bound in olive green morocco, signed "E. D." [i.e. Emily Daniel] on inside back cover; covers and spine tooled in gold (laurel wreaths on front and back, leaf ornaments and lettering on spine), top edge gilt. Untrimmed. No preface. Title-page: "By Diverse Kindly Hands." Bookplates of Clarence S. Bement and Morris Parrish. Penciled note on front pastedown: "Rachel Daniel's own copy bound by her mother." There is nothing resembling Emily Daniel's usual miniation; most of the initials are hand-lettered in standard roman and (occasionally) Lombardic letterforms, either dark purple or black; two are in red. There are no tendrils in the margins.

It is unclear who made the claim that this was Rachel Daniel's own copy; we suspect that the note is by a bookseller (perhaps Rosenbach?).[1] In any case, there is neither documentary evidence nor marks of ownership within the book itself to support the claim, and it should also be kept in mind that a solid family tradition identifies one of the copies now owned by Penny Tuerk as Rachel's copy [3.33]. We have therefore not listed this as the Rachel Daniel copy. The rather experimental, unfinished initials suggest that this copy, then unbound, was used by Emily Daniel in practicing her miniation shortly before publication in 1881, and then at about the turn of the century she turned to it again when she began her bookbinding.

---

1. But there is no reference to Rachel Daniel's alleged ownership in the Rosenbach catalogue (see PROVENANCE). Another plausible theory is that the penciled remark about Rachel Daniel may be in the handwriting of Bement; directly below, also in pencil, is a four-character formula that is perhaps a private shelf-mark (Bement's?).

DANIEL PRESS & GARLAND OF RACHEL

PROVENANCE: Rosenbach catalogue 17 (Philadelphia), November 1913, no. 154 [*Catalogue of rare and important books and manuscripts in English literature*] ($165). — Clarence S. Bement. — American Art Association (New York), 28 February 1923, lot 392 [*Private library of the late Clarence S. Bement*] (sold for $77.50). — Morris L. Parrish. — Princeton University Library (bequest from Parrish, 1944).

CLARENCE S. BEMENT (1843–1923) joined his family's Philadelphia machine tool company as a young man and eventually became its president, but he also had a broad range of collecting interests: coins, medals, stamps, minerals (these later acquired by J. P. Morgan for the American Museum of Natural History), and books. His library, mainly purchased from Rosenbach, displayed a heavy emphasis on illuminated manuscripts, prayer books, large paper editions, and prints; a substantial portion of it went to the Widener Library at Harvard.

MORRIS L. PARRISH (1867–1944), a member of the Philadelphia Stock Exchange, was one of the leading American book collectors of the twentieth century, with a library focused mainly on Victorian novelists. He was not particularly drawn to poetry, but he was willing to make exceptions—such as this copy of the *Garland*—when they were connected with his other great passion, Lewis Carroll. Unlike some collectors, Parrish generally did not pursue association copies or manuscripts; instead, the hallmarks of his library were superb condition ("Parrish condition" became a byword in the book trade during his lifetime) and completeness. He left his collection to his alma mater, where it is now the centerpiece of Princeton's Special Collections.[1]

---

1. Earlier, in the 1920s, there had been an unsuccessful attempt to donate his Carroll collection to Christ Church, Oxford. (See Imholtz.)

A CENSUS

EXHIBITION: Avery Library, Columbia University, April 1932 [*Catalogue of an Exhibition to Commemorate the One Hundredth Anniversary of the Birth of Lewis Carroll* (New York: Columbia University Press, 1932), no. 280].

REFERENCES: [BEMENT] Comparette, T. L. *A Descriptive Catalogue of Greek Coins, Selected from the Cabinet of Clarence S. Bement, Esq., Philadelphia*. New York: American Numismatic Society, 1921. — Dickinson. — Leach, Joseph G. *Chronicles of the Bement Family in America for Clarence Sweet Bement*. [N.p., 1928?] — McCall, G. J. H., A. J. Bowden, and R. J. Howarth, eds. *The History of Meteoritics and Key Meteorite Collections: Fireballs, Falls and Finds*. Bath: Geological Society, 2006. (See Denton S. Ebel, "History of the American Museum of Natural History Meteorite Collection," pp. 267–89.) — Peters, Joseph J., and Charles L. Peterson. "Clarence S. Bement, the Consummate Collector." *Mineralogical Record* 21 (January–February 1990): 47–62. R[osenbach], A. S. W. "Bement, Clarence Sweet," in *DAB*. ¶ [PARRISH] Dickinson. — Imholtz, August, Jr. "Parrish the Thought: Alice's Misadventures at Christ Church, Oxford." *Princeton University Library Chronicle* 72 (Spring, 2011): 752–60. — *A List of the Writings of Lewis Carroll (Charles L. Dodgson) in the Library at Dormy House, Pine Valley, New Jersey, Collected by M. L. Parrish*. [New York]: privately printed, 1928. — "Morris L. Parrish. Member of Philadelphia Stock Exchange a Book Collector." *New York Times*, 11 July 1944, p. 15. (Obituary.) — Parrish, Morris L. "Adventures in Reading and Collecting Victorian Authors." *Princeton University Library Chronicle* 3 (February 1942): 33–34. — Randall, David. "The Adventures of Two Bibliophiles." *New York Times Book Review*, 6 August 1944, pp. 14, 16. — Wainwright, Alexander D. "The Morris L. Parrish Collection of Victorian Novels." *Princeton University Library Chronicle* 62 (Spring, 2001): 361–75. — Wainwright, Alexander D. "Morris Longstreth Parrish," in *Grolier 75*. (See pp. 160–63.) — Weaver, Warren. "The Parrish Collection of Carrolliana." *Princeton University Library Chronicle* 17 (Winter, 1956): 85–91. — Wilson, Carroll A. "Morris L. Parrish: Trollope Collector." *Trollopian* 1 (Summer, 1945): 5–10. — A special issue of the *Princeton University Library Chronicle*—vol. 8, no. 1 (November 1946)—is devoted to Parrish and his collection.

3.31 ❦ MARK SAMUELS LASNER (PRIVATE)

Mark Samuels Lasner Collection (private), on loan to University of Delaware Library, Newark, Del.† ¶ Symonds–Samuels Lasner copy.

DANIEL PRESS & GARLAND OF RACHEL

Dark green morocco binding signed "Morley. Oxford." Elaborate gilt tooling front and back; gilt tooling and lettering on spine. With preface (laid in). Title-page: "By John Addington Symonds and Divers Kindly Hands." "$3,00.00" written in pencil of rear flyleaf. In a green morocco slipcase with gilt lettering on spine.

Despite the title-page, we have not listed this as John Addington Symonds's copy, since the letter cited below makes it clear that it was never owned by Symonds and was instead a gift from the Daniels to Symonds's cousin Horatio on the occasion of his marriage. For J. A. Symonds's copy, see [**3.15**].

RELATED MATERIAL (originally laid in): Emily Daniel to Horatio Symonds, 9 December 1892 [**4.47**].

PROVENANCE: Horatio Symonds (gift from the Daniels, 1892). — Blackwell. — Mark Samuels Lasner (purchased for £3,000 from Blackwell, 28 September 1988).

HORATIO PERCY SYMONDS (1850–1923), a lifelong resident of Oxford, was John Addington Symonds' cousin. Like his father Frederick (and several generations before him), he was a medical figure of considerable local reputation and in 1878 was elected surgeon of the Radcliffe Infirmary as the successor to Frederick Symonds. It was probably in that capacity that he came to know the Daniels, who, through the years, gave much moral and financial support to the institution very near Worcester College. Emily Daniel's letter to Symonds [**4.47**] also implies that he had treated Rachel during an illness. Symonds in 1892 married Marion Robinson Leckie, and after the death of his daughter Annie, the Horatio Symonds Studentship in Surgery was created at Oxford in 1938.

MARK SAMUELS LASNER (b. 1952), collector, bibliographer, and typographer, has formed a major private collection of books, manuscripts, and artworks by British cultural figures who flourished between 1850 and 1900. The Mark Samuels Lasner Collection, currently on loan to the University of Delaware Library, focuses on the Pre-Raphaelites and the writers and artists of the 1890s and includes other materials related to the Daniel Press. Samuels Lasner is the author of a number of books and exhibition catalogues (some in collaboration with Margaret D. Stetz) and is active in many bibliophilic and bibliographical organizations.

A CENSUS

REFERENCES: [SAMUELS LASNER] Samuels Lasner, Mark. *A Period Library: A Short-Title Catalogue of the Collection of Victorian Literature formed by Mark Samuels Lasner*. Washington, D.C.: privately printed, 1993. (See p. 50.) — Information from the collector. ¶ [SYMONDS] "Marriage of Mr. Horatio Symonds." *Reading Mercury*, 24 December 1892, p. 6. — "Mr. Horatio Symonds." *Spectator*, 27 January 1923, p. 13. (Obituary.) — "Radcliffe Infirmary: Election of a Surgeon." *Oxford Journal*, 8 June 1878, p. 6. — Symonds, John Addington. *On the English Family of Symonds*. Oxford: privately printed, 1894. — "University News." *The Times*, 22 June 1938, p. 10. — See also the REFERENCES under JOHN ADDINGTON SYMONDS [**2.15**].

3.32 ❧ UNIVERSITY OF SOUTH CAROLINA

Ewelm Collection, University of South Carolina Library. ¶ Parsons–Nowell-Smith copy.

Vellum binding. With preface (laid in). Title-page: "By Divers Kindly Hands." Bookplates of Alfred Parsons and Simon Nowell-Smith.

RELATED MATERIAL: Undated descriptive note by Simon Nowell-Smith.

PROVENANCE: Alfred Parsons. — Simon Nowell-Smith. — University of South Carolina (purchased as part of Nowell-Smith's Ewelme Collection in 1966).

ALFRED PARSONS, R.A. (1847–1920), a landscape painter and garden designer who spent his childhood in Frome, married Emily Daniel's sister-in-law and was closely connected with the Daniel family throughout their Oxford years. Parsons and his friend Edwin Austin Abbey, an American painter, were also associated with a group of painters and writers known as the "Broadway Group," which had strong ties with William Morris and the arts and crafts movement.

Parsons provided two ornaments for the *Garland* [*Pls. 4–5*] as well as the printer's device (all of which were also used in subsequent Daniel Press books). Emily Daniel explained in a letter to

Madan that "the figure of Daniel in the Printer's mark is drawn by E. A. Abbey R.S. Alfred Parsons drew everything but the figure."[1]

SIMON NOWELL-SMITH (1909–1996) was educated at Sherborne School—where his father was headmaster—and New College, Oxford. During the nineteen-thirties he supervised the back page of the *Times Literary Supplement* (i.e. its bibliographical section) and after the War became librarian of the London Library. But throughout his life he devoted most of his energy to building up a major collection of English literature of the nineteenth and early twentieth centuries, with emphasis on association copies. He had a particular interest in Robert Bridges, and this copy of the *Garland* was part of his Ewelme Collection—centered around the books and manuscripts of Bridges—named after the Oxfordshire village in which Nowell-Smith and his wife lived for many years. He was a frequent contributor to bibliophilic journals.

REFERENCES: [NOWELL-SMITH] Barker, Nicolas. "Simon Nowell-Smith: A Bibliophile with Wit and Generosity." *Guardian*, 5 April 1996, p. 17. (Obituary.) — Bell, Alan. "Smith, Simon Harcourt Nowell-," *ODNB*. — Fredeman, William E. "Two Uncollected Bibliographers: Simon Harcourt Nowell-Smith and Michael Trevanion of Erewhon." *Book Collector* 38 (Winter, 1989): 465–82. — Kable, William S., comp. *The Ewelme Collection of Robert Bridges: A Catalogue*. (Department of English Bibliographical Series, no. 2.) [Columbia, S.C.]: University of South Carolina, 1967. (See p. 27.) — Nowell-Smith, Simon. "Contemporary Collectors LXI: The Ewelme Collection." *Book Collector* 14 (1965): 185–93. — Preston, Claire. "Obituary: Simon Nowell-Smith." *The Independent*, 29 March 1966. — WWW. ¶ [PARSONS] Borenius, Tancred. "Parsons, Alfred William," in *ODNB*. — "Death of Mr. Parsons, R.A. Painter of Flowers and Gardens." *The Times*, 21 January 1920, p. 15. — WWW.

3.33 ❧ PENNY TUERK (PRIVATE) [1]

Penny Tuerk (private collection), England.† ¶ Daniel family copy.
Vellum binding. No preface. Title-page: "By H. D. and Divers Kindly Hands."
Slip of paper laid in, with this note in Henry Daniel's hand: "To

---

1. Emily Daniel to Falconer Madan, 31 May 1921 (JJC 2).

16 *Rachel Daniel Lee.*

PERFORMANCES OF
Alice's Adventures in Wonderland,
&
Through the Looking-glaſs
WILL BE GIVEN IN
THE GARDEN OF WORCESTER HOVSE
(ADJOINING WORCESTER COLLEGE)
ON THVRSDAY & SATVRDAY
June 13 & 15
at 3 and 8.30.
IN AID OF A LOCAL CHARITY.

THE FOLLOWING HAVE KINDLY CONSENTED TO TAKE PART:

MRS HVNTINGFORD	MR RVBENS
MISS FLETCHER	MR BRVCE
MISS ROWDEN	VISCOUNT SVIRDALE
MISS FARMER	MR COTTON
MISS PLAYFAIR	MR TAYLER
MISS P. FLETCHER	MR NEWMAN
MISS RVTH DANIEL	MR TALBOT PONSONBY
&	MR HOLLAND
MISS RACHEL DANIEL	MR PRYOR &
	MR NIGEL PLAYFAIR

The Management of the Play is under the direction of
MRS DOWSON

The Muſic ſpecially compoſed by MR RVBENS

Voluntary Donations—5/ 3/ & 1/ reſpectively according to place occupied—will be collected at each performance. Children's Donation (afternoon only) will be 2/6 & 1/6. Seats reſerved on application to *Mrs Daniel* or to any of the above.

17 *Rachel Daniel played the lead role in this performance (1894), and her sister Ruth was the Dormouse.*

A CENSUS

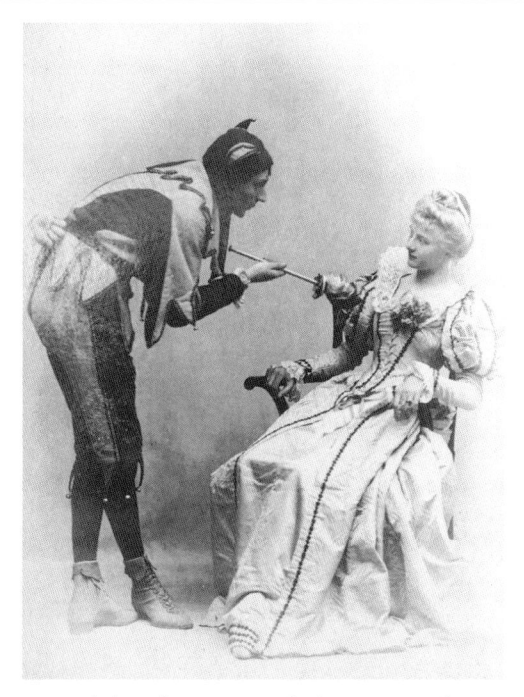

18 *Rachel as Olivia in an Oxford amateur production of* TWELFTH NIGHT, *February 1900.*

Rachel | setting out on her way through the world. | With the blessing and love of her father & mother. | Sept 27, 1901."

PROVENANCE: Henry and Emily Daniel. — Rachel Daniel (gift from her parents, 1901). — Ruth Joanna (Lee) Kirkman (by inheritance from her mother, 1937). — Penny Tuerk (by inheritance from her mother, 1986).

Since the paper slip is only loosely inserted, there is no irrefutable evidence that it has always been associated with this book, but Penny Tuerk describes a very strong tradition in the family that this copy of the *Garland* was given to Rachel by her parents on her twenty-first birthday.

For HENRY DANIEL, see Chapter 1; for EMILY DANIEL, see Chapter 1.

DANIEL PRESS & GARLAND OF RACHEL

RACHEL DANIEL (1880–1937) [*Fig. 16*], daughter of Henry and Emily, was an exceptionally attractive child with very light blond hair, and she and her sister Ruth (see below) seem to have enjoyed an idyllic childhood in Worcester House, where they shared a small sitting-room decorated with lively Morris wallpaper. Inevitably she attracted the attention of Lewis Carroll, who became a regular caller in the household, though on the one occasion that he tried to draw her, he found Rachel "too restless a subject" (*Diaries*, 2:418). Like her mother, she had strongly aesthetic impulses: Rachel drew and painted, occasionally participated in the family printing activities,[1] and, by the time she reached adolescence, became intensely involved in Oxford amateur theatricals [*Fig. 18*]. In June 1895 she played the role of Alice in a dramatized version of *Alice in Wonderland* and *Through the Looking-Glass* that was performed, as a fund-raiser for local schools, in the Worcester House garden [*Fig. 17*]. Contemporary accounts all agree that Rachel, with her long, rippling hair, made a convincing Alice, while Ruth was equally successful as the Dormouse.

Rachel appeared in a number of other plays, including a production of *Twelfth Night* sponsored by OUDS (the Oxford University Dramatic Society), the president of which was Reginald Lee, her future husband. Even *The Times* in London took notice of her performance: "Miss Rachel Daniel... played Olivia with grace and refinement, and was natural alike in her expression of passion and in repose. Her elocution was peculiarly clear, and her acting... left little need for her to plead the privileges of an amateur."

In June 1907 she married Reginald Lee (1878–1940), who was by then a military officer; the reception was at her parents' home, the Provost's Lodge, and one of her wedding gifts was an edition of Matthew Arnold's poems bound by Katharine Adams (*Bookbinding in the British Isles*, no. 293). In contrast with her quiet childhood, Rachel now found herself (in 1909) being presented at court and following Reginald Lee to various postings, including Ireland and India. Though she moved around a great deal through-

---

1. See David Chambers, "*The Lamb* Printed by Rachel Daniel, 1889," cited below.

out her marriage, Rachel continued to be involved in nonprofessional theatrical productions and, during these years, gave birth to two children, Joanna (1911–1986) and Veronica (1920–2006). There were also frequent visits to her mother and sister at Oxford.

Rachel Daniel Lee died of cancer at Odiham, Hampshire, in October 1937. Her family felt the loss very keenly, and for four years after her death this memorial appeared annually in *The Times*: "LEE.—In loving memory of Rachel Lee, wife of Reginald Tilson Lee. Oct. 1, 1937."

RUTH JOANNA KIRKMAN, *née* LEE (1911–1986) [*Fig. 19*], the elder daughter of Rachel Daniel and Reginald Lee, was born in the Provost's Lodge at Worcester College and always regarded Oxford as her home, though her father's military career meant that she had a peripatetic childhood. In 1937 the family was devastated by Rachel's sudden death at the age of 56. Rachel's will left her copy of *The Garland of Rachel* and various documents and books associated with the Daniel Press to Jo (as she was known in the family), many of which were subsequently donated to Worcester College. Jo Kirkman had inherited her parents' love of the theater and appeared in one of the earliest television dramas, but in 1940, following her father's death, she abandoned her acting career, moved to Cambridge with her younger sister Veronica (1920–2006), married Sidney Kirkman in 1946, and spent the rest of her life in Cambridge, though she maintained close ties with her aunt, Ruth Daniel, who had continued living in Oxford. On Ruth's death, Jo Kirkman inherited a second copy of the *Garland*, which she believed had once belonged to Emily Daniel (see below).

19 *Rachel Daniel Lee and her daughter Joanna.*

PENNY TUERK, *née* KIRKMAN (b. 1947), is the only child of

Rachel's elder daughter Ruth Joanna (Jo) and Sidney Kirkman. She was born and brought up in Cambridge and read history at the University of York. She joined the British Broadcasting Corporation on a graduate training scheme in 1968 and worked in the BBC World Service for more than 30 years, retiring as the head of the world-wide English language radio network. She is married to Laurence Tuerk. Like her mother and grandmother, Penny Tuerk is an enthusiast for the theater and is currently chair of the trustees of The Tower Theatre Company, one of Britain's busiest "little theaters." On her mother's death, she inherited all of Jo Kirkman's Daniel Press material, but only recently has she begun studying it in detail. Penny Tuerk regrets never having known her maternal grandmother, although she was close to Rachel's younger sister Ruth.

REFERENCES: Information from Penny Tuerk. ¶ [RACHEL DANIEL] *Bookbinding in the British Isles: Sixteenth to the Twentieth Century* (Maggs Brothers catalogue 1212, 1966). — Chambers, David. "*The Lamb* Printed by Rachel Daniel, 1889." *Private Library* 5 (1992): 99–102. — Dodgson, C. L. *The Diaries of Lewis Carroll*. Ed. Roger Lancelyn Green. 2 vols. New York: Oxford University Press, 1954. — "His Majesty's Court." *The Times*, 5 March 1909, p. 13. — Lovett, Charles C. *Alice on Stage: A History of the Early Theatrical Productions of Alice in Wonderland*. Westport, Conn., and London: Meckler, 1990. — Mackinnon, Alan M. *The Oxford Amateurs: A Short History of Theatricals at the University*. London: Chapman & Hall, 1910. — "'Twelfth Night' at Oxford." *The Times*, 22 February 1900, p. 6. — *Who Was Who* (for Reginald Lee). ¶ [KIRKMAN] "Marriages." *The Times*, 8 July 1946, p. 1. — Web sources.

3.34 ❧ PENNY TUERK (PRIVATE) [2]

Penny Tuerk (private collection), England.† ¶ Daniel family copy.
Vellum binding but with a different pattern of tooling on the front and back covers, lettering on the spine, and plain endpapers. Binding signed by Morley, Oxford. No preface. Title-page: "By Divers Kindly Hands."
PROVENANCE: Daniel family. — Ruth Daniel (by inheritance from her mother). — Ruth Joanna (Lee) Kirkman (by inheritance

A CENSUS

20 *Ruth Daniel at her sister's wedding in 1907.*

from her aunt). — Penny (Kirkman) Tuerk (by inheritance from her mother).

RUTH DANIEL (1883–1961) [*Fig. 20*], the Daniels' younger daughter, was overshadowed much of her life by her more glamorous sister Rachel, but Ruth was the one who stayed close to home and helped to preserve the legacy of the Daniel Press, and to many of her contemporaries she seemed to embody the Daniel family's qualities of culture and generosity. T. H. Warren, in 1895, tried to capture the magic of the Daniels by writing a poem about "Mistress Rachel, Mistress Ruth, | Dancing down the ways of youth | by the dancing rills of truth." However, the serenity of her early years was interrupted by an engagement to Compton MacKenzie, then an Oxford undergraduate, which came to an abrupt end in 1904 when Ruth and her mother suddenly decamped to Paris, and Ruth sent him back his ring. Mackenzie was so furious that he burned Ruth's hundreds of letters addressed to him and threw the ring into a pool. The cause of the breakup was apparently Ruth's growing religious seriousness.

Ruth had a reputation for charming eccentricity (she annoyed the usually patient Madan by asking him to store her collection of Daniel Press books at the Bodleian every summer while she was out of town), and she also displayed some of the same literary impulses seen in her parents. Between 1902 and 1904 she published and edited an amusing little Oxford periodical entitled *Sheaf: A (Perhaps) Quarterly Magazine* that included contributions from some of the old Daniel Press authors such as Robert Bridges and F. W. Bourdillon; a few years earlier she had also created a similar magazine called *The Scarlet Runner*.

After her father's death she shared a house on Iffley Road, Oxford, with her mother ("The peace of your house is very great," John Betjeman wrote after a visit in 1947[1]), lovingly preserved the books and papers of the Daniel Press, and was active in the nearby Church of St. John the Evangelist—a very high Anglican parish church that her father would have approved of but not her grandfather.

For RUTH KIRKMAN, and PENNY TUERK, see above.

REFERENCES: [RUTH DANIEL] "Deaths." *The Times*, 17 April 1961, p. 1. — Linklater, Andro. *Compton Mackenzie: A Life*. London: Chatto & Windus, 1987. — Mackenzie, Sir Compton. *My Life and Times*. 10 vols. London: Chatto & Windus, 1963–71. (See vol. 3.) — Masterman, J. C. *On the Chariot Wheel: An Autobiography*. London and New York: Oxford University Press, 1975. (See pp. 48–49.) — Correspondence (JJC 2, Houghton Library [T. B. Mosher papers], Worcester). — Information from Penny Tuerk.

3.35 ❧ WORCESTER COLLEGE

Worcester College, Oxford University, Oxford, England.† [Yc. 4. 47] ¶ Madan copy.

Vellum binding. Ownership stamp of F. Madan, Brasenose College, Oxford, with annotation: "£3/- bought Sept. 12 1882." With preface (tipped in). Title-page: "By Divers Kindly Hands."

The following note (in ink) appears on a blank leaf of the preface: "The poems in the ensuing volume are signed by their authors,

---

1. Betjeman to Ruth Daniel, 23 December 1947 (Worcester).

except (p. 9) the first, which is by the Printer. | p. 11. 'W.' is the Rev. Albert Watson | p. 31 'Lewis Carroll' is the Rev. Charles Lutwidge Dodgson. | p. 67. 'C. J. C.' is C. J. Cruttwell, uncle of the Printer. | F. Madan | June 1898."

PROVENANCE: Falconer Madan (purchased for £3, 12 September 1882). — Worcester College (gift from Madan, between 1932 [see first exhibition catalogue below] and 1935).[1]

FALCONER MADAN (1851–1935), a Fellow of Brasenose College, was Sub-Librarian of the Bodleian for more than thirty years (1880–1912) and Librarian for seven years (1912–1919). At Brasenose he knew Humphry Ward, Walter Pater, and Albert Watson, all of whom had ties with Henry Daniel, and by the 1880s Madan—always fascinated by Oxford printing past and present—had begun collecting every scrap produced at the Daniel Press; in fact, he insisted that he personally owned each item described in his later bibliography and claimed, accurately, that no other Daniel Press collection in the world equalled his. The note in his copy of the *Garland* shows that he purchased it in September 1882, perhaps directly from the Daniels or from the Oxford bookseller Gee.

During that decade he became a confidant of both Daniels, but especially Emily, who consulted him frequently about bookish matters and regarded him as a close family friend. In this way, Madan made himself the gatekeeper of the Daniel Press, and throughout his lifetime it was impossible, in either England or America, to assemble a solid collection of the Press's imprints without advice, encouragement, and inside information from Madan. He traded and gave duplicates from his own collection to favored bibliophiles (especially Andreini in New York), kept an extremely close watch on everything issued by the Daniel Press, and in 1904 published anonymously in the *Times Literary Supplement* an ex-

---

1. Most of Madan's other Daniel Press books were given by his son Francis to the Bodleian in 1940.

haustive list of all the Press's titles. (This was then privately printed by Andreini in book form and thus became the definitive record of the Daniel Press until Madan's even more comprehensive bibliography appeared seventeen years later.) In a characteristic letter to Emily Daniel in 1911, he wrote that "I still hope that some day if the Press ever thinks of really ceasing (long distant may the day be!), I shall be allowed to print a full and proper Bibliography of the Frome Press and it [i.e. the Daniel Press in Oxford].

"So pray never throw away any proofs or fragments of Daniel Printing—they may fit, in some unforeseen way, into the history of it all."[1]

When Henry Daniel died in 1919, Madan intervened and took over the cataloguing of Daniel's library for auction, and about this time he also began to put the finishing touches on the ambitious Daniel Press bibliography that he had been preparing for many years. C. H. Wilkinson (a Daniel Press collector himself, though on a more modest scale),[2] Daniel's younger colleague at Worcester, was making arrangements for what he envisioned as a volume of tributes to the Provost—a Garland of H.D., in effect—but Madan's bibliography, initially intended to be a sort of appendix, simply swamped the volume by the time it was published in 1921. It was awkwardly entitled *The Daniel Press: Memorials of C. H. O. Daniel with a Bibliography of the Press, 1845–1919*, but despite the emphasis of the title-page, the tributes from friends became merely a brief prelude to the very substantial bibliography.

Except for one serious blunder about the identity of Daniel's second press, Madan's scholarship was meticulous and beyond reproach, and in 1922 and 1923 he published two small lists of addenda and corrigenda. He was rather humorlessly boastful about his own high standards as a bibliographer and was dismissive of ri-

---

1. Madan to Emily Daniel, 1 April 1911 (Worcester).
2. For two accounts of Wilkinson's collecting interests, see C. H. Wilkinson, "Contemporary Collectors IX: A Small Collection at Oxford," *Book Collector* (Summer, 1956): 127–36; and Richard Sayce, "Another Oxford Bibliophile: C. H. Wilkinson (1888–1960)," in *The Warden's Meeting: A Tribute to John Sparrow*, ed. Anthony Davis (Oxford: Oxford University Society of Bibliophiles, 1977), pp. 86–89.

A CENSUS

val claims by other collectors. When Edmund Gosse announced to him in 1893 that "almost everything Daniel ever printed is here [i.e. in Gosse's home]," Madan wrote in the margin of the letter, "Stuff! The conceit of a collector" and proceeded to list on a blank leaf all the titles that Gosse lacked.[1] And on a clipping of one review of his bibliography he scrawled a contemptuous response: "Not one word of original criticism or new idea anywhere."[2] To Constance Astley he complained that "not one of my reviewers, not even C. T. Jacobi, has noted any one of the really distinctive features of the book" and proceeded to enumerate the ways in which he thought it was superior to any other descriptive bibliography that had ever been published [4.78].

EXHIBITIONS: *Lewis Carroll Centenary Exhibition, London: 29 June–31 July, 1932* (London: Bumpus, 1932), p. 26 (with Madan described as owner). — *The Typographical Adventure of William Morris: An Exhibition Arranged by the William Morris Society 1958* [London: William Morris Society, 1958], no. 29.

REFERENCES: [MADAN] C[ooke], G. A. "Falconer Madan." *Bodleian Quarterly Record* 8, no. 86 (2nd quarter, 1935): 73-74. — *The Daniel Press: Memorials of C. H. O. Daniel, with a Bibliography* [by Madan] *of the Press, 1845-1919.* Oxford: Printed on the Daniel Press in the Bodleian Library, 1921. — [Gibson, Strickland]. "Bodley's Librarian, Emeritus." *Papers of the Bibliographical Society of America* 13, no. 2 (1919): 148-50. (Includes "Works of Falconer Madan," pp. 149-50.) — Madan, Falconer. *C. H. O. Daniel vs. Thomas B. Mosher: A Letter from F. Madan to R. W. Rogers.* San Francisco: Roxburghe Club, 1983. — [Madan, Falconer.] "The Daniel Press." *TLS*, 20 February 1903, pp. 55-56. (Reprinted as *The Daniel Press* [Wausau, Wis.: The Philosopher Press, Van Vechten & Ellis, 1904.]) — [Madan, Falconer.] "The Daniel Press." *Bodleian Quarterly Record* 2 (November 1919) 269-70. — [Madan, Falconer.] "The Daniel Press at Frome and Oxford." *The Library* 4th ser., 1 (September 1920): 65-68. — Madan, Falconer. *The Madan Family and Maddans in Ireland and England.* Oxford: Printed for subscribers at the University Press by J. Johnson, 1933. — Madan, Falconer. "Some Experiences of a Bibliographer, a Presidential Address." *The Library* 1 (December 1920): 129-40. — "Mr. Falconer Madan. 39 Years at the Bodleian." *The Times*, 23 May 1935, p. 18. (Obituary.) — Roberts, R. Julian. "Madan, Falconer," in *ODNB*. — [Waters,

---

1. Gosse to Madan, 22 December 1893 (JJC 4).
2. JJC 3. The review appeared in the *Church Times*, 20 January 1922.

DANIEL PRESS & GARLAND OF RACHEL

W. G.] "The Daniel Press." *TLS*, 12 January 1922, p. 23. (Review of *Memorials*.) — *WWW*. — Correspondence (Worcester, JJC, Bodleian [Don. d.94 and Don. e.227]).

Proofs, Manuscripts, etc.

3.36 ❧ TUERK MANUSCRIPT

Penny Tuerk (private collection, England).†

Green morocco binding with gilt lettering on spine: "MSS. OF GARLAND OF RACHEL".

This volume consists of manuscripts of the poems in *The Garland of Rachel*, presumably those used in typesetting the book, with four letters. It has been handed down through several generations of the family.

It includes the following poems: Henry Daniel (early draft), Watson, Dobson, Lang, Symonds, Bridges [*Pl. 1*], Dodgson (both versions) [*Pl. 3*], Harington (two drafts), Robinson, Gosse, Bourdillon, Henley, Locker (with a short, undated note at the top, apparently to Willert), Ward, Myers, Woods, Cruttwell. These letters to Henry Daniel also appear in the volume: Symonds, 13 March 1881 [**4.18**], written at the top of his poem; Dodgson, 11 May 1895 [**4.48**]; Myers, 6 December 1880 [**4.7**], Cruttwell, 20 December 1880 [**4.11**].

PROVENANCE: Daniel family. — Rachel Daniel. — Ruth Joanna (Lee) Kirkman (by inheritance from her mother). — Penny Tuerk (by inheritance from her mother).

For the DANIELS, see Chapter 1, above; for RUTH JOANNA (LEE) KIRKMAN and PENNY TUERK, see **3.33**.

3.37 ❧ GETTY PROOFS

Mark Getty, England (private collection, Wormsley Library).†

Rust morocco binding, with "THE GARLAND OF RACHEL" on spine. (The binding is not signed, though Colin Franklin has conjectured that it may have been by Emily Daniel. Another likely possibility is Katharine Adams, who bound the set of proofs at the Huntington Library [3.38].) Bookplate of Arthur A. Houghton, Jr. A full set of proofs, including all of the poems and the preface, and consisting of 29 leaves, with manuscript corrections by Henry Daniel and some of the contributors—the most extensive corrections coming from Henley. In several instances there is a note by Daniel to a contributor indicating that the proofs are "rough" and not yet leaded. (But some of the other proofs are in fact leaded.) On Bourdillon's proof, he complains, in a note dated 18 March 1881, about the typographical arrangement of his poem. The only instance of miniation by Emily Daniel is in Woods' poem; in some of the other poems the initial is recorded in pencil.

For another bound set of proofs in a somewhat similar binding, apparently representing a later state in the book's production, see **3.36**.

Tipped into the volume are fifteen letters, mostly from contributors: Harington to Henry Daniel, 31 March 1881 [4.20]; P. F. Willert to Daniel, 12 April [1881] [4.21]; Thomas Hutchinson to Bridges, 30 May 1895; Myers to Daniel, 2 October 1917; Henley to Daniel, [early 1881?] [4.13]; Locker to Daniel, 4 November 1881 [4.33]; Ward to Daniel, 10 December [1880] [4.8]; Ward to Daniel, 23 October [1881] [4.27]; Lang to Daniel, [c. December 1880] [4.5]; Lang to Daniel, [c. December 1880] [4.6]; Gosse to Daniel, 26 February 1881 [4.14]; Gosse to Daniel, 16 November 1881 [4.36]; Willert to Daniel, 13 December [1880] [4.9]; Bridges to Daniel, 25 November 1880 [4.4]; Dobson to Daniel, 10 March 1881 [4.17].

PROVENANCE: Daniel family. — Arthur A. Houghton, Jr. — Houghton sale, Christie (London), 13 June 1979, no. 153 (sold to Colin Franklin for £400). — Colin Franklin (sold to J. Paul Getty). — J. Paul Getty (Wormsley Library). — Mark Getty (by inheritance).

For the DANIELS, see Chapter 1. For ARTHUR A. HOUGHTON, Jr., see Bridges copy [3.2]. For J. PAUL GETTY and MARK GETTY, see 3.24.

DANIEL PRESS & GARLAND OF RACHEL

3.38 ❧ HUNTINGTON PROOFS

Huntington Library, San Marino, Calif.† [Rare Books 19712]

Red morocco binding [*Pl. 6*] by Katharine Adams (signed "KA"); gilt lettering on spine ("THE GARLAND OF RACHEL | DANIEL PRESS | 1881"). With preface (tipped in). Title-page: "By Lewis Carroll and Divers Kindly Hands." Clearly a full set of bound proofs; many of the pages are smudged.

RELATED MATERIAL: [*Tipped in at front*] Robert Bridges to Daniel, 1 March 1881 [**4.15**]; Dodgson to Daniel, 22 November 1880 [**4.1**]; Dodgson to Daniel, 7 March 1881 [**4.16**]; Walter H. Pater to Daniel, 23 November [1880] [**4.3**]; Pater to Daniel, 18 December [1880] [**4.10**]; Frederick Locker to Daniel, 14 September 1881 [**4.22**]. ¶ [*In separate provenance folder*] Correspondence between Leslie Chaundy & Co. and the Huntington Library, 23 June–12 October 1921.

PROVENANCE: Emily Daniel. — Leslie Chaundy & Co. (London) catalogue 49 [1921], no. 176 (£140). — Huntington Library (purchased from Chaundy in the summer of 1921).

Despite the misleading title-page, it is most unlikely that this proof copy was ever in Dodgson's hands. Dodgson died in 1898, and his copy of the *Garland* was sold by the auction firm of Brooks in Oxford that year; it is now at New York University [**3.7**]. The most plausible explanation of the proofs is that when they were brought together by the Daniel family—no doubt from scraps in the pressroom—a stray proof of the title-page with "By Lewis Carroll" happened to be at hand. Probably at about the turn of the century Emily Daniel persuaded Katharine Adams to bind it.

Chaundy's catalogue (see PROVENANCE above) offers the explanation that "books in this list consist of recent purchases, including some unique volumes from the Daniel library, which were not included in the main library which we bought in 1919, as they were not at that time in Worcester College." (Chaundy—the Oxford office, that is—had sold Henry Daniel's library in 1919.)

When the book was delivered to the Huntington, it lacked the Bridges letter, and a representative of Chaundy wrote on 23 June 1921: "With reference to the Garden of Rachel the autograph let-

A CENSUS

ter of Robert Bridges will follow in a week or two. This book belonged to Mrs Daniel and the Bridges letter happened to be in her private house at the time we bought the book. Mrs Daniel has been away from home, but she promises to hand it over to us in a week or two on her returning home. Under the circumstances we are sending you the book rather than keep it until the letter arrives." On 9 September, Chaundy wrote again, "With reference to your letter of July 9th we now have pleasure in sending you the letter by Robert Bridges which was lacking from 'The Garland of Rachel.' The volume is now in its complete form as catalogued."

A note in the Huntington's provenance folder for the book indicates that the Bridges and Locker letters were tipped in much later, in March 1985.

REFERENCES: Ayres, Harry Morgan. "Lewis Carroll and The Garland of Rachel." *Huntington Library Quarterly* 5 (October 1941): 141–45. — Chaundy correspondence (Huntington).

3.39 ❧ TUERK PROOFS

Penny Tuerk (private collection, England).†

A volume of proofs of *The Garland of Rachel*, which were later bound with this lettering on the front cover: "THE | GARLAND OF RACHEL | DANIEL PRESS | 1881". (The binding is very similar to that of the Getty collection of proofs: see **3.37**.) The poems are miniated by Emily Daniel in various styles, suggesting that she used these proofs for practice. The proofs do not include the poems by Dobson and Gosse and the preface. More interestingly, the proof of Dodgson's poem is the rejected first version [**4.3**; *see also Pl. 2*]. The only correction is in Locker's poem (where his name was misspelled *Lockyer*).

Laid in the volume is a letter from Rachel Daniel to her father on Worcester House stationery, undated (but in very immature handwriting): "My Dearest Dad | I will try and be a very good girl to morrow and try my very hardest [?] at my lessons and try to read Mr M nicely. and can you paint on any sort of china in china paints if you can I have gott some thing that I should [?] like to paint good

DANIEL PRESS & GARLAND OF RACHEL

| bye from your loving | little Rachel | p.s I do love you so *Dearest*".

PROVENANCE: Henry and Emily Daniel. — Rachel Daniel. — Ruth Joanna (Lee) Kirkman (by inheritance from her mother). — Penny Tuerk (by inheritance from her mother).

For the DANIELS, see Chapter 1; for RUTH JOANNA (LEE) KIRKMAN and PENNY TUERK, see 3.33.

3.40 ❧ THE FALCONER FACSIMILE

Mark Getty, England (private collection, Wormsley Library).†

A facsimile of the *Garland*: the poems are in the hand of C. M. Falconer, who created the volume; the title-page is a type-facsimile; and the printer's device and ornaments are reproduced by lithography. Bound in blue levant morocco (top edge gilt) by Zaehnsdorf (signed). Bookplate of Arthur A. Houghton, Jr.

Because Falconer attempted to secure the autographs of all the contributors, the following documents are tipped in: Henry Daniel to Falconer, 23 December 1896 [4.50]; Watson to Falconer, 4 March 1897 [4.62]; MS of three-stanza poem with note by Falconer ("Received 8th January 1897 from Mr Andrew Lang at St Andrews in my ms copy of The Garland of Rachel C. M. Falconer"); Gosse to Falconer, 19 January 1897 [4.51]; signature of Symonds with note by Falconer ("Sent by Edmund Gosse"); Daniel to Falconer, 19 January 1898 [4.64]; Dodgson to Emily Daniel, 27 January 1894; Harington to Falconer, 11 February 1897 [4.57]; Harington to Falconer, 14 February 1897 [4.58]; Francis Robinson to Falconer, 13 February 1897; Mary Robinson to Gosse, 3 March 1887; Robinson to Falconer, [24 February 1897] (postcard) [4.60]; Gosse to Falconer, 25 January 1897 [4.53]; Gosse to Falconer, 9 October 1897; Henley to Falconer, 22 January 1897 [4.52]; Henley to Falconer, 26 January 1897; Courthope to Falconer, 27 January 1897 [4.54]; Daniel to Falconer, 18 September 1897 [4.63]; Locker to Daniel, 15 March [1881] [4.19]; Augustine Birrell to Falconer, 22 February [1897] [4.59]; Ward to Falconer, 29 January 1897 [4.55]; Myers to Falconer, 6 February 1897 [4.56]; Myers to Falconer, 9 February [1897]; Daniel to Falconer, 1 March 1897 [4.61]; signature of Cruttwell ("sent by C. Henry Daniel").

A CENSUS

PROVENANCE: C. M. Falconer. — Sotheby, 11 December 1907, lot 80 [*Select and valuable library of the late Mr. C. M. Falconer, Esq. of Dundee*] (sold to J. Bumpus for £10). — Constance Astley (purchased 1908). — Charles J. Sawyer catalogue (October 1941), no. 119 (£25). — Arthur A. Houghton, Jr. — Christie (London), 13 June 1979, lot 154 [*Library of Arthur A. Houghton, Jnr.*] (sold to Colin Franklin for £400). — Colin Franklin. — J. Paul Getty/Wormsley Library (purchased from Franklin). — Mark Getty.

CHARLES MCG. FALCONER (1845–1907), a rope manufacturer in Dundee, had long been a collector and reader of nineteenth-century books, but in the early 1880s he became extremely enthusiastic about the poetry of Andrew Lang and began to form an ambitious Lang library, eventually with the assistance of Lang himself. In 1894 Falconer issued (privately and rather tentatively, as with all of his publications) a Lang bibliography, based on his own collection, and while he was preparing it for the press, he got in touch with Henry Daniel asking for help in locating and borrowing certain Oxford periodicals to which Lang had contributed during the 1860s.[1]

Falconer obviously was first attracted to the *Garland* because of Lang's poem in it. The story of what happened next was recounted by Falconer himself, writing anonymously in a local newspaper: "Mr. C. M Falconer, of Dundee, who despaired of ever meeting with a copy [of the *Garland*] in the way of trade, or of being able to buy it though it did turn up, was so desirous to obtain one to complete a certain section of his library that he hit upon the happy thought of making one for himself. Fortunately he was on friendly corresponding terms with Mr. Daniel—he has not a few examples of Mr. Daniel's private press—who generously lent him Rachel's own copy, and permitted him to make what use of it he pleased. The book was copied in exact facsimile, so far as writing goes, every word, line, verse, space, margin being reproduced; the writing is in an open style to make it as easily read

---

1. Falconer to Henry Daniel, 7 March 1894 (Worcester)

DANIEL PRESS & GARLAND OF RACHEL

as print. The miniation, or red lettering, was also done as closely as possible, but it lacks the neatness of the original. A local printer was called in, and set up a perfect copy of the title-page and dedication, while a young Dundee artist copied Parsons' designs with absolute fidelity, and reproduced them by lithography—the three designs being repeated five or six times. The book was then bound in pure vellum, limp, and forwarded to Mr. Daniel for his approval. The gentleman called it 'an admirable transcript' and added, 'If my printed copies are a treasure to the collector, your MS. is ten times more so. And the copies of the head pieces are perfect, while your printer has caught the look of the somewhat artless volume quite admirably'" (*Dundee Advertiser,* 23 May 1898).

The correspondence published below (in Chapter 4) shows that, with the assistance of Henry Daniel, Falconer went to considerable lengths to secure autographs of all the contributors to the *Garland*. Falconer also sent a copy of the *Dundee Advertiser* article to Mosher in America, who was then in the midst of laying plans to reprint the *Garland* [**3.29**]; Mosher reprinted the article in its entirety in his introduction.

CONSTANCE ASTLEY (1867?–1940), daughter of Sir Vincent R. Corbet, 6th Baronet, successively married Sir Richard Sutton, 5th Baronet, and, in 1895, Hubert D. Astley, a noted ornithologist. The Astleys lived at Brinsop Court, a medieval moated manor house in Herefordshire, which Wordsworth's brother-in-law had once leased for farming for nearly two decades. Constance Astley was an ambitious book collector with a strong interest in natural history and in modern English private presses, as the *Catalogue* (1928) of her library demonstrates.

Falconer Madan was aware of the existence of Falconer's facsimile (which had been mentioned by Mosher in his reprint) and alluded to it in his Daniel Press bibliography (*Memorials*, p. 89), but he was pleasantly surprised in early 1922 to learn from Astley that she was its current owner. "It must be of very considerable interest and value," he remarked in a letter to her [**4.78**; *see also Pl. 9*].

He immediately asked for more details, and Astley responded by sending him partial transcriptions of the various letters bound into the volume; he in return sent her a set of the extra ten illustrations that had appeared in the de luxe edition of *Memorials*, arranged for her election to membership in the Oxford Bibliographical Society, and lavished a good deal of flattery in his subsequent letters to her. In the *Addenda & Corrigenda* for his bibliography (1922) Madan duly noted that "Mr. Falconer's transcript of the *Garland* is now in the possession of Mrs. Astley of Brinsop Court, Hereford, having been purchased by her in 1908."

Some years later, in January 1930, C. H. Wilkinson of Worcester College and Herbert Warren, President of Magdalen College, called upon Constance Astley to examine the prized document, and Wilkinson immediately arranged for Emily Daniel to see the facsimile as well.[1] Within a few days Astley sent the facsimile through the post to Emily Daniel, who declared that "I have enjoyed looking at it very much & it brought back many happy memories of nearly 50 years ago" [4.81].

For ARTHUR A. HOUGHTON, Jr., see Bridges copy [3.2].

REFERENCES: [ASTLEY] *Burke's Peerage* (1914). (See p. 970 for Hubert Delaval Astley.) — *Catalogue of the Library of Constance Astley at Brinsop Court, Herefordshire*. London: Printed by George W. Jones, 1928. (See p. 6.) — "Deaths." *The Times*, 4 September 1940, p. 1. — S., W. L. "Obituary. Mrs. Constance Edith Astley." *The Ibis* 5 (January 1941): 187–88. — Correspondence (Honnold Library, JJC 2). ¶ [FALCONER] [Falconer, C. M.] *Catalogue of a Library Chiefly the Writings of Andrew Lang*. Dundee: privately printed, 1898. — [Falconer, C. M.] "The Garland of Rachel: Unique Copy in Dundee." *Dundee Advertiser*, 23 May 1898. — Falconer, C. M. *The Writings of Andrew Lang, M.A., LL.D., Arranged in the Form of a Bibliography, with Notes by C. M. Falconer.* Dundee: privately printed, 1894. — Franklin [1]. — Green, Roger Lancelyn. *Andrew Lang: A Critical Biography*. Leicester: E. Ward, 1946. (See pp. 196–97.) — "Mr. C. M. Falconer." *Dundee Advertiser*, 19 December 1907. (Obituary.) — Murray, Francis Edward. *A Bibliography of Austin Dobson*. Derby: Francis Murray, 1900. — Reid, Alan. *The Bards of Angus and the Mearns: An Anthology of the Counties*. Paisley, Scotland: J. and R. Parland, 1897. (See p. 194.) — Correspondence (Getty, Worcester).

---

1. Wilkinson to Astley, 13 January 1930 (Honnold Library).

4. CORRESPONDENCE

THE following letters are mostly either laid or tipped in individual copies of *The Garland of Rachel* (or the Falconer facsimile), though in some instances we have added correspondence from other sources that sheds light on the history of the production of the book. On the other hand, we are not reproducing every letter found in a copy of the *Garland*, because a few of them deal only tangentially (if at all) with the book.

4.1 ❧ C. L. DODGSON TO HENRY DANIEL, 22 NOVEMBER 1880[1]

Dear Daniel,

I am much complimented by your wish to include verses of mine in your little 'livre de luxe'—and profoundly puzzled to know what the subject is to be. And as Mrs. Daniel has set you on to puzzle me, I enclose, in revenge, certain puzzles for her. Verses written on a set subject, even when one knows something about it, & [i.e. are] pretty sure to be rubbish: but, when one knows *nothing*!

Is it the Old Testament Rachel—of whose infancy nothing is known? Or is it the actress—of whose infancy nothing is known either?

Yours sincerely | C L Dodgson

Nov. 22/80

---

1. With Huntington proofs [3.38].

DANIEL PRESS & GARLAND OF RACHEL

4.2 C. L. DODGSON TO HENRY DANIEL, 23 NOVEMBER 1880[1]

Rev. C. Dodgson, | Christ Church, | Oxford. | Nov. 23 / 80

My dear Daniel,

I shouldn't have thought it— There *did* appear some slight hope of a new idea occurring about the Actress as an Infant: but, as to the typical human Baby, what hope is there? The subject is exhausted, I fear—(parenthetically, I hate babes, but that is irrelevant). And I suppose you want something serious—not *this* style, for instance:—

> "Oh pudgy podgy pup!
> Why *did* they wake you up?
> Those crude nocturnal yells
> Are *not* like silver bells:
> Nor ever would recall
> Sweet Music's 'dying fall'.
> They rather bring to mind
> The bitter winter wind
> Through keyholes shrieking shrilly
> When nights are dark & chilly:
> Or like some dire duett,
> Or quarrelsome quartette,
> Of cats who chant their joys
> With execrable noise,
> And murder Time and Tune
> To vex the patient Moon!["][2]

However, I will, as a German lady once said to me, 'put it into my mind'—& see if anything comes of it. Candidly, I don't expect anything will.

Sincerely yours | C L Dodgson

---

1. Parrish Collection, Princeton University Library.

2. There are two surviving proofs of this poem (Tuerk and Princeton), both in Fell type on Henry Daniel's usual paper; Madan later claimed that it was typeset by someone other than Henry Daniel (Emily, presumably).

CORRESPONDENCE

4.3 ❧ WALTER PATER TO HENRY DANIEL,
23 NOVEMBER [1880][1]

B. N. C. | Nov. 23.

My dear Daniel,

I shall prize the "Colloquies," which you so kindly brought me, greatly. It is, I suppose, the most exquisite specimen of printing I have seen. Accept my best thanks.

I am much tempted to take part in the making of your proposed baby-house, and like the idea of it very much, but at the moment feel very barren on the subject. Perhaps however if my contribution was to be by way of preface, it might be actually printed last, so that I might tell you in or after the vacation, and have a preliminary look at the other contents—only, of course, you must not delay your plan on my account. Have you ever seen Colvin's very pretty book on "Children in Italian and English Design"?[2] Earle's "Microc"[3] I have not read, but should be glad to. Has Dodgson of Ch. Ch. occurred to you as a possible contributor?

Yours very sincerely | W. H. Pater

4.4 ❧ ROBERT BRIDGES TO HENRY DANIEL,
25 NOVEMBER 1880[4]

52 Bedford Square London.

My dear Sir

Thank you very much for your offer, which it wd be most agreeable to me to accept, but I am afraid that I cannot make a *promise* of this sort. If I do write anything you shall have it. I happen to have a poem on the subject which I had intended to print with my last series, but I was dissatisfied with it and tore it up. I would try and get that finished but it is in blank verse and will be over 80 lines

---

1. With Huntington proofs 1 [**3.38**].
2. Sidney Colvin, *Children in Italian and English Design* (1872).
3. Bishop John Earle, *Microcosmographie* (1628), from which Daniel printed an excerpt in his preface to the *Garland*.
4. Getty.

long and having failed at it once it will require some courage to try it again. So unless you do not think of printing for some time yet I think you will have to do without me.

Andrew Lang wrote to me the other day asking me if I thought you would be persuaded, and if I was disposed to aid in trying to persuade you "to print a little book of poems on sleep, English French Greek and perhaps Latin, which (he said) it is the ambition of my life to select. Of course it is too recondite for publishers. I think it wd make such a pretty book, with an etching of the bronze head of Sleep in the British Museum"[.]

I submit Lang's proposition to you now. He is a great admirer and coveter of your 'publications'[.]

Perhaps you will tell me when you mean to bring out Rachel, when you answer Langs proposal.

Believe me yours truly | Robert Bridges

Nov. 25th 80

PS. I shd be glad to hear if the blank verse wd be out of the question, and of course you reserve the acceptance till you see the work itself.

4.5 ANDREW LANG TO HENRY DANIEL, [C. DECEMBER 1880][1]

1, Marloes Road, | Kensington. W. | Wednesday

Dear Daniel

I am sorry Lord Salisbury's choice did not fall aright.[2] However, it is better than having a school-master. I enclose a French ballade by W. E. Henley.

Yours very truly | A Lang

---

1. Getty.
2. Henry Daniel had hoped to be chosen as Provost of Worcester, but the Prime Minister, Robert Cecil, 3rd Marquess of Salisbury, instead selected William Inge.

4.6 ❧ ANDREW LANG TO HENRY DANIEL, [C. DECEMBER 1880][1]

1, Marloes Road, | Kensington. W.

My dear Mr Daniel

I don't know how to thank you for the Erasmus; it is a beautiful little book. If I can, I will contribute to the *Berçeau*, or *Guirlande*, but I am almost as bad at writing on a given topic, as at algebra. Gosse, on the other hand, is very clever at it. I only know Bridges, who strikes the chorded shell, besides Gosse and Dobson, but if I make acquaintance with a poet, I will entreat his aid. Perhaps Miss Mary Robinson or O'Shaughnessy[2] could send a stanza or two.

I send you a pamphlet of Theocritus,[3] which is at least very scarce; it would be better for me if it were scarcer, as it is full of blunders.

Yours very sincerely | A Lang

4.7 ❧ ERNEST MYERS TO HENRY DANIEL, 6 DECEMBER [1880][4]

Wadham | Dec. 6.

Dear Daniel

I fear the accompanying fragment wd. make a poor show beside the contributions you have got, & if you take my advice you won't add it.

Yrs very truly | E. Myers.

---

1. Getty.
2. See **4.14**.
3. Lang, *Specimens of a Translation of Theocritus* (1879?).
4. Tuerk.

4.8 ~ T. H. WARD TO HENRY DANIEL, 10 DECEMBER [1880][1]

Dec 10. | 5, Bradmore Road, | Oxford.

My dear Daniel

The charming Miss Robinson writes—"Here is a lullaby which I have written *to* Baby Rachel & not *at* or *of* Baby Rachel—so you must measure it by her standard of appreciation & not by yours". The verses are not her best, but I think they will do!

So your old Provost is gone![2] QVOD FELIX FAVSTVMQVE SIT![3] if that is good Latin: or QVOD FELICITER VORTAT![4] if you like it better.

I came in town yesterday & saw Dick[5] & we conspired a good deal about the future.

Ever yrs | THW.

4.9 ~ P. F. WILLERT TO HENRY DANIEL, 13 DECEMBER [1880][6]

Exeter College. | Oxford. Dec. 13.

Dear Daniel

I wrote to & said the lines wouldn't do— Yesterday mornings post brought me an impassioned address to Mrs. Langtry!! wh[ich] I sent back at once explaining that however great her innocence she could scarcely be considered a *child*. This afternoon the enclosed arrived— It seems to me pointless & I suspect does not at all meet your requirements— If I am right in surmising that it will

---

1. Getty.
2. The Rev. Richard Lynch Cotton, Provost of Worcester College, died 8 December 1880.
3. "May it be favorable and prosperous."
4. "May it turn out happily." The phrase appears in a Latin passage above the entrance to the Bodleian Library.
5. Richard Thursfield.
6. Getty.

not do, would you please send it back to Locker yourself & explain *why* it does not suit your collection.

If you are not going to press in a great hurry I think we are sure to get something from Courthope— I will send a reminder to Theodore Martin— I might perhaps get something from old Henry Taylor— His wife is a great friend of mine, though I suspect the old gentleman would not care greatly to oblige me—

Yours in haste | F. Willert

4.10 ❧ WALTER PATER TO HENRY DANIEL, 18 DECEMBER [1880][7]

22 Bradmore Road. | Dec. 18.

My dear Daniel,

I have been thinking over your proposal, and find that I liked the notion of it so much as to be tempted to keep the matter open when I ought, in fairness to you, to have declined what there is such a small prospect of my being able to fulfil. It would take me a long time to satisfy myself in this little composition you require—long time, in proportion to the due brevity of the result; and meantime yourself, who have conceived the whole pretty design, would I am sure be better able than any one else to introduce your composers gracefully. I should have been pleased and proud to contribute, had I seen my way; but must, in justice to you, ask you to take the will for the deed, together with my best wishes for Rachel—the infant and the book.

I had written the above more than a week ago, but did not send it because I fancied you would be very busy just then. I must now add my sincere good wishes for yourself, and remain

Very truly yours | W. H. Pater.

---

7. With Huntington proofs [3.38].

4.11 ❦ C. J. CRUTTWELL TO HENRY DANIEL, 20 DECEMBER 1880[1]

Newhaven Lodge, S.W. | 20 Dec. 1880.

My dear Henry

On the other half I send the sonnet bespoke by your letter; but am apprehensive it will not please you as that in the 'Little Book'[2] of which you speak so flatteringly. I was minded to write out some lines composed on your Cousin Maria's[3] christening as better than my latter day productions; but besides poaching on another's manor, I should have seemed indolent or indifferent to Benedick & Beatrice of W.H[4] & their young hope, & this at any rate my new bantling[5] will disprove. [...]

Ever yr affect. Cousin | C. J. Cruttwell

4.12 ❦ C. J. CRUTTWELL TO HENRY DANIEL, 31 DECEMBER 1880[6]

Newhaven Lodge, | 15 Thistle Grove, | S Kensington: | Dec. 31. '80

My dear Henry

I trouble you—rhymers are troublesome to the point of bore[dom]— with a substitution for the last 2 lines of "Rachel", which I am sure cannot have pleased you, & only found place because its concetto[7] pleased me on the score of dear mamma. The following is better but will thank its amender:

> Precious ewe-lamb, & sprinkle, we discern
> The Heavenly Shepherd's arms, which thee engird.

---

1. Getty.
2. Probably Cruttwell's poem *The Tomb of Bonaparte*, published by Pickering in 1842.
3. C. J. Cruttwell's daughter.
4. Worcester House. Benedick and Beatrice were Cruttwell's usual nicknames for Henry and Emily Daniel.
5. Illegitimate child, i.e. his poem.
6. Worcester.
7. Concept (Italian).

CORRESPONDENCE

I add with Littleton "Blest be the amending hand."[1] [...]

Your affectionate uncle | C. J. Cruttwell

Revd C. H. O. Daniel

4.13 ❧ W. E. HENLEY TO HENRY DANIEL, [EARLY 1881?][2]

51 Richmond Gardens | Shepherds Bush W | Monday

My dear Sir

I am afraid I am sending you back a very dirty proof.

In the first refrain I should like quotation marks, if you can permit them. And in all three of the refrains I should like three dots (...) in place of the second dash.

Will you kindly consult a big dictionary for me, & see if "Mozambique" is masculine or feminine? I haven't such a thing in the house, & I rarely go to the Museum; or I would not trouble you.

I never heard of the Guenon you have discovered. I must look him up, if its only for curiosity's sake. My guenon, with a small g, is the ancestral she-ape, the Eve of our wretched race, the common mother of us all.

Please put *Sonata Pathétique* in italics. If you have no quotation-mark it might be as well to put the first refrain in italics also. I suppose that the lack of accents is of no sort of consequence, is it?

I wish the verses were better worth your care.

Very faithfully yours | W. E. Henley

---

1. A saying attributed to Sir Thomas de Littleton (1407?–1481), a celebrated English jurist.

2. Getty.

DANIEL PRESS & GARLAND OF RACHEL

4.14 ❧ EDMUND GOSSE TO HENRY DANIEL, 26 FEBRUARY 1881[1]

29, Delamere Terrace, | Westbourne Square. W. | Feb. 26. 81.

My dear Sir

I have no corrections to make in the proof which you have been so good as to send me. I should be glad if my name might have short s's instead of long ones. There was an Elizabethan poetaster called Goffe.[2]

My poor friend Arthur O'Shaughnessy[3] designed a contribution to the "Garland of Rachel," but his sudden death has made it impossible to find out whether he had or had not written it. His executor tells me that he finds no such poem among his MSS.

I am looking forward with much pleasure to the volume, which will be exquisite in its material part, at all events.

Yours vy faithfully | Edmund W. Gosse

C Henry Daniel Esq

4.15 ❧ ROBERT BRIDGES TO HENRY DANIEL, 1 MARCH 1881[4]

52 Bedford Square   March 1. 81

My dear Sir,

I got your letter on Saturday, and now send you the verses. If you are not better pleased with them than I was on seeing them again pray do not print them. They will however I think suit the size of your pages, & have the advantage of being unlike any others in the book: unless there shd be quite a miraculous coincidence. If you do make use of them do not take the trouble to send me a proof as I will write them out (or try to do so) in an intelligible manner[.]

I suppose that I am not wrong in understanding that the idea of

---

1. Getty.
2. Thomas Goffe (1591–1629).
3. O'Shaughnessy died on 30 January 1881.
4. With Dodgson copy [3.7].

your book was to have all the poems on the subject of "the infant". Otherwise I cd send you a much better lyric, and shd be glad to do so for I feel that you cannot but be disappointed with my attempt on this theme. I hope all the others may be much better.

yours very truly | Robert Bridges

Rev C H Daniel Worcester Coll Oxford

4.16 ❧ C. L. DODGSON TO HENRY DANIEL, 7 MARCH 1881[5]

Ch. Ch. Mar. 7 / 81

My dear Daniel,

Your note was quite a pleasant surprise—I had made up my mind that I was under the displeasure of Mrs. Daniel & yourself for having ventured to write such outrageous stuff on such a theme as your child! And I had thought I had better hold my tongue & let the whole thing pass into oblivion. I am penitent now, and ready to do what I can. Give me a week's law & I will see if any happy thought occurs.

Sincerely yours | C L Dodgson

4.17 ❧ AUSTIN DOBSON TO HENRY DANIEL, 10 MARCH 1881[6]

Board of Trade | Mar. 10. 1881.

My dear Sir,

I return the proof, in wh:, as you will see, I have made but little alteration. As to the note, will it not be best to put "To R. D." —if those are the correct initials? This I leave to you. With every good wish for the book, and the subject of it,

Believe me | Faithfully yours | Austin Dobson

---

5. With Dodgson copy [**3.7**].
6. Getty.

4.18 ❧ J. A. SYMONDS TO HENRY DANIEL, 13 MARCH 1881[1]

Hotel Buel, Davos Platz | Graubünden, Switzerland |
March 13 1881

My dear Sir

I should be very glad to send you something in the right key for your guirlande. And it so happened that just before your letter came last night, Miss Poynter (a sister of the painter)[2] had been amusing us by telling how the dolls of the period have assumed a serious & care-worn look. This tickled my fancy, & I scribbled the lines wh.[ich] I now send you. I don't feel sure they will do. But pray take them as a sign of my goodwill, & believe me to be very faithfully yours

John Addington Symonds

I cannot remember whether you are in Orders, & had no Calendar.[3] Pray excuse me, if I am wrong.

4.19 ❧ FREDERICK LOCKER TO HENRY DANIEL, 15 MARCH [1881][4]

25 Chesham Street | 15 March

My dear Sir

I return the Verses, with many thanks[.] I have only made one suggested Correction[.] I wish the Verses were more worthy your acceptance[.] I write in haste[.]

Vy truly [?] yrs | F Locker

Could you kindly send me another revise, at yr. leisure[.]

---

1. Written at the top of the manuscript of his poem (Tuerk).
2. Sir Edward Poynter had three sisters; Symonds is probably describing Henrietta Poynter.
3. *The Oxford Diocesan Calendar and Clergy List*, an annual publication.
4. With Falconer facsimile [3.40].

CORRESPONDENCE

4.20 ❧ SIR RICHARD HARINGTON TO HENRY DANIEL, 31 MARCH 1881[1]

Whitbourne Court. | Worcester. | 31 March 1881

Sir Richard Harington presents his compliments to Mr. Daniel, & referring to the lines which he enclosed to him yesterday at Charles Dodgson's request, would venture to suggest, if it is not too late that the 13th line should altered by substituting "Carmine soletor tener Philomela dolentes". [...]

He must apologise for the delay which his (after all very unsuccessful) attempt to render Dodgson's lines into Latin worthy of them must already have caused.

But his version which was he must admit very full indeed of faults in the first instance has been subjected to a good deal of criticism by Mr Onions,[2] & as these could only be answered or obviated by a reference to authorities, & as Sir Richard Harington's time is very closely occupied, the delay which he very much regrets has been unavoidable.

He must apologise also for having sent the lines yesterday unaccompanied by a letter. He only arrived at home late in the afternoon after having been about since 5:30 in the morning of the day before & then had to write pressing business letters & to attend to domestic matters also.

The Revd C. H Daniel

4.21 ❧ P. F. WILLERT TO HENRY DANIEL, 12 APRIL [1881][3]

Nelson House | Mount Ephraim | Tunbridge Wells. | Ap. 12.

Dear Daniel

Enclosed is Courthopes contribution—tho' pessimist & reac-

---

1. Getty.
2. Probably John Henry Onions (1852–1889).
3. Getty.

tionary (with a flavour of jingoism[)] I hope you will consider it pretty & appropriate. [...]

Yours ever sincerely | F. Willert

4.22 ❧ FREDERICK LOCKER TO HENRY DANIEL, 14 SEPTEMBER 1881[1]

Riby Grove, | Gt. Grimsby | 14 Sept 81

Dear Sir

Your letter has reached me here where I have come for Doncaster. I regret that my sterility has given you so much trouble. I ought to have written you off some verses at once to [*illegible*] fit the young lady, whoever she may be! but I am v[er]y glad that you have been able to make mine fit pretty well.

Wishing you all success | Believe me truly yrs | F Locker

Perhaps they had better be signed Frederick Locker[.]

4.23 ❧ MARGARET L. WOODS TO HENRY DANIEL, [C. OCTOBER 1881][2]

28, Holywell, | Oxford.

Dear Mr Daniel

So many thanks to you & Mrs Daniel for the "Garland," which I found this afternoon. I am sure you must both feel well content with your work, & I hope many more equally beautiful will issue from the same press. I am so pleased to find the charming bit of Earls in the beginning[.] We shall both always value the book much, & tell Gilbert about it when he is older. With love to Mrs Daniel,

Believe me | yrs very sincerely | M L Woods

---

1. With Huntington proofs [4.21].
2. Tuerk.

CORRESPONDENCE

4.24 ❧ ANDREW LANG TO HENRY DANIEL,
[C. OCTOBER 1881][1]

Hall Grove. | Bagshot. | Sunday

Dear Daniel,
What a lovely book you have sent me. I wish the poetry deserved the printing. Bridges and Dobson are best. Courthope could not forget the General Election! I wish I had written a more excellent song. You should do my sleep book, about the same size, after all, and let Pickering or some one sell it, and make a lot of coin. I am glad the child of so many rhymes has recovered.

Yours truly | A Lang.

4.25 ❧ ROBERT BRIDGES TO HENRY DANIEL,
[C. OCTOBER 1881][2]

52 Bedford Square

My dear Sir,
I do not know when your handsome present arrived, but I found it on my table yesterday on my return to London after an absence of a month. The expectation of having it had been a long pleasure, but the binding was quite a surprise, and it demands my especial thanks. I think the book is very pretty indeed, and does great credit to your household press: and I wish that my verses were more worthy of the trouble and care that has been spent on them. I was glad however to find that they make the variety which I hoped they might. I was sorry not to find, what someone told me there was to be, a preface by Mr Pater—this is a loss .. but Ernest Myers has supplied the place of M. Victor Hugo most admirably: His skilful evasion of the difficulty is most dignified. On first reading I give him the prize. The whole garland seems to me better than other garlands I have seen.
 I was sorry to read in the advertisement that you had been ill. I

---

1. Tuerk.
2. Tuerk.

myself have spent this glorious summer in bed with acute illness, and am only just recovering my strength. I leave tomorrow for the Continent which must excuse the haste of this letter, as I am 'troubled about many things'.[1] I hope that I may meet you some day soon after my return in the spring. If you should ever again wish to print a pamphlet of my verse, or to undertake the "Oxford garland" which I once proposed, you have only to apply to me.

 Yours very truly | Robert Bridges

P.S. | I hope that Lang and Mr Dobson and others will not reprint their verses elsewhere. I shd hope that you have secured this as it must add to the value of your book.

Rev. H. Daniel | Oxford

4.26 ❧ EDMUND GOSSE TO HENRY DANIEL, 20 OCTOBER 1881[2]

 29 Delamere Terrace | W. | 20. 10. 81.

My dear Sir

 Allow me to offer you my best thanks for a copy of your exquisite "Garland of Rachel", one of the prettiest books which ever passed from an English press. I am proud to have a share in so delightful an enterprise.

 I wish I might venture to send a kiss to Rachel herself! Do you think I might?

 Yours sincerely | Edmund W. Gosse

---

1. Luke 10:41.
2. Tuerk.

CORRESPONDENCE

4.27 ❧ T. H. WARD TO HENRY DANIEL, 23 OCTOBER [1881][1]

61 Russell Sq. | Oct 23.

My dear Daniel

This note is from Gosse, who does not know your address. From him I learn that Rachel's Guirlande is ready. May I have my copy, sent in a manner to be quite safe from postal worry? It would be better if you would send it, with Miss Robinson's, to *84 Gower St W.C.*, where we are all quartered for a few days till our home is ready.[2] It is her house, & her people will send her copy to Italy where she is staying.

I don't know whether Gosse asks in his letter to you what he wishes me to ask you—whether the book may be shortly noticed (not reviewed) in the bric-a-brac column of Scribner?[3] "The publisher" he says "wd be so much delighted to secure it. I wd have it noticed from my copy. If moreover he would spare proofs of A. Parson's headpiece for Scribner to facsimile, a cry of joyous gratitude would rise to heaven from the Office."

We hope to get settled this week, & that will bring to an end a most tiresome interlude in my life. Lodgings are horrid, & we have been tossed about from one to the other for weeks.

Ever yrs | T H Ward

4.28 ❧ ALBERT WATSON TO HENRY DANIEL, 27 OCTOBER 1881[4]

My dear Daniel

---

1. Getty.
2. Humphry Ward had recently left Oxford for London in order to take up a journalistic career, and he and his family were about to move into a house on Russell Square.
3. "Bric-a-brac: The Garland of Rachel," *Century Illustrated Monthly Magazine* 23 (February 1882): 639–40. The piece was written by Austin Dobson, but Gosse arranged for its publication in the magazine.
4. Tuerk.

Please accept for yourself and Mrs. Daniel my best thanks for your beautiful present.

I am only afraid that my poor little offering will feel ill at ease in such distinguished company.

Always truly yours | Albert Watson

Brasenose College | Oct. 27. 1881

4.29 ❧ T. H. WARD TO HENRY DANIEL, 27 OCTOBER [1881][1]

61 Russell Square | Oct 27.

My dear Daniel

The book is a masterpiece, within & without. I think it does credit to the bards, & I am sure that it does credit to the printer, miniatress, the paper-maker & the binder. In future years it will be collected with strange passion, some Rothschild or Bodleian will give fabulous prices to complete the collection of the 17 different titlepages. What is to happen to the other 19 copies? The Brit. Mus. & Bodley & Cambridge ought really to have one each.

Dobson's, Mrs Woods', Lang's are charming; Henley's fearfully & wonderfully idiomatic; C.J.C's pleasingly quaint; Courthope's good but o! how gloomily Tory. Symonds is very much on the spot in this his third venture: and what shall be said of the nameless one who leads the dance in that sweet Caroline measure?

Farewell. We are just on the point of getting in town here after a long struggle. But it will be the climax of discomfort.

Ever yrs | THW.

P.S. On reading over I find I omitted Bridges' poem. It is surely the best? Tennyson might own it; would be glad to own it I should think. And C.J.C. is really a great sonnet-writer.

---

1. Tuerk.

CORRESPONDENCE

4.30 ❧ SIR RICHARD HARINGTON TO HENRY DANIEL, 30 OCTOBER 1881[1]

Whitbourne Court, | Worcester. | 30 Oct 1881

My dear Sir,

I postponed thanking you for the Garland of Rachel until I should have had an opportunity of reading it. I have now done so & have to combine my thanks & congratulations. Many thanks to you for what is a very nice book both inside & outside, & my congratulations to you on having so many friends who have been able to express their good wishes to you in so pleasant a way.

Dodgson's lines I always thought very pretty—& of the others if I may venture choose amongst so many that are meritorious, I think that those by Austin Dobson[,] A. M. F. Robinson & T. Ward are the nicest. Indeed, there is a certain gratification of the pleasure with which I read so many compositions in the feeling that the imperfections of my own poor attempt to translate Dodgson are rendered especially conspicuous by the glare in which they will be viewed. And I feel this somewhat the more, because I am afraid that I must have omitted to send you one or two emendations, which would, I thought, have had the effect of rendering my attempt a little less like a second rate schoolboy's exercise.

Your typographical labours have produced a most decided success—& as I do a little in a very common plain way of that myself, excite my envy.

I enclose you a copy en Anglais et Latin of a prologue to some favourite theatricals we had here last Christmas, that you may see how very far inferior my production is to yours. I should rather like to know what sort of press you use. My own is merely a shallow wooden box with a lever to shut down the lid & press. I bought it for 25/ from an advertising man named Wightman at Leeds about six years ago. Before I had had it very long the box broke & the screws which screwed the fulcrum broke in the wood. I forged myself an iron bar, & made a strap of iron to fit under the bottom of the press, which stood pretty well for strength but it is very diffi-

---

1. Tuerk.

cult to get the pressrun [?] evenly distributed over the whole of the forme. [...] I can conclude I think with no better wish than those expressed the 8th & last stanzas of Mr. Ward's lines[.]

 Yours faithfully | Richard Harington
Revd. C. H. Daniel

4.31 ❧ W. E. HENLEY TO HENRY DANIEL, [C. NOVEMBER 1881][1]

 51 Richmond Gardens, | Shepherds Bush W.
My Dear Sir,
 I owe you many apologies for the abominable way in which I have neglected to acknowledge the receipt of your charming gift. The fact is, however, that I was away from home when the book came in & that ever since my return I have been very busy—so busy, indeed—& so tired in the intervals of being busy—that, often as I have remembered my debt, I have never once had an opportunity of paying it off, by writing to thank you. Now that at last I do so, I hope you will be generous & accept my excuses. I assure you they are both humble & sincere.

 The book is a delightful one, & it gives me great pleasure to think that I am [sic] for a little in its composition. I shall value it much; & always. I have seen nothing so pretty & so graceful in conception, & nothing so attractively & finely wrought, this many a day.

 I hope that the heroine of so many charming songs will live happily & long, & that our verses will give pleasure to her & her's until the end. For my part, I could wish that I had been content to speak plain English, & had left French to my betters. But the thing is done now, & I mustn't complain. I only hope that posterity will not find too many mistakes in my French, or miscall me very bitterly for those they do find. They have only to turn to Austin Dobson's English, & the charming ballads signed "Andrew Lang" to

---

1. Tuerk.

forget that I even existed. And this, I doubt not, they will not fail to do.

With kind regards & best wishes, | Very sincerely yours | W. E. Henley.

4.32 ❧ ERNEST MYERS TO HENRY DANIEL, 1 NOVEMBER 1881[1]

12, Hereford Gardens. | W. | Nov. 1. 1881.

Dear Daniel

Lang has shown me a beautiful copy of 'The Garland of Rachel' & tells me he believes you meant to send one to all contributors. I hope I am to be allowed one, though I feel it will be Χρυσεα Χαλκειων[2] after my meagre contribution. But in case it should be tarrying from ignorance of my address, I send you this line.

I was sorry not to be able to come to the Club last time but hope I may be next.

Yours very truly, | Ernest Myers.

4.33 ❧ FREDERICK LOCKER TO HENRY DANIEL, 4 NOVEMBER 1881[3]

Warwick Castle | Warwick | 4 November 1881.

Dear Mr. Daniel

I fear that inadvertently I made a v[er]y stupid mistake when I wrote to you the other day, to thank you for your very interesting little book. I hope you will pardon me. I wonder if it will ever be my fate to see the young lady who has so many laureates! If I had seen the Collection before I sent you my verses I think I could have sent you something much more appropriate.

Faithfully yrs | F Locker

---

1. Tuerk.
2. Gold of the coppersmiths (or bronzesmiths), meaning probably inferior or counterfeit coins with a gold veneer (Greek).
3. Getty.

4.34 ⇒ HENRY DANIEL TO FREDERICK LOCKER, 5 NOVEMBER 1881[1]

Worcester House, | Oxford. | Nov. 5. 1881

My dear Sir,

I am afraid that the letter of which you speak has miscarried— at all events it has not yet reached me. So, whatever the mistake referred to, it as yet unknown, but I am sure that it must be unimportant.

I am glad to find you got the little book safely. I owe you many apologies for the long delay in its production. The Bursar of a College, now a days, has not much time for such distractions. I wish it were more worthy of your pretty verses. For which I must again thank you. I didn't know whether you are likely to be tempted to Oxford: I should be proud to introduce you to "Rachel" who will some day realise upon what a pinnacle of fame she has been placed.

Believe me my dear Sir | Faithfully yours | C. H. Daniel.

4.35 ⇒ EDMUND GOSSE TO HENRY DANIEL, 6 NOVEMBER 1881[2]

29, Delamere Terrace, | Westbourne Square. W. | 6. 11. 81.

My dear Sir

I am very much obliged to you for your kind permission to speak of the Garland and reproduce the proofs in *The Century* (Scribner's Monthly).[3] I am sure that Parsons will have no objection. The reproduction will not in any way endanger your copyright: it will even, in case you have never published your printer's mark, ensure and protect it! I wish you could see your way to attempt another important work. No such beautiful book as the "Garland" has been produced in England for many years. If it were not that I fear to be troublesome, I should like to ask you the history of your types.

With many thanks | Yours very truly | Edmund W. Gosse

---

1. With Locker copy [**3.12**].
2. Hilary Martin Daniel.
3. See **4.27**.

CORRESPONDENCE

4.36 EDMUND GOSSE TO HENRY DANIEL, 16 NOVEMBER 1881[1]

29, Delamere Terrace, | Westbourne Square. W. | 16. 11. 81.

My dear Sir

My cupidity as a bibliophile is not proof against so tempting an offer as that of your earlier work, which, if you can indeed spare me a copy, I shall greatly value.[2]

A friendly hand—not mine—has written a very pretty notice of "The Garland of Rachel," wh.[ich] has been sent to New York.[3] You will not, I hope, let any one forestall us with an account of the book? We hope to facsimile nicely the designs you were so good as to send me.

Thank you for your very kind and interesting letter & believe me

Very faithfully yours | Edmund W. Gosse

4.37 ❧ ERNEST MYERS TO HENRY DANIEL, 18 NOVEMBER [1881][4]

12, Hereford Gardens. | W. | Nov. 18.

Dear Daniel,

Many thanks for the 'Garland', wh. has now arrived in all its beauty. Such a work of art must be too cheaply earned, I think, by any of the contributors, and especially by me.

I am glad that I only hear of the illness of 'the subject of our Muse' when you can also tell me that it is over; & I trust that these

---

1. Getty.
2. Daniel had published two small books at Oxford before the *Garland*: *Worcester College Library: Notes from a Catalogue of the Pamphlets in Worcester College Library* (1874) and *A New Sermon of the Newest Fashion* (1876). Both appear in *A Catalogue of the a Portion of the Library of Edmund Gosse* (London: privately printed, 1893).
3. See **4.27**.
4. Tuerk.

Σωστρα[1] may serve to exempt her from all such mischances in the future.

Sincerely yours | Ernest Myers.

4.38 ❧ C. J. CRUTTWELL TO HENRY DANIEL, 21 DECEMBER 1881[2]

Newhaven Lodge | 15 Thistle Grove, S.W. | 21 Dec. 1881.
My dear Henry
Very many thanks for the "Garland of Rachel—a tribute to a darling little child, such as has not been often seen; so luxuriously beautiful & so chastely classical; its topic at once & sentiment, that of infantine innocence, touched in many aspects by many minds, & exquisitely set off by 2 loving parents' loving toils—a gem of typography & ornamentation happily embodying a happy idea.

But I turn to the contents— Am I wrong in attributing to you the first on the list with its pretty picture of a crowing chickabid,[3] its "dimpled hands" stretched out to pull your whiskers; a reminiscence of my own boy Wilson? Mr Dobson's & Mr Lang's are both pleasant & to the point. "Merton ringdoves coo"[4] strikes a chord: I trace that quaint pen, methinks, in the Daily News. Mr Bridges' pretty lines are overweighted. Lewis Carroll is very sweet but his last line is literal Shelley. The Latin & French pass me. "Lullaby Baby" reminds of "Baby boy." Gifford's "Baviad"[5] spoils me for Mr Gosse, who I guess to be a son of Omphalos.[6] Mr Bourdillon's sonnet (you know my predilection for sonnets) is exquisite, as is the first half of Mr Courthope's. Mr Locker I cannot unriddle. I am

---

1. *Sostra*, reward (Greek). Henry Daniel had used this word in his preface to the *Garland*.
2. Tuerk.
3. *Chickabiddy* is a term of endearment for a child.
4. A phrase in Andrew Lang's poem.
5. *The Baviad* (1791) by William Gifford.
6. *Omphalos* (1857), a notorious book written by Gosse's father Philip Gosse, that argued against evolution.

afraid some frail fair damsel has played him a practical joke in his college garden. Are you in his secret? [...]

4.39 ☙ J. A. SYMONDS TO HENRY DANIEL, 9 JANUARY 1882[1]

Hôtel & Pension Buol | Davos-Platz | Jan: 9. 1882.

Dear Mr. Daniel

I wish to tell you with delight I received your quite uniquely dainty "Garland" yesterday, & with what interest I have read its contents. It is a most beautiful little book. Let me congratulate you on its being truly a sostra. I was so sorry to hear of Rachel's illness from my sister Mrs. Green:[2] for I need not say that, though I have never seen Rachel, I feel, as I suppose all her poets do, a sort of godfather to her, & imagine in her every grace & virtue deserving of long life.

What a delicate thought it was to put a fresh name on each title-page!

Some of the pieces are very pretty, & not least pretty are those by the unprofessional poets: espy. L. M. [sic] Woods', Ward's, & the first. Mary Robinson has written a really charming little nursery song.

Do you not think you could send also a photograph to Rachel's godfathers? It need not be put into the book so as to spoil it for bibliophiles. Yet it might lie loose within the pages.

I envy the power of printing as you print! But perhaps if I had it, I might spend too much time in too exquisitely printing to my own author's vanity by getting up my wretched verses in a form wh[ich] would compell [sic] the curious at least in lovely typography to regard them.

Believe me very truly yours | J. A. Symonds.

---

1. Tuerk.
2. Symonds' favorite sister Charlotte.

4.40 ❦ F. W. BOURDILLON TO HENRY DANIEL, 19 JANUARY 1882[1]

Hurlingham House, | Eastbourne. | Jan: 19th 1882

Dear Mr Daniell [*sic*],

I have just returned home, and find your beautiful "Garland of Rachel," which must have come immediately after I left; but was not sent on to me. Thank you very much for it. It is so charming in every way, that in admiration of printing, binding, and paper, I almost forgot to read the verses. However I have now done so, and like them,—some of them very much.

What a work it must have been to you and to Mrs Daniel, the "miniation" is so delightful, and adds much to the book. Personally I feel proud to be admitted as contributor amid so distinguished a gathering[.]

You may be interested to hear that I am going soon to be married, to a sister of one of my pupils, Miss Agnes Watson-Smyth. We hope to be married "next holidays" as the pedagogue needs say, "in April" as common folk speak.— My brother Gerard also is engaged, but has to wait for a living.

With kind regards and a respectful salutation (of whatever kind she will most appreciate) to "Rachel"—who, I much hope, is quite well again now.

believe me | Very sincerely yours | F. W. Bourdillon

[…]

4.41 ❦ P. F. WILLERT TO HENRY DANIEL, 20 JANUARY 1882[2]

Headington Hill, | Oxford. | Jan. 20. 82.

Dear Daniel

How shall I thank you for the book beautiful within & without & which is to be a perpetual memento of your great happiness &

---

1. Tuerk.
2. Tuerk.

mine? I am not a bibliophile as you know, a unique title page has no charms for me, but I am not such a philistine as to be unable to appreciate your beautiful type & paper. As to the binding I never saw anything prettier.

Once more many thanks from us both—may all good things prophesied for Rachel & many more befall her.

Yours very sincerely | P. F. Willert

4.42 ❧ HENRY DANIEL TO FREDERICK LOCKER, 15 FEBRUARY 1882[1]

Worcester House, | Oxford | Feb. 15, 1882.

My dear Sir

Allow me to thank you very much in my little daughter's name for the most charming and kindly Valentine which you have bestowed upon her. I need hardly say that as yet the Book pleases Father & Mother more than herself. But in time to come she will be very proud of the possession of your keepsake and of your autograph. As yet the child can hardly be said to have developed literary tastes, for though she asks to be taken to her fathers ă (the crude form of study) it is rather with an eye to prospective goodies than from a love for books.

Again thanking you on the behalf of Rachel, her Mother and myself

I am | Yours faithfully & obliged | Henry Daniel

4.43 ❧ W. J. COURTHOPE TO HENRY DANIEL, 18 FEBRUARY 1882[2]

Education Department | Whitehall | 18 Feby. 1882

My dear Mr. Daniel

I have to thank you very sincerely for so kindly sending me a pre-

---

1. With Locker copy [**3.12**].
2. Tuerk.

sentation copy of 'Rachel's Garland'. For my own part I am only sorry I did not know the 'child' about whom I was asked to write was your little girl—I would then have made a more auspicious contribution to the 'garland'.

I was only told that the subject was *a* child, and the birth of a little niece in winter suggested lines which I fear are rather too melancholy for the occasion.

The appearance of the book is beautiful. Thanking you once more for sending it to me

I am | yrs. truly | W J Courthope.

4.44 ❧ MARY ROBINSON TO HENRY DANIEL, 5 MARCH 1882[1]

84 Gower Street. London. | March 5th. 1882.

Dear Mr. Daniel

When I came back from Italy on Thursday night, I found your most rare and beautiful gift awaiting me. It is indeed an unexampled christening present; and even if, when little Rachel grows up, she shall hate the bards with all Mr Dobson's prophesied intensity she must still be proud of the book as an artistic production. The little frontispiece is, in its way, a perfect thing, to my mind. The poems are all very pretty & charming & full of delicate humour. I like Mr. Dobson's & Mr. Symonds's, & Mr. Henley's the best. But it is a complete 'Wits' Miscellany.'

Thanking you very sincerely for the prettiest return that I think was ever made for the saying of a nursery rhyme.

Believe me | Truly yours | Mary Robinson.

---

1. Tuerk.

CORRESPONDENCE

4.45 ❧ ANDREW LANG TO W. IRVING WAY, 26 NOVEMBER [1882][1]

1, Marloes Road, | Kensington. W. | Nov. 26

My dear Sir

I am very grateful for all the kind things you say of H. of T.[2] A sculptor has put new claws on your Mexican owl, which is now justly admired by all who have the privilege of his acquaintance.

It must be hard to get books when catalogues have to come from so far. Fortunately, as you are interested in the *Garland* of Miss Daniel, I can send you a copy, which, I hope, will reach you safely. You will find no merit in it, but rarity: it is nearly as rare as Hookes's *Amanda*.[3] I fancy only 35 copies exist. The printer is a Worcester Don, who has a small private press. What with the Sunderland, Beckford, and other sales, we have plenty of bookish entertainments here.[4] Paul[5] is bringing out quite a brood of his "parchment" volumes, of which Shelley's letters, and Saintsbury's French Lyrics should be the best.

Believe me | Yours very sincerely | A Lang.

I am going soon to look for your box of curiosities, which must soon arrive[.]

4.46 ❧ HENRY DANIEL TO C. L. DODGSON, 11 MAY 1887[6]

Worcester College | May 11. 1887.

My dear Dodgson

The first piece in the Garland of Rachel is the Printer's—the sec-

---

1. With Lang copy [3.11]. The date is supplied by the postmarked envelope, which is addressed to Way in Topeka, Kans.
2. Lang's *Helen of Troy* (1882).
3. Marginal note, apparently in Way's hand: "For an account of *Amanda* see Philoblion p. 187[.]"
4. The libraries of Charles Spencer (3rd Earl of Sunderland) and William Beckford were being auctioned in London in 1882.
5. Kegan Paul, a London publisher.
6. With Dodgson copy [4.29].

ond (signed W.) is Albert Watson's the present principal of B.N.C. and the final piece signed C.J.C. is by Charles James Cruttwell, uncle of the Printer, some of whose poems—notably "Massacre of Cabul" (Pickering) you will find in Bodley if not out on loan!—

Sincerely yours | C. Henry Daniel

4.47 ❧ EMILY DANIEL TO HORATIO SYMONDS, 9 DECEMBER 1892[7]

Worcester House, | Oxford | Dec 9th 1892

Dear Mr. Symonds

We are sending you with our very best wishes for your future happiness a copy of the "Garland of Rachel". We thought as you had done so very much for her you might like to have her book. I think you know its history & that it is regarded as a literary curiosity.

Believe me | yours very sincerely | Emily Daniel.

You will see that the special title page which differs with each copy has I may say a family appropriateness.

4.48 ❧ C. L. DODGSON TO HENRY DANIEL, 11 MAY 1895[8]

Ch. Ch. | May 11/95

My dear Daniell [sic],

I am preparing for the Press a reprint of some serious poems, & would be glad to know if it will be quite agreeable to you that I should include the verses written for the "Garland of Rachel".[9] If you feel any wish that they should be, so to speak, unique, in your book, and shd not appear in any other form, of course it shall be so.

Very truly yours, | C. L. Dodgson

---

7. With Samuels Lasner copy [3.31].
8. Tuerk.
9. This projected book never appeared.

CORRESPONDENCE

4.49 ❧ HENRY DANIEL TO C. M. FALCONER, 12 OCTOBER 1896[1]

Worcester House | Oxford | Oct 12. 1896.

Dear Sir

I am afraid the Garland of Rachel is *introuvable*.[2] I think only 36 copies were printed, one for each of the contributors—with independent title pages—and I think 6 were sold. If a copy came into the market, the price would probably range from £7 to £10.

But, luckily for your collection of Langiana, I found in a portfolio a rough proof of Lang's contribution to which you are welcome—as well as one of Robert Bridges' little Poems written for the collection years ago, Lang and I proposed to issue a little collection of poems on 'sleep'—but it came to nothing—and I do not suppose it will ever be carried out. Should I ever print anything for or in connection with him I will let you know.

"Rachel" is my daughter. Gosse, Dobson, Henley, Lewis Carroll, Mrs. Woods and other friends contributed to the Garland.

Yours faithfully | C. Henry Daniel.

4.50 ❧ HENRY DANIEL TO C. M. FALCONER, 23 DECEMBER 1896[3]

Worcester College, Oxford. | Dec 28. '96.

Dear Sir

I herewith return to you by Registered Parcel your very admirable transcript of the 'Garland of Rachel'—you have done the Book too much honour in taking such pains over it. If my printed copies are a treasure to the Collector, your MS is ten times more so. And the copies of the head pieces are perfect—while your printer has caught the look of the somewhat artless volume admirably.

I am sorry to have kept it so long, but I lay in ambush for

---

1. Getty.
2. Impossible to find (French).
3. With Falconer facsimile [3.40].

the one or two Oxford contributors—to obtain their signatures for you. Alas! I have been able to do next [to] nothing for you. Two—'W'[1] and Lewis Carroll[—]would not be won over. The former from modesty, the latter because even in this case he would not break his rule—never to give his signature. Mrs. Woods I got upon her return to Oxford and your humble servant has signed a production of his own for the first time. So that I am not quite re enfecta.[2]

But to atone to some extent for this failure I have hunted up and send you for your acceptance a copy of the missive which was despatched to each of the authors with his copy— I doubt if I have another of these myself.

With best Xmas wishes | I am | Yours faithfully | C Henry Daniel

4.51 ❧ EDMUND GOSSE TO C. M. FALCONER, 19 JANUARY 1897[3]

29, Delamere Terrace, | Westbourne Square, W. | 19. 1. 97

My dear Sir

Your transcript of the Garland of Rachel is a miracle of skilful and industrious ingenuity. I would fain add something to such a labour of love, and I therefore enclose the signature of my dear late friend, Mr. Symonds.

Believe me to be | Faithfully yrs | Edmund Gosse

C. M. Falconer Esq.

---

1. Albert Watson.
2. Without success (Latin).
3. With Falconer facsimile [3.40].

4.52 ❦ W. E. HENLEY TO C. M. FALCONER, 22 JANUARY 1897[1]

Stanley Lodge, | Muswell Hill. N. | 22/1/97

Dear Sir,

I wish the verses had been better; but I've signed them with pleasure all the same.

Your transcript deserves all that Mr. Daniel says of it. I'm glad to have seen it[.]

Very truly yours | W. E. Henley

C. M. Falconer Esq.

4.53 ❦ EDMUND GOSSE TO C. M. FALCONER, 25 JANUARY 1897[2]

Board of Trade, S.W. | 29 Delamere Terrace | W. | 25. 1. 97

My dear Sir

I know nothing of Mr. Bourdillon, and Mr. Ernest Myers (I believe) lives somewhere in the country. Mr. Lang would know his address. Miss Mary Robinson is the widow of the late Prof. Darmesteter and lives in Paris. I enclose her Mother's address, and that of Mr. Ward.

I signed your book & returned it this morning.

Mr. Lang's first work of 1863 I never heard of. It must be very curious, and I congratulate you on its possession.[3] I mean to write to you again about his editions of the Blue & White Ballads.[4]

Sincerely yrs | Edmund Gosse

C. M. Falconer Esq

---

1. With Falconer facsimile [3.40].
2. With Falconer facsimile [3.40].
3. Lang's first publication, a poem entitled "Sir Launcelot," appeared in the March 1863 issue of the *St. Andrews University Magazine*.
4. *XXXII Ballades in Blue China* (1881).

4.54 ❧ W. J. COURTHOPE TO C. M. FALCONER, 27 JANUARY 1897[1]

29, Chester Terrace, | Regents Park. | 27 January 1897

Dear Sir

I return your transcript of 'The Garden [sic] of Rachel' with my signature to my contribution. As Mr Daniel says the result of your labours does much honour to everyone who had a share in the volume[.]

Yrs faithfully | W J Courthope

4.55 ❧ T. H. WARD TO FALCONER, 29 JANUARY 1897[2]

25, Grosvenor Place, S. W. | Jan 29. 97.

Dear Sir,

I am much flattered by the tribute you have paid to the little volume, of which I believe I was the first to give the suggestion to Mr Daniel. I have signed with much pleasure. Your transcript is charmingly done: Mr Daniel's letter is not at all too strong.

The book goes back to you today, by registered post.

Yrs [*illegible*] | T H Ward

C. M. Falconer

4.56 ❧ ERNEST MYERS TO C. M. FALCONER, 6 FEBRUARY 1897[3]

Brackenside, | Chislehurst. | Feb. 6. 1897.

Dear Sir

I am returning by Registered Parcel 'Rachel's Garland' with my signature as you desire.

Mr Daniel must indeed be pleased at your admirable reproduc-

---

1. With Falconer facsimile [3.40].
2. With Falconer facsimile [3.40].
3. With Falconer facsimile [3.40].

tion of his little book, & at the pains you have thought it worth while to bestow on it.

 Sincerely yours | Ernest Myers.

Perhaps you wd. send a post-card to tell me of its safe return?[1]

4.57   SIR RICHARD HARINGTON TO C. M. FALCONER, 11 FEBRUARY 1897[2]

    Whitbourne Court, | Worcester. | 11 Feb 1897

Dear Sir,

 I have some little difficulty in putting my name to my very poor translation of my friend Lewis Carroll's very pretty lines in the Garland of Rachel, because there are two errors in them, as there are unfortunately in Mr Daniel's print[.]

 The word "occisos" in the 15th line should read "Exanimos", & the 17th & 18th lines should read

> "Dat voces turtur, Veneri devota moratu
> Quâ nova nupta diu."

The original draft was as your copy, but my attention being called to the bad grammar & clumsy expressions in the lines in question, I altered them, & sent to Daniel a corrected copy. Unluckily he by mistake printed from the wrong M.S. & didn't like to affirm blunders which I had endeavoured to correct.

 Allow me to add to Mr Daniels remarks my own appreciation of [the] very nice way in which your copy is got up. I retain it pending your reply[.]

 Yours faithfully | Richard Harington

[…]

---

1. Myers sent Falconer a second note on 9 February [3.40] expressing relief that the *Garland* facsimile had safely reached its destination.
2. With Falconer facsimile [3.40].

4.58 ❧ SIR RICHARD HARINGTON TO C. M. FALCONER,
14 FEBRUARY 1897[1]

Whitbourne Court, | Worcester. | 14 Feb 1897

Dear Sir,

It seems to me that the best way out of the difficulty will be to append footnotes in ink, as & when I have written them in lead pencil.

All I wish, is to escape responsibility for a clumsy epithet, & bad grammar.

In the faith that you will take care that this object is accomplished I have signed my lines.

The word you could not read was "devota". The lines run

> Dat voces turtur. Veneri devota moratur
> Quâ nova nupta diu.

Yours faithfully | Richard Harington

Falconer Esq

4.59 ❧ AUGUSTINE BIRRELL TO C. M. FALCONER,
22 FEBRUARY [1897][2]

30, Lower Sloane Street, | S.W. | Feb. 22.

My dear Sir

I am returning your beautiful book per registered post. I will look up a letter of Mr Locker,[3] but he generally wrote in pencil & only signed his initials, but if I haven't one I will write Mrs LL.

Yours | A Birrell

---

1. With Falconer facsimile [3.40].
2. With Falconer facsimile [3.40]. A postcard.
3. Birrell was Locker's son-in-law.

CORRESPONDENCE

4.60 ❧ MARY ROBINSON TO C. M. FALCONER, [24 FEBRUARY 1897][1]

Dear Sir   I feel much flattered by your kind request. I would advise you however not to send the book for the moment as, at this moment, I may be leaving for the South and I should not like so valuable a volume to run any risk during my absence—which may last at least a month.

M. J. Darmester   18 B[ouvelar]d de la Tour Maubourg

4.61 ❧ HENRY DANIEL TO C. M. FALCONER, 1 MARCH 1897[2]

Worcester College, Oxford. | March 1. '97

My dear Sir

I congratulate you on the success which has attended your hunt for signatures. Of C.J.C[3] who is now dead I have hunted up the signature which I herewith enclose. W. is the Rev. Albert Watson, Fellow (late Principal of Brasenose College, Oxford.) Although he refused me, he may perhaps change his mind under the circumstances. "Lewis Carroll"—the Rev C. Dodgson, Christ Church Oxford—you might try, but I do not think for a moment you will overcome his resolution never under any circumstances to give his autograph. I apprehend he will even take a sort of pleasure in being the only blank.

I am | Yours sincerely | C Henry Daniel

---

1. With Falconer facsimile [3.40]. A postcard sent from Paris; Falconer had earlier consulted Robinson's father about her address.
2. With Falconer facsimile [3.40].
3. C. J. Cruttwell.

4.62 ⁂ ALBERT WATSON TO C. M. FALCONER, 4 MARCH 1897[1]

Brasenose College | Oxford, March 4 | 1897

Dear Sir

I am afraid that the reasons which have led me to decline hitherto to allow my name to appear among those of the contributors to "the Garland of Rachel" are still in force.

I need, I hope, hardly assure that it is with much regret that I refuse a request made in such terms as yours, and by a friend of Mr. Andrew Lang, for whose literary taste I have such respect, and from whose works I have derived so much pleasure.

I hope that you will not object to my returning you the amount of the postage of the parcel, which I return herewith

I am | faithfully yours | Albert Watson

C. M. Falconer

4.63 ⁂ HENRY DANIEL TO C. M. FALCONER, 18 SEPTEMBER 1897[2]

Oxford | Sept 18. 97

My dear Sir

Many thanks for remittance for which I send receipt. I hope the Japanese things will reach you in a weeks time. They are being put into thin covers.

What odd forms modesty takes—as in Mr Watson's case. It is with him pure bashfulness, not as with Dodgson—a caprice.

I send you a 'Locker letter' without mutilations. As it refers to the little poem, you may set additional store by it—though the signature must face his Poem and not foot it.

Yours sincerely | C. Henry Daniel

---

1. With Falconer facsimile [3.40].
2. With Falconer facsimile [3.40].

CORRESPONDENCE

4.64 ❧ HENRY DANIEL TO C. M. FALCONER, 19 JANUARY 1898[3]

Jan. 19. '98 | Oxford.

My dear Sir

I enclose you a holograph of our lamented friend[4]—of some interest in itself—to which you are welcome

and am | Yours sincerely | C Henry Daniel

[*enclosure*]

Ch. Ch. Jan. 27 / 94

Dear Mrs. Daniel,

Your kind offer, to give me a photo of your children, was very nearly escaping my knowledge altogether: it remained behind in the big envelope, which I threw aside as empty, & by mere accident happened to take it up again & noticed it had something in it. Such small enclosures had better always be put across the top of the large one, to secure their being taken out. I will gratefully accept your offer, & will call some time (but not on Monday, the day mentioned to Mrs. Daniel) to see the photos.

I suppose you have taken to the 'dry' process. I wish some amateur would again take up the 'wet' process, which I worked for 25 years. Its results are far more delicate and artistic: this professionals admit, but cannot afford to adopt it, as it takes so much more time. Its only chance is with amateurs. I would take it up again myself, if I could, but expect the rest of my life will be none too much for the writing I have yet to do.

Believe me | sincerely yours, | C. L Dodgson

Many thanks for the printed verses.

---

3. With Falconer facsimile [**3.40**].
4. Dodgson died on 14 January 1898.

DANIEL PRESS & GARLAND OF RACHEL

4.65 &ev; HENRY DANIEL TO W. E. MOSS, 31 MAY [1898][1]

May 31

Dear Mr. Moss

The compliment you paid my book in expending so many shekels on its purchase deserves that I should equip you with the circular letter which accompanied each contributor's copy. [2] My wife has at last hunted up a specimen—which please accept. You know, no doubt that your copy is unique—no other bearing Lewis Carroll's name on the titlepage.

Sincerely yours | C. Henry Daniel

4.66 &ev; EMILY DANIEL TO T. B. MOSHER, 28 DECEMBER 1901[3]

Worcester House, | Oxford. | Dec 28th. 1901

Dear Sir

36 copies of The Garland [of] Rachel were printed in 1881. of these 18 copies were bound in white vellum & given to the 18 contributors to the Garland—one of these only (so far as we know) has come in to the market i.e. Lewis Carroll's copy[.] This copy was bought at the sale of Lewis Carrolls books by a Mr. Moss for £12: 12.

The other copies were issued in various bindings (all the copies were bound, there were no paper wrappers). I am now at Mr. Williams & Norgate[']s request sending a copy, (the last we have,) in sheets absolutely as it came from the press.[4] If you do not like it you are at liberty to return it, as we have had another application for it

---

1. With Dodgson copy 2 [4.29].
2. Moss purchased Dodgson's copy of the *Garland*—now at New York University—on 11 May 1898, but it did not include the preface.
3. With Newberry Library copy [3.29]. Part of this letter was quoted by Mosher in his reprint of the *Garland*, p. xxvi.
4. This phrase has been underlined, presumably by Mosher, with two exclamation points in the margin. Williams & Norgate were London booksellers and publishers, but they had an Oxford office as well.

since I have been in communication with Messrs. Williams & Norgate about it.

Believe me | Yours faithfully | Emily Daniel.

4.67 & NOTE BY EMILY DANIEL, 20 FEBRUARY 1902[1]

Worcester House. | Oxford. | Feb 20th: 1902.

An account of the "Garland of Rachel" appears in the Century Magazine Vol. xxiii—49. Feb: 1882. pages 438 & 439. I do not know whether this is the account to which your client refers. I do not remember any other account in an American Magazine—

An account of the "Daniel Press" appeared in the September 1900 number of "The Library" [Kegan Paul Trench & Co) in which there is a short account of the Garland of Rachel.[2]

E. Daniel

4.68 & C. M. FALCONER TO T. B. MOSHER, 1 MARCH 1902[3]

Falconhurst Terrace, | Hyndford Street, | Dundee. | 1st March 1902

Dear Sir

Your letter and Catalogue of the 14th ult. was delivered to my brother, who is a local antiquary and collector, but it is meant for me.

I am afraid Mr Shorter's note in the "Sphere" has misled you. I sent him a newspaper cutting, like enclosed, giving a description of my unique copy of "The Garland of Rachel" (which was written by myself for our principal local newspaper)[4] and in his hurry he has

---

1. With Newberry Library copy [3.29]. Apparently sent to Williams & Norgate in response to a query from Mosher.

2. Henry R. Plomer, "Some Private Presses of the Nineteenth Century." *The Library* NS 1 (September 1900): 407-28.

3. With Newberry Library copy [3.29].

4. "The Garland of Rachel: Unique Copy in Dundee," *Dundee Advertiser*, 23 May 1898.

written as if I had *reprinted* Mr Daniel's book—a course which it would have been impossible for me to take.

This description of a famous book, is the fullest I know of and has been reprinted by several papers, and made use of, among others, in Mr Frank Murray's Bibliography of Austin Dobson's Works, where, doubtless you have seen it. I have a short account of the original cut from *The Century Magazine* (I think) of some years ago, but it does not contain any additional information

Many thanks for your Catalogue which is very interesting

 Yours truly | C. M. Falconer

Thos. B. Mosher Esq.

4.69 ·❧ C. M. FALCONER TO T. B. MOSHER, 29 MARCH 1902[1]

Falconhurst Terrace, | Hyndford Street, | Dundee. |
29th March 1902

My Dear Sir,

You are very good to send me such a handsome book as "Aes Triplex"[2] and I thank you for it. It is a charming reproduction of [a] very charming work. I have the Scribner "Christmas Sermon" also sent me by an American friend.[3] Your dainty booklet is a worthy neighbor.

I am sorry I cannot assist you to any more information about "The Garland of Rachel." I am afraid you will have some difficulty in picking up the pamphlet preface, for being separate it would not be kept by the owners with the same care as the book. My copy was Mr Daniel's own: he had no other, and it was very good of him to let me have it. I would not have known of its existence otherwise.

---

 1. With Newberry Library copy [**3.29**].

 2. Robert Louis Stevenson, *Aes Triplex and Other Essays* (Portland, Me.: Thomas B. Mosher, 1902).

 3. Stevenson, *A Christmas Sermon* (New York: Charles Scribner's Sons, 1900).

If I had an original copy such as yours I should keep it in the original binding: it was different with mine, for it had to be bound.

Sincerely yours | C. M. Falconer

Thomas B. Mosher Esq

4.70 ☙ CLEMENT SHORTER TO T. B. MOSHER, 9 APRIL 1902[1]

The Sphere | The Tatler | Great New Street, | Fetter Lane, E.C. | April 9, 1902.

T. B. Mosher, Esq., | Portland Maine, U.S.A.

Dear Mr. Mosher,

I have been a long while answering your enquiries, but so far as that author is concerned I have not been able to trace him, and now I have, unhappily, mislaid your letter.

With reference, however, to "Rachel's Garland," I put the matter into the hands of a great friend of Mrs. Daniels [*sic*]—the daughter [*sic*] of Rachel, and, as you know, the wife of the printer of the Daniels Press books, of Worcester College, Oxford. This friend spent Easter with the Daniels, and came away with the following suggestions.

First; Mrs. Daniels thinks that as you have already printed two of their books, if you are going to print any more you should put them on the free-list of all your publications.

Secondly. Mrs. Daniels is an enthusiast for several Oxford charities. It was she who did the illuminated letters on each of the copies of "Rachel's Garland." The fact that you have not got illuminated letters upon yours proves that it was not one for which she engaged to do this. She would undertake to put the letters on your copy of the book if you send her Five Guineas, which she would devote to one of her charities.

Thirdly; the enquiry was in reference to an article that appeared on "Rachel's Garland," and I understand was in a Number of the

---

1. With Newberry Library copy [**3.29**]. Shorter (1857–1926) was a well-known English journalist and editor.

CENTURY some twenty years ago, and was written by Edmund Gosse.[1]

I think I now have answered all your queries, except the reference to that mysterious author. By the way, you sent me the other day a little book with an inscription to Fiona Macleod.[2] I forwarded it to Mr. William Sharp, Fiona Macleod's cousin. I imagine the copy intended for me went to her, in which case I shall doubtless get it soon.

I am, Dear Mr. Mosher, | Yours very truly, | Clement Shorter

4.71 ❧ EMILY DANIEL TO T. B. MOSHER, 3 AUGUST 1902[3]

Worcester House, | Oxford. | Aug 3rd. 1902.

My dear Sir,

I am sorry to have left your letter so long unanswered.

I am now sending you a specimen letter (a view of Oxford)[.] I shall be happy to put in letters after this manner for your copy of the "Garland of Rachel" if you approve of the manner of letters & like to send me your copy.

With regard to your kind offer of sending me copies of your book in return for the copies of the "Daniel Press" books I could not ask this of you as our books are issued so very seldom & we never know when another will be forthcoming. I am however much obliged to you for the copies of Aes Triplex & Doris an Idyll[4] both of which I am very glad to have & especially the latter as Dr. Jessop is a Fellow of our College & I have a very great admiration for his writing.

The Stevenson essays are also delightful.

---

1. The article was in fact by Austin Dobson: "Bric-a-brac: The Garland of Rachel," *Century Illustrated Monthly Magazine* 23 (February 1882): 639–40.

2. Fiona Macleod was the *nom de plume* of William Sharp. Mosher reprinted a number of his books.

3. With Newberry Library copy [**3.29**].

4. Mosher reprinted both Stevenson's *Aes Triplex* and Augustus Jessopp's "Doris: An Idyl of Arcady" in 1902, the latter in *The Bibelot*.

Believe me with many apologies for delay in answering your letter

Yours sincerely | Emily Daniel

I do not want the specimen returned.

[*Note by Mosher at the bottom of the page*]

Nov 15 02 | 5 R | 1 R [illegible] of towers D | 1 promises to illuminate— | £5. 5. | as to books opening line?

4.72 ❧ EMILY DANIEL TO T. B. MOSHER, 30 NOVEMBER 1902[1]

Worcester House, | Oxford. | Nov: 30th. 1902

Dear Sir

Very many thanks for your letter & cheque for £5: 5 & also for the most interesting parcel of books. The Garland of Rachel (original copy) arrived quite safely & I will put in the water colour letters & return as soon as I can, but our days are too dark & foggy at present time & there is not light enough for fine work.

"The Garland of Rachel" brought out by you is a very pretty book, & we shall find the list of books at the end most useful as it is the only printed list of "Daniel Press Books". My daughter is going to write you her own thanks for your gift. The other 5 copies you mention as having sent have not yet arrived. Of course we shall be very glad to have them—& also another 5 copies which you are kind enough to say you will send if we should like to have them. We should be very glad to have them. I have also to thank you for your kindness in sending Shakespeare's Sonnets & Michael Angelo's 'Sonnets' & the little book of Stevenson's Essays, all these books are charming—& very beautifully printed.[2]

I am going to leave the latter part of your letter in which you

---

1. With Newberry Library copy [**3.29**].

2. *Shakespeare's Sonnets* (1901), *The Sonnets of Michael Angelo Buonarroti* (1897), *Aes Triplex* by Robert Louis Stevenson (1902), all published by Mosher.

kindly offer to be agent for Daniel Press books in America, for my husband to answer, as he is better able to do this than I am—

 With renewed thanks | Believe me | yours sincerely | Emily Daniel.

4.73 ❧ RACHEL DANIEL TO T. B. MOSHER, 30 NOVEMBER 1902[1]

 Worcester House, Oxford. | Sunday Nov. 30. 1902

Dear Sir,
 Thank you very much for sending me a copy of "The Garland of Rachel" printed so charmingly on Japanese vellum. I am very glad to have it. It is also nice to have a complete list of the Daniel Press Books.
 I think it would be delightful to have the five copies you so kindly suggest sending us.

 Yours sincerely | Rachel Daniel

4.74 ❧ EMILY DANIEL TO T. B. MOSHER, 4 JANUARY 1903[2]

 Worcester House, | Oxford. | Jan 4th. 1903

Dear Sir
Very many thanks for your last letter. I am glad to say the 2d five copies of the "Garland of Rachel["] arrived safely a few days before Christmas—& the first five copies you sent arrived from London a day or two later so I have now received all ten copies you so kindly sent.
 I am getting on the initial letters of your original copy of the Garland & I shall hope to send it (carefully packed & registered) before very long. I am most obliged to you for saying I need not hurry over it. I am trying to put in an appropriate view of Oxford to each contributor's poem—i.e. so far as I am able to do a view of the

---

1. With Newberry Library copy [**3.29**].
2. With Newberry Library copy [**3.29**].

College to which the Contributor belonged. I will send a list of the views with the book. I hope you will like them.

Believe me with many thanks for the 10 copies of the Garland & with all good wishes for 1903

Yours sincerely | Emily Daniel

4.75 &❧ EMILY DANIEL TO T. B. MOSHER,
21 FEBRUARY 1903[1]

Worcester House, | Oxford | Feb 21st 1903

Dear Sir

I am today sending you, your copy of "The Garland of Rachel" with the initial letters put in. I hope you will like them, I am sorry to have been so long in doing them, but you kindly said you were in no hurry for them.

I am enclosing a list of the views, thinking you may like to know the places they represent. As far as possible I have tried to give the poet a picture of his college & have underlined the college in the list where this is the case. I am sending you the sheets carefully packed & registered as you sent them to me.

Hoping that they will arrive safely & that you will like them

Believe me | yours faithfully | Emily Daniel

4.76 &❧ MARGARET L. WOODS TO C. H. WILKINSON,
[C. 1920][2]

Dear Mr Wilkinson

You have asked me to do a very difficult thing—[3] I never can write a poem deliberately. The poem in Rachel's 'Garland' was an

---

1. With Newberry Library copy [3.29].
2. With Symonds copy, Fales Library [3.15].
3. Wilkinson had asked for a contribution to the *Memorials* volume. Instead of a poem, Margaret Woods sent him an essay on "Henry Daniel and His Home" (*Memorials*, pp. 22–31).

exception, because children are so easy to write about. But I should not like to be absent from any gathering of friends, in any form, to do honour to the memory of Henry Daniel, & therefore I will do my best, & only regret that the tribute is not likely to be worth much. When would you want to have it?— Please send me a line to | Highlands | North Parade | Southwold | Suffolk—

yrs sincerely | Margaret L. Woods

4.77 ❧ EMILY DANIEL TO DAME KATHERINE FURSE, 3 JANUARY 1920[1]

Oddington | Moreton-in-Marsh | Jan 3. 1920

Dear Dame Katherine

I opened your letter to my husband which was forwarded to me here yesterday: He died on Sept. 6. There were notices of his death in all the papers—the Times article which appeared Sept. 7th was headed "Treasures of the Daniel Press". I conclude your copy of the "Garland of Rachel" is the copy which belonged to your father, Mr. John Addington Symonds, in which case it will bear his name on the title page and which will add to its value its having been his copy. Every contributor to the "Garland of Rachel["] has his name on the title page thereby appearing the principal contributor, so out of the 36 copies there are no two title pages alike. Only two or three copies have ever come into the market—Lewis Carroll's (I do not remember what his sold for)[2] and one or two more, at most—a copy was for sale after my husband's library was sold in October, for which £40 was asked. I expect this is already sold. I should think you would get more than this sum for it in America as there is, I believe, only one copy in America.[3]

My husband's press has gone to the Bodleian & is in the Long Gallery with a case of books one of which is the "Garland of Ra-

---

1. With Symonds copy [**3.15**].

2. Dodgson's copy was sold by Brooks of Oxford, 11 May 1898, for £12 10s.

3. She seems to be thinking of Poor's copy, but W. I. Way also owned the *Garland*.

chel". Some of the Poets of today are making a "Garland" of Verse in memory of my husband. Masefield has written a most charming poem for him which I received from him on Christmas Day.[1]

I very much rejoice in Mr. Furse's portrait of my husband, or rather in a reproduction of it as the original is not mine.[2]

Believe me | Yours sincerely | Emily Daniel

4.78 ❦ FALCONER MADAN TO CONSTANCE ASTLEY, 16 FEBRUARY 1922[3]

Brasenose College | Oxford. | Feb. 16. 1922

THE DANIEL PRESS.

Dear Madam,

I was delighted to receive your letter. I had no idea where the Falconer Garland of Rachel had found a home. Oddly my name is Falconer! I only know the details given by Mosher, and trust that what I have printed about it is correct[4]. It must be of very considerable interest and value.

Certainly you shall receive the Addenda and Corrigenda.[5]

Not one of my reviewers, not even C. T. Jacobi,[6] has noted any one of the really distinctive features of the book, that is to say, in hap-hazard order:—

1. The book describes itself on p. 136—which is very rare[.]

2. The original leaves, as many as twelve, of Daniel printing. That is a very rare feature—and *three* is the utmost ever given before.

---

1. John Masefield's "The Dream," in *Memorials*, pp. 17–21.

2. The portrait of Daniel by C. W. Furse, reproduced as the frontispiece of *Memorials*, now hangs in Worcester College hall.

3. Getty. The first page of the letter is reproduced in Pl. 9.

4. In his bibliography Madan made only a passing reference to Falconer's manuscript transcription of the *Garland* (*Memorials*, p. 89).

5. Madan, *The Daniel Press: Addenda and Corrigenda* (Oxford: Oxford University Press, 1922).

6. Charles T. Jacobi, "Dr. Daniel and the Fell Types," *Bookman's Journal and Print Collector* NS 5 (February 1922): 163–66.

3. The Details given are far more elaborate than ever attempted before.

4. No one has before *attempted* to give prices, much less to separate them into decades.

5. The method of identifying small undated pieces by first words &c., I do not remember elsewhere.

6. Given a press producing 724 pieces, I doubt if any author of an account of it has possessed *all* its *known* issues.

I hope you secured one of the Édition de Luxe copies.[1]

Of course we shall be delighted to have you as a member of the Oxford Bibliographical Society. Your election shall be notified to you. […]

    I am | Very truly yours | F. Madan

Mrs Astley

Of the Memoirs of Dr. Daniel in the book, *Mrs. Woods's* is really firstrate, for intimacy, expression and humour; I hope you agree.

    Thanks indeed for your kind expressions about the book[.]

4.79 ❧ FALCONER MADAN TO CONSTANCE ASTLEY, 19 MARCH 1922[2]

    94, Banbury Road, | Oxford. | March 19. 1922

Dear Mrs. Astley,

I am very grateful for a detailed account of your wonderful copy of the *Garland of Rachel*. Your list of contents in excellent, and you are to be congratulated on possessing such a treasure, and I on knowing where it is. I wonder if you know *why* this Mr Falconer was so keen about that particular book.

You are fortunate also in having the printed preface, which is rather rarer than the Garland itself.

The Édition de Luxe will be difficult to pick up in the future. We

---

1. The de luxe edition of *Memorials* included some original leaves of Daniel Press books.
2. Getty.

did not anticipate a rush for it. It is quite *possible* that Messrs. Quaritch (11 Grafton Street, New Bond Street, London, W.1) has a copy, still, but at an enhanced price.

In my list of corrections and additions, I will mention (if I may) where the volume is: but of course not you unless have no objection. To save you time, I will assume that you give leave, if you do *not* write to me. My corrections will be out in July, see p. 40 of the *Daniel Press*.[1]

I am with very many thanks | Very truly yours | F. Madan

4.80 ❧ FALCONER MADAN TO CONSTANCE ASTLEY, 2 APRIL 1922[2]

94, Banbury Road, | Oxford | April 2. 1922

Dear Mrs. Astley,

That is very good of you, to offer me a copy of parts of your letters in that manuscript *Garland of Rachel*.

I should be very glad indeed to receive any sentences which bear on the *Daniel Press*, that is to say criticism or notes, such as Dr. Daniel's opinion of your manuscript, or any view expressed about individual contributions to it or about any other Daniel volume.

And in order that I may not be under a too heavy weight of obligation to you, I think I could spare you a set of the extra ten illustrations of the Édition de Luxe of the *Daniel Press*, if you fail to obtain a copy from Quaritch. You would thus have, *with* a copy of

---

1. ". . . I possess every Daniel piece printed at Frome or Oxford mentioned in the List which follows, and every variety of each piece. But there must be other minor pieces which have either perished or, if in existence, have not come to my notice, and I should welcome additions and corrections of any kind. Such as reach me before the end of June 1922 shall be summarized as Corrigenda, and shall be sent out soon after on a printed sheet to any subscriber who will signify that he wishes to receive it at a given address" (Memorials, p. 40). Madan's list of *Addenda & Corrigenda*, dated 1922, duly notes that "Mr. Falconer's transcript of the *Garland* is now in the possession of Mrs. Astley of Brinsop Court, Hereford, having been purchased by her in 1908" (p. 5).

2. Getty.

the guinea edition (which can I believe still be got from the "Controller, Clarendon Press, Oxford", though very few copies are left), all that is really valuable of both editions. I still have *one* set of the illustrations.

I am away for a fortnight from now, and there is no *urgency* about receiving what you so kindly offer. I am sure you will kindly give the *date*, *place* where written, and *signature*, in each extract: and will indicate by ... the place of omissions or any words left out.

I am with renewed thanks | Very truly yours | F. Madan

4.81 ❧ EMILY DANIEL TO CONSTANCE ASTLEY, 20 JANUARY 1930[1]

67, Iffley Road, | Oxford. | Jany 20. 1930.

Dear Madam

We returned this morning, your copy of the "Garland of Rachel"[2] with very many thanks. I have enjoyed looking at it very much & it brought back many happy memories of nearly 50 years ago— I am enclosing a snap shot of Rachel & her younger sister Ruth. I wish I had a copy of one taken this spring at Sialkot Railway Station,[3] with Rachel & her daughter, a replica of herself, garlanded!

If I do not hear from you to the contrary I shall conclude the "Garland" has reached you safely so please do not bother to write: again thank you[.]

Believe me | yours truly | Emily Daniel

4.82 ❧ LEONARD MOUNTENEY TO CHARLES H. SLOAN, 12 MARCH 1949[4]

5021 Dorchester Ave. | Chicago, Illinois | 3.12.49

Dear Mr. Sloan:

---

1. Getty.
2. The Falconer facsimile [**3.40**].
3. A city in the Punjab province of Pakistan.
4. With Newberry Library copy [**3.29**].

[...] You are most kind to invite me to spend my summer vacation with you & Mr. Abel, I know you would have many interesting things to show me & I would enjoy myself. I don't quite know what I will do when I get my vacation. If my health does not improve, I may go to St. Joseph's Hospital, Hot Springs, Ark. for two or three weeks.

I have done the greater part of the tooling on your Rachel. I hope to ship it next Thursday, there's a little more work on it than I expected, there's a solid & an outline heart shaped leaf all over the cover, the outline leaf was inlaid in the Riviere pattern, so I have treated your book in the same manner, 50 separate pieces of inlay on each cover. I know you will be glad to get it. I really expected to get it finished last week. I have a [sic] many visitors, a lady brought several calf books in & said she just wanted me to show her how to restore them, so she could do the work herself. Then she said she would stay & look over my shoulder, while I was inlaying your book, of course she promised not to talk to me, but she did not keep the promise. A friend of Mr Cuneo's brought two leather bound books in, she only wanted a name put on each book while she waited, those are the kind of hindrances I have to contend with, however I feel sure I will be able to ship your book next Thursday "God" willing[.]

Very best wishes to both Mr Abel & yourself
yours most sincerely | Leonard Mounteney

5. BOOKBINDERS

IN this chapter we describe the bookbinders who are associated with the known copies of *The Garland of Rachel*. The major difficulty here is that most of the copies—including, significantly, the contributors' copies—are in a white vellum binding, with simple gilt tooling and marbled endpapers, that is unsigned [*Fig. 21*].[1] However, we can see no reason to attribute this binding to any firm or individual bookbinder other than Morley & Sons in Oxford. Morley was the Daniel family's favorite local bindery, and the firm was especially celebrated for its work in vellum. "My binder is Morley, Long Wall Street—Oxford," Henry Daniel later commented in a letter,[2] and it seems highly unlikely that the Daniels would have entrusted the contributors' copies to any other bindery.

5.1 KATHARINE ADAMS

Katharine Adams (1862–1952) was born in Bracknell, Berkshire. In her early childhood, her father, the Rev. William Fulford Adams, became the incumbent of the estate church at Little Faringdon near Lechlade. He had been a friend of William Morris both at Marlborough and Oxford, and the move brought his family close to Kelmscott and the Morris family. (He had also known Henry

---

1. Emily Daniel's most precise description is in a letter to T. B. Mosher, 28 December 1901: "36 copies of the Garland were printed in 1881, of these 18 copies were bound in white vellum to give to the 18 contributors of the Garland" [**4.66**] What is slightly misleading about her comment is that, in addition to the contributors' copies, we have also found many other copies in the vellum binding.
2. Daniel to Charles Elkin Mathews, 7 October 1890 (Reading University Library).

Daniel when they were both Fellows of Worcester College.) From childhood onward, Katharine had connections with the Arts and Crafts community, including the Morris family, Sydney Cockerell, and Emery Walker.

Marianne Tidcombe has described her early attempts at bookbinding, from making simple books as a child to more complex youthful projects. It was not until her thirties, after lessons with Sarah Prideaux and Douglas Cockerell, that she took up bookbinding as a professional, and because of her friendship with the Daniel family (Emily in particular), some of her earliest bindings in the 1890s were on books published by the Daniel Press. Her first studio was in Lechlade, but by 1901 she had moved it to Broadway and named it Eadburgha after the parish church. The bindery was active until 1915.

On 8–9 March 1901, Emily Daniel opened her own home, Worcester House, for an exhibition of Katharine Adams' bindings. Fifty-six books were on display, fourteen of them Daniel Press publications. The variety of leathers and binding techniques was impressive: brown chrome calf, all colors of morocco, painted vellum, white pigskin, Niger goatskin. And the lenders of the bound books indicate that her customer base included many of the William Morris circle, such as Emery Walker, C. H. St. J. Hornby, Jane Morris, and F. S. Ellis.[1] She continued to exhibit her bindings, often with the Arts and Crafts Exhibition Society, and in galleries in London and abroad, partic-

---

1. A list of the items on display at the exhibition was issued under the title *Bookbindings by Katharine Adams at Worcester House, Oxford, on March 8th and 9th, 1901*. The list, set entirely in the Fell types and ornaments, closely resembles the Daniel Press style but was printed by Horace Hart at the University Press.

ularly during the early decades of the twentieth century. In 1935 she served as president of the Women's Guild of Art.

In 1913, at the age of 50, Katharine Adams married Edmund James Webb (1853-1945), a scholar presumably in retirement. After the marriage, the couple, who seemed to live only on the money Katharine Adams earned from bookbinding, sank increasingly into poverty as they moved deeper into the English countryside. Although Katharine continued binding, she gave up her studio and her two employees. By 1944, because of her shrinking income, she agreed to sell her collection of her own bindings at Sotheby's. The sale, which raised more than £2,000, alleviated her financial problems, and at the same time the high prices for individual books also demonstrated a widespread admiration for her work. Although she continued to bind occasional books after her husband's death in 1945, she found the work more difficult. She died at the age of 90 in 1952, leaving behind some uncompleted tasks: Sangorski & Sutcliffe finished the tooling on the Ashendene Press *Don Quixote* and the Lucretius now in the British Library. During her lifetime Katharine Adams bound a total of around 300 books, of which approximately a third were for St. John Hornby.

Today her books can be found in many major libraries, particularly in England and America. A number of her bindings are in the British Library's online Bookbinding Database. Her reputation has been growing in recent decades, and she is now regarded by many as one of the most accomplished English bookbinders of her generation.

COPY BOUND: Huntington Library (proofs) [**3.38**; *see also Pl. 6*].

WORCESTER HOUSE EXHIBITION: "Bookbindings at Oxford." *The Times*, 12 March 1901, p. 11. — F., H. H. "Bookbinding as a Fine Art." *Country Life* 10 (14 December 1901): 784-85. — "Notes and News." *Oxford Magazine* 19 (6 March 1901): 250.

REFERENCES: [Cockerell, Sir Sydney.] "Mrs. Edmund Webb. A Notable Bookbinder." *The Times*, 20 October 1952, p. 8. (Obituary.) — Corley, P. M. S. "Katharine Adams, C. H. St John Hornby and the Ashendene Press" (October 2000). (Typescript in Bridwell Library.) —Nixon, Howard M. *Five Centuries of English Bookbinding*. London: Scolar Press, 1978. (See pp. 220-21.) —*Proceedings: A Collection of Papers from the June 2000*

DANIEL PRESS & GARLAND OF RACHEL

Conference Celebrating the Installation and Opening of the Bernard C. Middleton Collection of Books on the History and Practice of Bookbinding. Rochester, N.Y.: Rochester Institute of Technology, Cary Graphic Arts Press, 2002. (See Marianne Tidcombe, "Women Bookbinders in Britain before the First World War," pp. 53–70.) — Tidcombe, Marianne. *Women Bookbinders, 1880–1920.* New Castle, Del.: Oak Knoll Press; London: British Library, 1996. (See "Katharine Adams," pp. 131–46, and "Katharine Adams' Tools, and a List of her Bindings, 1901-1916," pp. 199–204.) — Web sources. — Correspondence (British Library [with Sydney Cockerell], Bridwell Library [with St. John Hornby]).

5.2 ❧ EMILY DANIEL

Emily Daniel (1852?–1933) [*see Frontispiece*], wife of Henry Daniel and mother of Rachel and Ruth, worked busily in the background of the Daniel Press. She assisted with the printing, acted as secretary, and corresponded with booksellers and potential customers, some of whom were American. She had a close, friendly relationship with Falconer Madan, providing everything from memories to receipts so that his bibliographical history of the press would be correct and complete.

But she was also an artist: she created delicate miniations and (in one instance) watercolor illuminations in copies of the *Garland* [*Pls. 4–5*]. And she even became a bookbinder. In a letter to Katharine Adams, dated 28 March 1900, when her husband was recovering from an accident and objected to her working alone in the printing room, she inquired about taking lessons in bookbinding.[1] Several months later, probably in the autumn of 1900, she actually had the lessons. Not surprisingly, many of the bindings were done on the readily available publications of the Daniel Press. Her work is deliberately simple: often vellum bindings with ties or leather with gold tooling, and occasionally silver clasps. Some of her bindings were shown at the seventh exhibition of the Arts and Crafts Exhibition Society in 1903.

COPY BOUND: Princeton University Library [**3.30**].

---

1. This letter is in private hands and will be published in Marianne Tidcombe's forthcoming biography of Katharine Adams.

REFERENCES: "Funeral of Mrs. Daniel. A Friend's Tribute to Her Memory." *Oxford Times*, 28 April 1933. — Masefield, John. "Mrs. Henry Daniel." *The Times*, 21 April 1933, p. 17. (Tribute.) — "Mrs. Henry Daniel: Work for a Famous Press." *The Times*, 20 April 1933, p. 15. (Obituary.) — Tidcombe, Marianne. *Women Bookbinders, 1880–1920*. New Castle, Del.: Oak Knoll Press; London: British Library, 1996. (See pp. 165–66.)

5.3 ❦ MORLEY & SONS

Thomas Morley (*c.* 1811–1897), who had been apprenticed as a bookbinder to William Hayes & Son about 1845, joined with his business partner Edward Brewer in 1853 to buy the bookbinding operation of Messrs. Thomas and George Shrimpton in Ship Street, Oxford. The firm was known as Morley & Brewer, and in 1864 it moved to the yard behind 15–17 Long Wall Street, Oxford. By the 1871 census, Edward Brewer (d. 1875) and his family lived in number 16, and Thomas Morley, who employed nine men, lived in number 17. In that same year the partnership was dissolved, and the firm became Messrs. Morley & Sons, for two of Thomas Morley's sons had joined their father's business: William (b. 1840) and Henry (1843–1930). In 1897, after their father's death, the firm became Messrs. Morley Brothers. Although the Morleys no longer lived in the building after 1901, the business seems to have continued in the yard until 1935–36.

The firm advertised that it did "high class" binding, and it was known both for its vellum work and for intricate morocco commemorative bindings. One of the most celebrated of Thomas' bindings was for presentation to the Queen in 1883. The book was an enormous folio edition of a series of poems by Edward Eastwick in honor of "the Empress of India," bound in blue morocco with elaborate tooling. Similarly (though on a less spectacular scale), Henry Daniel commissioned a special binding by Morley of *A New Sermon of the Newest Fashion* (Daniel Press, 1876) [Madan no. 2] for presentation to Prince Leopold, son of Victoria and Albert, when the Prince visited the Daniel Press.[1]

---

1. Henry Daniel to Charles Elkin Mathews, 8 July 1899 (Berol's Daniel Press papers, box 1, folder 1, Fales Library, NYU).

21 *Most copies of the* GARLAND *were bound in vellum by Morley. (This is the Library of Congress copy.)*

The Morleys bound regularly for the Daniel Press, including the majority of copies of *The Garland of Rachel* [*Fig. 21*]. (As the list below shows, we have identified six signed copies of the *Garland* bound by Morley and nineteen unsigned copies in vellum.) The endpapers of the vellum copies were furnished by a local printer, Edward Webster Morris, based on some models that Morley had acquired earlier from northern England or Scotland.

COPIES BOUND: *The following copies are signed:* Claremont Colleges (green morocco) [**3.22**]; Mark Samuels Lasner Collection (blue levant) [**3.31**]; University of Melbourne (russia) [**3.27**]; Emily Daniel copy, Penny Tuerk [2] (vellum) [**3.34**]; Getty (blue levant) [**3.24**]; Myers copy, unlocated (olive morocco) [3.13]. ¶ *The following are all vellum, unsigned:* Bridges copy, Getty [**3.2**]; Henry Daniel copy, unlocated (probably by Morley), variant binding [**3.5**]; Dobson copy, Yale University [**3.6**]; Dodgson copy, New York University [**3.7**]; Gosse copy, British Library [**3.8**]; Harington copy, unlocated [**3.9**]; Lang copy, University of Minnesota [**3.11**]; Locker copy, Columbia University [**3.12**]; Symonds copy, New York University [**3.15**]; Ward copy, private collection [**3.16**]; Watson copy, University of San Francisco [**3.17**]; Woods copy, University of Texas [**3.18**]; Birmingham Public Libraries [**3.19**]; Oxford University [**3.20**]; Cambridge University [**3.21**]; Hilary Martin Daniel [**3.23**]; Library of Congress [**3.25**]; John Lindseth [**3.26**]; Armour–Berol copy, New York University [**3.28**]; Parsons copy, University of South Carolina [**3.32**]; Rachel Daniel copy, Penny Tuerk [1] [**3.33**]; Worcester College [**3.35**].

REFERENCES: "Passed Away." *Newspaper World*, 9 August 1930, p. 35. (Death of Henry Morley.) — "Partnerships Dissolved." *Bookseller*, 3 April 1871, p. 282. (Morley and Brewer.) — *Printing Times and Lithographer* 9 (15 November 1883): 286. (About the presentation binding for Queen Victoria.) — *The Victoria History of the County of Oxfordshire.* 17 vols. London: Oxford University Press, 1907–2011. (See 2:239.) — Census reports.

5.4 ❧ LEONARD MOUNTENEY

Leonard Mounteney (1881–1971) was born in Nottingham, England. Although no one in his family had been connected with the book trade (his father was a journeyman butcher), at a very young age he served as an apprentice to G. and J. Abbott, bookbinders in Nottingham, and seemed to take immediately to the work. While still an apprentice, he studied at the School of Art and Design on a scholarship and completed a course at the Leicester School of Art by the time he had finished his apprenticeship. He then found employment in London as a finisher for Rivière & Son. T. J. Cobden-Sanderson and Douglas Cockerell soon became role models as he pursued his strong interest in inlaid bindings.

After a stint in the Royal Navy during the First World War, followed by another five years at Rivière (for a total of twenty-five), Douglas Cockerell recommended him for a job in Chicago at the newly established Extra Binding studio of the Lakeside Press. Thus in 1924, almost 43 years old, he boarded the ship Leviathan for New York. After working for the Lakeside Press for eighteen months, he found himself suddenly without a job. According to Tom Conroy, who interviewed Bill Anthony sixty years later, Mounteney had a union background and as soon as he arrived began to organize, despite the fact that his employer, William Donnelley, was adamantly anti-union. Although there are no written records, certainly a clash seemed inevitable, and this would explain why Mounteney became unemployed. It was then, Conroy suggests, that he walked down the street to the Cuneo Press and convinced Mr. Cuneo that he could set up an extra bindery at Cuneo that would rival the Lakeside establishment. Evidently Mr. Cuneo was convinced, and Mounteney worked at Cuneo for more than thirty years.

During his tenure at the Extra Binding department at Cuneo, Chicago in 1933–34 celebrated its centennial with a World's Fair along the lakefront. The fair was known as the Century of Progress Exposition and included a very popular exhibition of bookbindings in which Mounteney participated in historic costume [*see photograph above*]. Among the notable books that he had bound in America was one that was described at the exhibition as the world's smallest book (a claim that has since been superseded), as well as the world's largest book, a guest book that he had bound for the Schlitz Brewery in Milwaukee. The majority of his bindings, however, were more serious. He is probably best known for his intricate inlaid bindings, but he also did beautiful tooling and even experimented with fore-edge paintings on several books. Mounteney's methodology and his views on bookbinding were explained in his two-part article in *Reading and Collecting*.

When Mounteney left England, Douglas Cockerell made him promise that he would always maintain the high standard of English bookbinding. The paradox of Mounteney's career is that although he was widely respected in the trade, both in England and America, during his lifetime, he is almost unknown today.

COPY BOUND: Newberry Library [**3.29**; *see also Pl. 8*].

REFERENCES: "American Hand Binders: Leonard Mounteney of Cuneo Press." *Book Production* 61 (February 1955): 33–34. — "Bookbinding Expert to Demonstrate His Art at Cordon Club." *Chicago Daily Tribune*, 18 March 1949, p. A8. — *Catalogue of an Exhibition of Handtooled Bindings Designed and Executed under the Direction of Alfred de Sauty, Formerly of London, Including Some Choice Examples of the Work of Leonard Mounteney, Formerly Exhibition Finisher at Riviére's [sic], London, December 9 to 13, 1924*. Chicago: The Lakeside Press, R.R. Donnelley & Sons Company, 1924. — "Former Cuneo Press Binder Mounteney Dies." *Chicago Tribune*, 9 February 1971, p. B19. — Miller, Julia, ed. *Suave Mechanicals: Essays on the History of Bookbinding*. Vol. 2. Ann Arbor, Mich.: Legacy Press, [forthcoming]. (See Tom Conroy, "Binding at Midcentury: The Rivers of America Competition of 1946.") — Mounteney, Leonard. "Extra Binding," *Reading and Collecting* 1 (December 1936): 8, 21; 1 (January 1937): 8, 25. — Mounteney, R. H., comp. *The Mounteney Family: A Miscellany*. London: privately printed, 1977. — Thompson, Lawrence S. "Hand Bookbinding in the United States since the Civil War." *Libri* 5, no. 2 (1954): 97–121. (See pp. 98, 100, 115.) — "Tradition-Plus-Progress Keynote of Two-Year Exhibit at Century of Progress." *Bookbinding Magazine* 20 (November 1934): 16, 18. — Census reports. — Correspondence (Newberry Library, Northwestern University Library [Cuneo archive]). — Information supplied by Tom Conroy.

6. CATALOGUES

WE have attempted to list here, in chronological order, all the copies of *The Garland of Rachel* that are known to have appeared in auction and dealers' catalogues since 1881. We have also included catalogue listings of C. M. Falconer's facsimile of the book [3.40] and a few proofs.

We have quoted and paraphrased the catalogue descriptions whenever they seemed to shed light on the book or its provenance. Catalogues are issued in London unless otherwise indicated.

1898

6.1 Edmund J. Brooks (Oxford), 11 May 1898, lot 413 [*Property of the late "Lewis Carroll"*] (sold to W. E. Moss for £12 10s.). ¶ *Now at Fales Library, New York University* [3.7]. (See also 4 March 1937 below.)

1903

6.2 Sotheby (London), 17 June 1903, lot 10 [*Property of a well-known amateur*] (sold to J. Bumpus for £10). ¶ Vellum extra, silver clasps, uncut. *Unlocated.*

1904

6.3 Sotheby (London), 20 June 1904, lot 150 (sold to Parker for £10 10s.). ¶ Olive morocco super extra t.e.g. by Morley; enclosed in a linen case. *Unlocated.*[1]

---

1. Described as the Myers sale in *Book Prices Current*, but there is no reference to Myers in the catalogue.

1906

6.4 Merwin-Clayton Sales Company (dealer, New York), 16 May 1906, no. 241[*Catalogue of extremely rare books*] ($66). ¶ Title-page: "By Divers Kindly Hands." Vellum binding, with preface. *Unlocated.*

1907

6.5 Sotheby (London), 11 December 1907, lot 80 [*Select and valuable library of the late C. M. Falconer, Esq. of Dundee*] (sold to J. Bumpus for £10). ¶ Facsimile reproduction of the original manuscript. Pale blue morocco super extra, t.e.g. uncut, by Zaehnsdorf, in his best manner. Inserted in the volume are several interesting and valuable autograph letters and signatures of C. H. Daniel, J. A. Symonds, etc. MS verses of Andrew Lang, proofs of Lang's contribution to the work and other matters. *Now at Wormsley Library* [**3.40**]. (See also 26 April 1939, October 1941, and 13 June 1979 below.)

1909

6.6 Anderson Galleries (New York), 23 February 1909, lot 136 [*Catalogue of the library of Henry W. Poor*, part 4]. ¶ *Unlocated* [**3.9**]. (See also 28 February 1923 and 1972 below.)

1913

6.7 Rosenbach (dealer, Philadelphia), catalogue 17 (1913), no. 154 [*Catalogue of rare and important books and manuscripts in English literature*] (sold for $165). ¶ Green levant morocco, gilt back, gilt wreaths on sides. *Now at Princeton University Library* [**3.30**]. (See also 28 February 1923 below.)

CATALOGUES

1920

6.8 Sotheby, 4 March 1920, lot 252 [*The property of a gentleman*] (sold to Thorp for £22 10*s*.). ¶ With preface and two letters from Henry Daniel. "The following pencil note appears on flyleaf: 'This Mr. D. wrote and asked me to write some verses for a book he was printing. I said I would do so, but I did not understand the character of the book, or I hope I might have done something a little more to the point. F. L. L.'" *Now at Columbia University Library* [**3.12**].

6.9 Leslie Chaundy, Bookseller (Oxford), catalogue 39 (1920), no. 108 [*Catalogue of the library of the late Dr. Daniel*] (sold to the Huntington Library). ¶ Title-page: "By Lewis Carroll and Divers Kindly Hands"; a collection of proofs. Morocco, super extra. "The book is of EXCESSIVE RARITY." *Now at Huntington Library* [**3.38**].

1922

6.10 Sotheby, 13 March 1922, lot 38 [*Property of the late Austin Dobson*] (sold to Maggs for £26). ¶ Vellum, enclosed in a cardboard cover. With preface. *Now at Beinecke Library, Yale University* [**3.6**]. (See also 15 February 1927, 17 November 1937, and 20 April 1979 below.)

1923

6.11 American Art Association (New York), 28 February 1923, lot 392 [*Rare and valuable books, original drawings, mezzotints and engravings from the private library of the late Clarence S. Bement*] (sold for $77.50). ¶ *Now at Princeton University Library* [**3.30**]. (See also 1913 above.)

6.12 Anderson Galleries (New York), 10 December 1923, lot 2302 [*The library of John Quinn*, part 2] (sold for $175). ¶ Original vellum in a crushed green levant morocco solander case; with the H. W. Poor bookplate. *Unlocated* [**3.9**]. (See also 23 February 1909 above and 1972 below.)

1927

6.13 American Art Association (New York), 15 February 1927, lot 369 [*The notable library of Major W. Van R. Whitall, of Pelham, New York*] (sold for $135). ¶ Vellum gilt binding. Austin Dobson's bookplate on verso of front cover. Tipped in to end-leaf is a printed circular giving a bibliographical account of this work. *Now at Beinecke Library, Yale University* [**3.6**]. (See also 13 March 1922 above and 17 November 1937 and 20 April 1979 below.)

6.14 Edgar H. Wells (dealer, New York), November 1930, inside front cover [*A catalogue of books on a variety of interesting subjects including English literature, topography, and travel, some of which are finely illustrated with coloured plates*] ($1500). ¶ Proof copy. Full morocco in slipcase. By H.D., etc. Inserted are 15 A.L.S., 12 by contributors, Henley, Locker, Ward (2), Lang (2), Gosse (2), Bridges, Dobson, Harrington, and Myers. Also preface, 4 leaves. *Now at Wormsley Library* [**3.37**].

1932

6.15 Samuel Marx (New York), 19 October 1932, lot 512 [*The Fine Library of Joseph Manuel Andreini (deceased)*] sold for $135. ¶ Vellum binding; by Robert Bridges, with his autograph. *Now at Wormsley Library* [**3.2**]. (See also 13 June 1979 below.)

1934

6.16 Thornton (dealer, Oxford), catalogue 276 (November 1934), no. 1308 (£45). ¶ Blue levant morocco binding with gold design. Loose preface. *Now at Wormsley Library* [**3.24**].

1935

6.17 Elkin Mathews (dealer), May 1935, no. 631 (£20). " A Collection of Rare Leaves from this press given to Mr. John Drinkwater by Mr. C. H. Wilkinson of Worcester College, Oxford, with a signed note from the former to that effect. Bound and mounted

CATALOGUES

in a buckram volume on hand-made paper, with Mr. Drinkwater's bookplate, and his notes throughout. V. Y." Contains various pages from the *Garland*, including four different title-pages and proofs of parts of several poems. *Unlocated.*

1936

6.18 American Art Association (New York), 18 March 1936, lot 94 [*The library of Abel Cary Thomas, New York City*, pt. 2] (sold for $130). ¶ By John Addington Symonds, with bookplate. Original vellum, uncut, in full crimson levant morocco slipcase. Accompanying the book are 8 A L.s. by contributors to the work: Symonds, C. L. Dodgson, and 6 by other contributors. *Now at Fales Library, New York University* [**3.15**].

1937

6.19 Sotheby, 4 March 1937, lot 537 [*Catalogue of the very well-known and valuable library: the property of Lt.-Col. W. E. Moss of the Manor House, Sonning-on-Thames, Berks., who is changing his residence*] (sold to Maggs for £170). ¶ Original vellum binding. Woodcut head-pieces, initials supplied in red by Mrs. Daniel. By C. L. Dodgson. This copy has written into it by Dodgson (in pencil on the last fly-leaf) an alternative version of two lines in the Latin rendering of his poem. Accompanying the volume are an A.L.s., 1½ pp., from C. H. Daniel to C. L. Dodgson, with the latter's serial receipt number in violet ink, and three documents relating to the present owner's acquisition of this copy, all mounted on cards. *Now at Fales Library, New York University* [**3.7**]. (See also 11 May 1898 above.)

6.20 American Art Association (New York), 23 April 1937, lot 235 [*The library of the late George Allison Armour*] (sold for $300). ¶ Autograph inscription on the front fly-leaf: "C. Henry Daniel October 25, 1887." Preface included. "No special title page printed, as Daniel apparently did not consider it necessary." *Now at Fales Library, New York University* [**3.28**]. (See also autumn, 1937, and 1940 below.)

6.21 Walter M. Hill (dealer, Chicago), catalogue 160 (autumn, 1937), no. 20 (sold for $450). ¶ Vellum binding with gilt borders and design in gilt on front cover. Autograph inscription on front fly-leaf: "C. Henry Daniel October 25, 1887." *Now at Fales Library, New York University* [**3.28**]. (See also 23 April 1937 above and 1940 below.)

6.22 American Art Association (New York), 17 November 1937, lot 113 [*Splendid library of the late Parke E. Simmons, Evanston, Illinois*] (sold for $190). ¶ Original vellum presentation binding with the preface. Dobson bookplate and W. Van R. Whitall bookplate. Includes a copy of *Memorials*. *Now at Beinecke Library, Yale University* [**3.6**]. (See also 13 March 1922 and 15 February 1927 above and 20 April 1979 below.)

1939

6.23 Park-Bernet, 26 April 1939, lot 238 [*The renowned library of the late John A. Spoor*, part 1] (sold for $155). ¶ Full vellum, with all over single leaf pattern in gilt. Metal hinges, g.t. uncut. Initials H. D. [Henry Daniel] on title, with *Bibliography of Daniel Press*, 1921. On inside of first end-leaf is the following note: "exceedingly rare, only 6 copies printed." *Unlocated* [**3.5**]. (See also 1945, 23 March 1954, and 19 May 1989 below.)

1940

6.24 Walter M. Hill (dealer, Chicago), catalogue 168 (1940), no. 20[*Catalogue of English literature of eighteenth and nineteenth century authors from the library of the late John A. Spoor and other recent purchases*] (sold for $390). ¶ Vellum binding with gilt borders and design in gilt on front cover. Autograph inscription on front fly-leaf: "C. Henry Daniel October 25, 1887." *Now at Fales Library, New York University* [**3.28**].

1941

6.25 Charles J. Sawyer (dealer), October 1941, no. 119 (£25). ¶ Bound in full blue levant morocco, top edges gilt by Zaehnsdorf. C. M. Falconer's manuscript copy. Most of the poems are signed by contributors. Proof sheets of Andrew Lang's poem and of Robert Bridges' poem. *Now at Wormsley Library* [3.40].[1] (See also 11 December 1907 above and 13 June 1979 below.)

1945

6.26 Goodspeed's Bookshop (Boston), catalogue 383 (1945), no. 47 ($250). ¶ "The books described in this catalogue were formerly in the collection of the late Frank B. Bemis, and contain his bookplate." *Unlocated* [3.5]. (See also 26 April 1939 above and 23 March 1954 and 19 May 1989 below.)

6.27 Sotheby, 31 July 1945, lot 591 (sold to Ludford for £65). ¶ *Unlocated.*

6.28 Sotheby Parke-Bernet (New York), 29 October 1945, lot 113 [*Selections from the library collected by the late Robert Hartshorne, of Highlands, New Jersey*] (sold for $150). ¶ Vellum binding. Preface accompanies volume. Unidentified calligraphic bookplate (EHF?). *Now at Library of Congress* [3.25].

1948

6.29 Sotheby Parke-Bernet (New York), 10 May 1948, lot 80 [*Library of the late Thomas Bird Mosher, Portland, Maine*, pt. 1] (sold for $80). ¶ Sheets, uncut. Includes 13 A.L.s by C. Henry Daniel, Rachel Daniel, and others. Also an autograph manuscript poem by Austin Dobson "From the 'Garland of Rachel.'" *Now at Newberry Library* [3.29].

---

1. On 4 November 1941 Sawyer wrote to C. H. Wilkinson offering him this document (Worcester College).

1954

6.30 Sotheby Parke-Bernet (New York), 23 March 1954, lot 340 [*English and American first editions and other books . . . collected by Jean Hersholt, Beverly Hills, California*] (sold for $250). ¶ Title-page: By H.D. and Divers Kindly Hands. F. B. Bemis bookplate. Vellum, gilt, uncut. Morocco-backed case. Tipped in: 4-page preface. Mosher reprint of the *Garland* (1902) accompanies book. *Unlocated* [**3.5**]. (See also 26 April 1939 and 1945 above and 19 May 1989 below.)

1960

6.31 Philip C. Duschnes (dealer, New York), catalogue 150 (1960), no. 62 ($600). ¶ Margaret Woods copy; with preface. *Now at Harry Ransom Center, University of Texas* [**3.18**].

1961

6.32 Bernard Quaritch (dealer), catalogue 823 (1961), no. 126 (£1150; no. 4 in a collection of 72 of Daniel Press items). ¶ "This copy was issued without the MS capital letters supplied in red; full green levant morocco, gilt top, other edges uncut, by Morley." No preface. *Now at Honnold Library, Claremont College* [**3.22**].

6.33 Sotheby, 15 February 1961, lot 724 [*Property of Capt David O. Fairlie, Myres Castle, Auchtermuchty*] (sold to Quaritch for £95). ¶ Vellum binding, with preface. *Unlocated.*

6.34 Sotheby, 27–29 March 1961, lot 752 [*Library of English Literature of the late Colonel C. H. Wilkinson, O.B.E, M.C., T.D., Fellow of Worcester College, Oxford*] (sold to Parker for £82). ¶ A collection of proof sheets of the *Garland*: 7 impressions of the title and half-title, dedication with following leaf; 8 full sheets of the text; 6 proofs on single leaves (3 showing pencilled corrections), loose in a cloth folder. *Unlocated* (evidently not the set of proofs now at Wormsley Library [**3.37**]).

CATALOGUES

1962

6.35 Philip C. Duschnes (dealer, New York) catalogue 152 (1962), no. 53 ($600). ¶ By M. L. Woods. With preface. White bevelled vellum binding with gold tooling. Now at *Harry Ransom Center, University of Texas* [**3.18**].

1963

6.36 Bernard Quaritch (dealer) catalogue 843 (1963), no. 124 (£100/$280). ¶ Green levant morocco, gilt top, other edges uncut, by Morley. This copy was one issued without the capital letters supplied in red. *Now at Honnold Library, Claremont College* [**3.22**].

1969

6.37 Sotheby, 26–28 January 1969, lot 575 [*Property of Mrs. Virginia Surtees*] (sold to Blackwell for £300). ¶ Original vellum. In green morocco pull-off type case (spine faded). *Unlocated.*

6.38 Sotheby (Hodgson's Rooms), 16 May 1969, lot 363 [*Catalogue of printed books comprising publications of the Middle Hill Press from the celebrated collection formed by Sir Thomas Phillipps, bart. (1792–1872)*] (sold to Blackwell for £95). ¶ A collection of proof sheets, "comprising 9 impressions of the half-title and title (eight bearing the names of individual contributors, one a general title), the dedication and following leaf (with the 'Misit' mark), 10 full sheets of the text (eight with stanzas by Thomas Humphry Ward), and 9 proofs on single leaves (three with pencilled emendations), in cloth folder." *Unlocated.*

1970

6.39 Blackwell (dealer, Oxford) catalogue (1973), no. 43 (£160). ¶ A collection of proofs; see description above. *Unlocated.*

1972

6.40 Colin & Charlotte Franklin (Culham, Oxfordshire) catalogue 5 (1972), no. 55 [*Privately printed*] (£560). ¶ White vellum binding with gilt, in green morocco slipcase, probably by Morley. Bookplate of Henry William Poor. *Unlocated* [3.9]. (See also 23 February 1909 and 28 February 1923 above.)

1979

6.41 Christie (New York), 20 April 1979, lot 226 [*Property of Mrs. Etienne Boegner*] (sold for $3,400). ¶ 8-page preface tipped in. Bookplates of Austin Dobson, W. Van R. Whitall, and John Saks. (The binding is reproduced in the color frontispiece of the catalogue.) *Now at Beinecke Library, Yale University* [3.6]. (See also 13 March 1922, 15 February 1927, and 17 November 1937 above.)

6.42 Christie, 13 June 1979, lot 152 [*Books and manuscripts from the library of Arthur A. Houghton, Jr.*] (sold to Colin Franklin for £2,200). ¶ Robert Bridges copy. Bookplates of John Manuel Andreini and Arthur A. Houghton Jr. *Now at Wormsley Library* [3.2]. (See also 19 October 1932 above.)

6.43 Same sale, lot 153 (sold to Colin Franklin for £400). ¶ Proof copy (29 leaves) with corrections by Daniel and in some cases by the contributors. Tipped into beginning of volume are 15 autograph letters, 12 by contributors. *Now at Wormsley Library* [3.37].

6.44 Same sale, lot 154 (sold to Colin Franklin for £400). ¶ Manuscript copy made by C. M. Falconer, in calligraphic script with decorative capitals in red on handmade paper, many of the poems signed by the contributors, containing 22 autograph letters from contributors and an unpublished autograph poem by Lang. *Now at Wormsley Library* [3.40]. (See also 11 December 1907 and October 1941 above.)

1989

6.45 Christie (New York), 19 May 1989, lot 2239 (sold for $6,000). ¶ From the Estelle Doheny collection. "By H.D." on title-page. No preface. Vellum binding. J. A. Spoor bookplate. *Unlocated* [**3.5**]. (See also 26 April 1939, 1945, and 23 March 1954 above.)

2005

6.46 Bertram Rota (dealer) catalogue, Summer, 2005, no. 1430.
¶ The T. H. Ward copy. "Original bevelled vellum, ruled, lettered and decorated in gilt, marbled end-papers, top edge gilt, others uncut. Binding just a little soiled and with one small scratch and just a few trivial spots and marks internally, but a very nice copy." *Now in private collection, U.K.* [**3.16**].

APPENDIX: TEXT OF THE GARLAND

WE have transcribed here the complete text of *The Garland of Rachel*. Though we have attempted to reproduce its main typographical features, we did not emulate the long s's of the Fell type, nor are we are reproducing Emily Daniel's miniation (which of course differs from one copy to another). The centered ornament below does not appear in *The Garland*; we are merely using it to indicate page breaks.

❧

[SEPARATELY ISSUED PREFACE BY HENRY DANIEL]

I have the pleasure of sending you at last a copy of the 'Garland of Rachel', *to which you so kindly contributed. A long illness of the subject of your Muse together with claims of business caused the suspension of the work till within the last month. So it is by chance at once* 'Genethliacon' *and* 'Sostra'.

One or two points are perhaps of typographical interest. The number of copies is 36; the title-page of each copy bears the name of a several author; the type is that given to the University by Dr. Fell *in the 17th Century; the whole of the Printer's work has been done by myself, the miniation by my Wife; the Printer's mark and the head-pieces are a contribution by Mr.* Alfred Parsons.

The Contents are all of present date: but for that I should have borrowed of Bp. Earle *a Preface, which I cannot refuse myself the pleasure of recalling to your memory.*

H. D.

Oct. 18, 1881.

A **Child** is a Man in a small letter, yet the best copy of *Adam* before he tasted of *Eve* or the apple; and he is happy, whose small practice in the world can only write his character. He is Nature's fresh picture newly drawn in oil, which time and much handling dims and defaces. His soul is yet a white paper unscribbled with observations of the world, wherewith at length it becomes a blurred note-book. He is purely happy, because he knows no evil, nor hath made means by sin to be acquainted with misery. He arrives not at the mischief of being wise nor endures evils to come by foreseeing them. He kisses and loves all, and when the smart of the rod is past, smiles on his beater. Nature and his parents alike dandle him, and tice him on with a bait of sugar to a draught of wormwood. He plays yet, like a young Prentice the first day, and is not come to his task of melancholy. All the language he speaks yet is tears, and they serve him well enough to express his necessity. His hardest labour is his tongue, as if her were loath to use so deceitful an organ; and he is best company with it when he can but prattle. We laugh at his foolish sports, but his game is our earnest; and his drums rattles and hobby-horses but the emblems and mocking of men's business. His father hath writ him as his own little story, wherein he reads those days of his life that he cannot remember, and sighs to see what innocence he has out-lived. The elder he grows, he is a stair lower from God; and like his first father much worse in his breeches. He is the Christian's example, and the old man's relapse; the one imitates his pureness, and the other falls into his simplicity. Could he put off his body with his little coat, he had got eternity without a burden, and exchanged but one heaven for another.

[*Half-title*]

THE
GARLAND OF RACHEL

TEXT OF THE GARLAND

[*Title-page*]

THE
GARLAND OF RACHEL
BY
DIVERS KINDLY HANDS

PRINTED AT THE PRIVATE PRESS OF
H. DANIEL : OXFORD.
1881.

☙

[*page v*]

TO MY DAUGHTER RACHEL ANNE OLIVE BORN SEPTEMBER XXVII MDCCCLXXX ON HER FIRST BIRTHDAY HER FATHER AND HER VNKNOWN FRIENDS THESE GREETING

☙

[*By Henry Daniel, pages 9–10*]

RACHEL! babe, whose frolic smile
Might a stoic's frown beguile,
Thou small quintessential thing,
That dost heaven to mortals bring,
Cradled from the world's alarms
In a mother's tender arms,
Stretch thy dimpled hands and crow—
Voiceless love finds passage so.

Maiden blithe and debonair
Tangling hearts in golden hair,
Fancy lurking in thine eye

DANIEL PRESS & GARLAND OF RACHEL

Genders care and lover's sigh:
ANNE, dear vision from above,
Ere thou spread they wings and rove,
Shed upon this house the grace
Of a girl's angelic face.

Matron sphered in virtuous calm,
Manhood's worship, sorrow's charm,
Of ready wit, of lofty soul,
Balanced in a well-poised whole,—
OLIVE, ere a stranger own
Thy fond smile and stately frown,
Bind a father for thy thrall,
And thy mother's reign recall.

❧

[*By Albert Watson, page 11*]

AD PATREM τῆς ʻΡαχήλ¹

Quam tibi promittunt cunabula prima: futuram
   Si referet flavæ matris adulta decus,
Indignam soceri fraudem duplicataque lenti
   Tædia servitii, vix feret acer amor.
               W.

❧

[*By Austin Dobson, pages 13–16*]

How shall I sing you, Child, for whom
   So many lyres are strung;
Or how the tone assume
   That fits a Maid so young?

---

1. To (or for) the father of Rachel (Latin and Greek).

TEXT OF THE GARLAND

What rocks there are on either hand!
    Suppose—'tis on the cards—
You should grow up with quite a grand
    Platonic hate for bards!

How shall I then be shamed, undone,
    For ah! with what a scorn
Your eyes must greet that luckless One
    Who rhymed you, newly born;—

Who o'er your 'helpless cradle' bent
    His idle verse to turn;
And twanged his tiresome instrument
    Above your unconcern!

Nay,—let my words be so discreet,
    That, keeping chance in view,
Whatever after-fate you meet
    A part may still be true.

Let others wish you mere good looks,—
    Your sex is always fair;
Or to be writ in Fortune's books,—
    She's rich who has to spare:

I wish you but a heart that's kind,
    A head that's sound and clear;
(Yet let the heart be not too blind,
    The head not too severe!)

A joy of life, a frank delight,
    A moderate desire;
And—if you fail to find a Knight—
    At least—a trusty Squire.

Austin Dobson.

DANIEL PRESS & GARLAND OF RACHEL

[*By Andrew Lang, pages 17–19*]

'Tis distance lends, the poet says,
    Enchantment to the view,
And this makes possible the praise
    Which I bestow on you.
    For babies roseate of hue
I do not always care,
    But distance paints the mountains blue,
And Rachel always fair.

Ah Time, speed on her flying days,
    Bring back my youth that flew,
That she may listen to my lays
    Where Merton ring-doves coo;
    That I may sing afresh, anew,
My songs, now faint and rare,
    Time, make me always twenty two,
And Rachel always fair.

Nay, long ago, down dusky ways
    Fled Cupid and his crew.
Life bring not back the morning haze,
    The dawning and the dew.
    Nay, other lips must sigh and sue,
And younger lovers dare
    To hint that Love is always true,
And Rachel always fair.

TEXT OF THE GARLAND

ENVOY

Princess, let Age bid Youth adieu,
Adieu to this despair,
  To me, who thus despairing woo,
And Rachel always fair.

Andrew Lang.

❧

[*By John Addington Symonds, pages 21–23*]

LES POUPEES DE NOS JOURS

A rumour reached me that the dolls
  Are heavy-eyed and wan to-day,
Like wearied girls with frizzled polls
  And artificial fringes grey,
Pale lips, wan foreheads which foresee
Class-lists and lecturers to be.

They tell me too that roseate wax,
  One plumply rounded into cheeks,
Where curled the old familiar flax,
  Is out of date. Your dollman seeks
At something subtle, sad, supreme,
To mould an æsthetician's dream.

'We old men born but yesterday,'
  De Musset cried. On him, on me,
Tired wanderers of life's stony way,
  Hath weighed, 'tis true, world-misery:
But why need dolls be over-wrought,
Plagued with our malady of thought?

DANIEL PRESS & GARLAND OF RACHEL

Oh, Rachel! in thy cradle thou
    Canst laugh or scold, as likes thee best:
Thou hast no care; upon thy brow
    Thy silky curls unfrizzled rest:
Smith then—art, fashion, culture pass—
Smile, sleep, or scold, thou English lass!

But when those tiny feet are free
To toddle o'er thy nursery floor,
Send me a message over sea:
I'll find for thee that doll of yore,
The flaxen waxen simpering miss
My baby sweetheart bade me kiss.

John Addington Symonds.

[*By Robert Bridges, pages 25–27*]

Press thy hands and crow,
Thou that know'st not joy:
Raise thy voice and weep,
Thou that know'st not care:

Thou that toil'st not, sleep:
Wake and wail nor spare,
Spare not us, that know
Grief and life's annoy.

Tine unweeting cries
Passion's alphabet,
Labour, love and strife
Spell, or e'er thou read:
But the book of life
Hard to learn indeed,

Babe, before thee lies
For thy reading yet.

Thou, when thou hast known
Joy, wilt laugh not then:
When grief bids thee weep,
Thou wilt check thy tears:
When toil brings not sleep,
Thou, for others' fears
Fearful, shalt thine own
Lose and find again.

Robert Bridges.

❧

[*By Charles L. Dodgson, pages 29–31*]

What hand may wreathe thy natal crown,
   O tiny tender Spirit-blossom,
That out of Heaven hast fluttered down
   Into this Earth's cold bosom?

And how shall mortal bard aspire—
   All sin-begrimed and sorrow-laden—
To welcome, with the seraph-choir,
   A pure and perfect Maiden?

Are not God's minstrels ever near,
   Flooding with joy, the woodland mazes?
Which shall we summon, Baby dear,
   To carol forth thy praises?

With sweet sad song the Nightingale
   May soothe the broken hearts that languish
Where graves are green—the orphans' wail,

DANIEL PRESS & GARLAND OF RACHEL

The widow's lonely anguish:

The Turtle-dove with amorous coo
    May chide the blushing maid that lingers
To twine her bridal wreath anew
    With weak and trembling fingers:

But human loves and human woes
    Would dim the radiance of thy glory—
Only the Lark such music knows
    As fits thy stainless story.

The world may listen as it will—
    She recks not, to the skies up-springing:
Beyond our ken she singeth still
    For very joy of singing.

Lewis Carroll.

[*By Sir Richard Harington, pages 33–35*]

IDEM LATINE REDDITUM

Qua tibi natalis nectenda tenelle coronæ
    Floscule serta manu?
Lapsus ut e cælo volitansque per aera terræ
    Decidis in gremium.

Quis, dum dedecorat scelus heu! mortale poetam,
    (Triste doloris onus,)
Cælesti comitante manu te casta puella
    Commemorare queat?

En divinus adest semper chorus! invia sylvæ

TEXT OF THE GARLAND

Gaudia cui resonant:
Anne ex his unum laudes celebrare decebit
    Rite adamata tuas?

Carmine soleteur tenero Philomela dolentes
    Quâ nova busta jacent,
Quâ planctu occifos orbata caterva parentes
    Flent, viduæque viros:

Datque graves turtur, Veneri devota, susurros,
    Quâ nova nupta manet,
Virgineam digitis iterum nexura coronam
    Mollibus ac tremulis.

Ast humanus amor dolor et sub nubilia condunt
    Hoc tenebrosa jubar!
Sola quidem famâ musam meditatur alauda
    Immaculata tuâ

Dignam: cui non cura silens quin audiat orbis,
    Æthera dum repetit,
Humano visu quærens sublimior ipsis
    Gaudia carminibus.

        Ricardus Harington Baronettus.

[*By A. Mary F. Robinson, pages 37–38*]

A NURSERY RHYME

Lullaby, Baby, and dream of a rose,
The reddest and sweetest that Eden knows.
There flowers in Eden a rose without thorn
For every baby that ever is born.

Some bloom completely,
    Some white and small,
And some smell sweetly,
    Some not at all.

Lullaby; listen, a viol string
Is leading the voices of angels that sing,
And every spirit that lives on the earth
Is a note of music in heavenly mirth:
    Some clear as a harp,
        Some low as a lute,
    Some sweet, some sharp,
        Some only mute.

A. Mary F. Robinson.

[By Edmund W. Gosse, pages 39–41]

'To be the Laureate of a child
    Unseen, unknown, beyond your care,'
Quick-witted Bavius asked, and smiled,
    'How can you dare?'

Unknown, unseen; and I know—
    I see—the Mother's eye-lids burn,
The unreasonable tears that flow,
    The lips that yearn.

The growing form, the steps that creep,
    Each new word warbled more than said,
The gay limbs folded up to sleep
    Where she has prayed.

I watch the fresh unclouded eyes,

> The sparkling lights, the glancing flowers,
> Shades of mysterious thoughts that rise
> In pensive hours.
>
> Nor less the blithe and hurrying wings
> Of ripening girlhood hail with glee,
> Nor grieve because her spring-tide brings
> Its snows for me.
>
> Until the violet garland fade
> Around the expanded virgin-brow,
> And to the full majestic maid
> I humbly bow.
>
> But what the conquest, what the fate?
> Ah! these, my Bavius, who can tell!
> And Life will ring, if we but wait,
> His own strange bell.
>
> *Edmund W. Gosse.*

❦

[*By Francis W. Bourdillon, page 43*]

'WE CANNOT TELL'

Life lies before thee!—Is it friend or foe?
God gave us life, and God made all things well;
Yet, for the sin and shame our own lives shew,
What shall we answer, save 'we cannot tell!'

Death lies before thee!—Is it friend or foe?
For all men fear it; yet, if Death comes well
To aching hearts, and many a lifelong woe,
What shall we answer, save 'we cannot tell!'

Yet, child, sleep softly! For the sweet buds swell
And sweet birds sing for thee; and on the shore
For thy delight lies many a fairy shell.

And, seeing thy happiness, our hearts rebel
No more at their own griefs; nor any more
Our lips shall answer thee 'we cannot tell!'

Francis W. Bourdillon.

[*By William E. Henley, pages 45–47*]

Ballade Rachel

(*En forme de Petition*)

Rachel, enfant au noble nom,
   Au nom amoreux et mystique,
Aie en pitié—ne dis pas non!
   Le pauvre poëte lyrique,
   Qui, n'ayant rien de fatidique,
S'en vient causer sur ton appel,
   Et s'ecrie, presq' en tragique:—
'Causons—ah! mais... de quoi, Rachel?'

Tu ne sais rien sur le canon,
   Rien sur l'économie antique;
Don parlons Darwin et guenon.
   Nenni? Ma foi—et l'esthétique?
   Pas plus, dis tu, que de l'optique,
Pas plus que du bon feu Vatel!
   Rachel, à tout tu fais la nique.
Causons—ah! mais... de quoi, Rachel?

TEXT OF THE GARLAND

Si nous discutions la Ninon!
   Me mettrai-je sur la statique?
Que penses tu d'Agamemnon?
   Aimes tu bein la Mozambique?
   Non, vraiment? mais las méchanique,
Et le dessin de Raphaël,
   Et la *Sonate Pathetique*?
Causons—ah! mais... de quoi, Rachel?

ENVOI

C'est une chasse à la moustique
A faire pester Sain-Michel.
   Bon! voilà de l'amphigourique!
Causons—ah! mais... de quoi, Rachel?

              W. E. Henley.

༄

[*By William J. Courthope, page 49*]

Babe, of a bitter year the early birth!
Loud roars the tempest round thy dreamless head,
The frozen linnet on the snow lies dead,
The sapless boughs confess the season's dearth:

Yet Spring shall stir fresh blood in bird and tree,
The linnet wake the fields to wonted mirth,
The sail shall whiten on the windless sea,
The seed shall grasp its firm paternal earth:

But from what Spring shall Nature nourish *thee*,
Upraise thy spirit, and thy soul refine,
Born in this winter age of Loyalty,

And Faith's decrepitude, and Art's decline?

God sends all seasons to all things. May He
Renew thy country's life, and perfect thine!

William John Courthope.

❧

[*By Frederick Locker, pages 51–52*]

HYPNEROTOPHANTASIA
ANNI 1900

Alone she stood by the garden wall;
Her veil was white; she was fair and tall;
And I gave my heart—I gave it all
    To that Lady mine.

I knew not the hue of her eyes or hair,
I spoke no word to that Lady fair
By the garden wall—she was always there,
    That Lady mine.

I stole to the garden yesternight;
How pale she looked in the pale moonlight!
And she drooped her head—she was veiled in white—
    That Lady mine.

Frederick Locker.

❧

TEXT OF THE GARLAND

[By Thomas Humphry Ward, page 53–57]

They say that, when in Cretan cave
    The Olympian baby lay,
A thousand priests in order brave
    Did service night and day.

To drown his cries their drums they beat,
    Their silver trumpets blew,
And made around that dim retreat
    Most musical ado.

Not otherwise *thy* priests, fair child,
    Around thy cradle throng,
And, by thy infant charm beguiled,
    Beat out the harmonious song.

Thy cast of feature, turn of limb,
    They fondly celebrate,
And chant in antistrophic hymn
    Thy face, thy form, thy fate.

But I, the humblest of the band,
    Whose notes are faint and few,
What ministry of voice or hand
    Shall I, thy servant do?

I cannot praise or prophesy,
    I cannot crown thy spring
With garlands fair of poetry,
    Or costly offerings bring,

Or pay the vows that Poets pay
    In measures framed to please,
But only on thy cradle lay
    My lowly wishes—these:—

I wish thee all that child can shew,
　　Or mother can desire,
Of health and movement, life and glow,
　　Of frolic, fun, and fire;

An average of naughtiness,
　　Warm temper, quick to cool,
A spirit rather more than less
　　Obedient to rule;

A head that's tolerably quick,
　　And that the imperious sway
Of Grammar and Arithmetic
　　Will not too much dismay;

A hand that can, when eve is still,
　　The homely needle ply,
And with hereditary skill
　　Obey the artist's eye;

But most, a tender heart and true,
　　A character sincere;
… These, dressed in verse nor fine nor new,
　　These are my wishes, dear!

　　　　　T. H. Ward.

[By Ernest Myers, page 59]

'Too shadowy form, what would'st thou to evoke
　　(I said) too stern a lyre?'
The shadow, melting like a blue-wreathed smoke,
　　Past on at my desire.

TEXT OF THE GARLAND

Yet, as it swept beside me, low and mild,
    One note came murmuring:
I turned; the tiny finger of a child
    Had touched—no more—the string.

Ernest Myers.

[*By Margaret L. Woods, pages 61–65*]

[*Little* GILBERT *speaks:—*]

Rachel! tell me what you know,
Tell me where the shadows go;—
For before I'm sent to sleep
I can watch them run and creep,
Rock and spring and fly and fall
On the ceiling and the wall,
Troops of shadows at their games
Dancing to the dancing flames.
Soon as I have done with sleep
All about I look and peep,
But the shadows steal away,
Hide themselves before the day.

Rachel! you must know of it,
For they say you often sit
Wide awake through all the hours
As the bells do in the towers.
You must see the shadows hide,
Though there *is* so much beside
That you have to keep in sight,
Things of day and things of night,—
Sheep and elephants in herds,
Woolly dogs and fluffy birds,

Jugs and mugs and Pretty Polls,
Dolls with caps and caps with dolls,
Little drawers with little handles,
Chairs and tablets, stars and candles:
These, and then the angels four
That at midnight cross the door,
Standing silent in their places
With bird-wings and mother-faces:—

Things to watch on every side,—
But your eyes are very wide,
Every thing I'm sure they see
Though they will not answer me.
Tell me where the shadows go,
And I'll tell you all I know—
Tell the slow awakening
Of the sleepy buds in spring,
How the winds and streams and horses
Race and leap along their courses,
How the flame outspeeds the thunder
And the rain comes rushing under:—

Tell you what my garden grows,—
There they stand and nod in rows,
Creatures, call them what you please,
Perhaps they're people, perhaps they're trees.
If you saw them in their places
With their great round yellow faces,
Nodding, bowing solemnly,
Staring so at you and me,
Though you'd meant to cry before
I would have to laugh I'm sure.

You are smiling, looking wise,
Listening, listening with your eyes;
You will tell me where they go,
And I'll tell you all I know:—

What the birds say to their mother
And the leaves to one another,
What the wind says to the tree,
What the ships say to the sea
And the wide sea to the sky.—
I will dance and by and by
Sing to you, and after this
  Give you all I have—a kiss.

M. L. Woods.

[*By Charles James Cruttwell, page 67*]

Rachel Christened

Young Rachel with her sheep stood at the well,
  But Jacob's arm to fray the boors and move
  The stone came timely, and behind came Love:
Kissed, wept, and sped the future Israel.

But childless was his Rachel; and he strove
  Till God gave Joseph whom high change befell,
  And him born in her death, who bore her knell,
Benoni, as her spirit passed above.

For Rachel twice seven years which seemed one day
  To his great love served Jacob, nor did spurn
  His motley wage from greedy Laban's herd.

They rest.—Dear little Rachel, as we pray,
  Precious ew-lamb, and sprinkle, we discern
  The Heavenly Jacob's arms, which thee engird.

C. J. C.

INDEX

Abbey, Edwin Austin, 99–100
Abbott, G. and J., 181
Abel, Allison, 92, 94, 173
Adams, Rev. William Fulford, 175–76
Adams, Katharine, 104, 112, 114, 175–78
Albion press, 6, 7, 8, 20, 21, 23, 67
Allen, Hervey, 64
Allen, Susan M., 84
American Art Association, 63, 77
American Museum of Natural History, 96
Andersen, Hans Christian, 61
Anderson Galleries (auction house), 70n
Andreini, John Manuel, 56–57, 109–110, 194
Andrews, Verity, viii
Angennes, Julie d', 27
Anglo-Catholicism, 4, 9
Anthony, Bill, 182
Armour, George Allison, 89–90, 189
Arnold, Matthew, 50, 104
Arts and Crafts Exhibition Society, 19, 176, 178
Ashendene Press, 10, 12, 64, 87, 177
Astley, Constance, 111, 117, 118–19, 169–72, Pl. 9
Astley, Hubert D., 118

Balliol College, Oxford, 45, 47
Barker, Nicolas, 82
Barlow, William P., Jr., 79
Baskin, Lisa, viii
Bath, 1
BBC World Service, 106

Beardsley, Aubrey, 18
Beckford, William, 149
Beinecke Library, Yale University, 63, 187–88, 190, 194
Bement, Clarence S., 95–96, 187
Bemis, Frank Brewer, 60–61, 192
Bennett, Rev. William, 3–4
Berol, Alfred Charles, 66–68, 7678
Berol, Kenneth R., 66, 77
Berol, Madelein Rossin, 66, 77
Betjeman, Sir John, 108
Bible, 121, 136n
Bibliographical Society of America, 79
Bidwell, John, viii
bindings, 175–83, Pls. 7–8
Birmingham Public Libraries, 80–81
Birrell, Augustine, 116, 156
Bishop, Philip R., 91, viii
black letter type, 10, 31
Blackwell's bookshop, 17
Blake, William, 38, 63, 67
Board of Trade, 36
Bodleian Library, 14, 18n, 22–23, 32, 51, 67, 81–82, 108–09, 126n, 138, 150, 168, viii
Bodley Head, 17–19
Boegner, Margaret (*née* Phipps), 64–65, 194
Book Club of California, 79
Book Prices Current, 76n, 86, 185n
Borrow, George, 63
Bourdillon, Francis William, 20, 29–30, 56, 77, 108, 112–13, 144, 146, 153, 209–10
Bourdillon, François, viii
Bourdillon, Gerard, 146

[219]

INDEX

Bourdillon, Peter, viii
Bradford, William, 78
Brasenose College, Oxford, 27, 50, 52, 108–09, 150, 157
Brewer, Edward, 179
Bridges, Robert, 17, 18, 30–33, 36, 39, 56–58, 75–77, 86, 93, 100, 108, 112–15, 119, 123–25, 130–31, 135–36, 138, 144, 151, 188, 191, 194, 204–05, Pl. 1
Brinsop Court, 118–19
British Library, 177
British Museum, 40, 124, 129, 138
Broadway Group, 99
Brooks, Edmund J. (auction house), 114, 168n
Brown University Library, 37
Brown, Phil, viii
Browne, Rev. Charles, 13
Browning Society, 68
Browning, Robert, 40
Broxbourne Library, 81–82
Bruce, Rosslyn, 23
Bruce, Verily Anderson, 16
Buchanan, Anne, viii
Bunn, Thomas, 1
Burges, William, 10, 13
Burgoyne, Vivienne, 86
Burne-Jones, Sir Edward, 85
Buscot, Oxfordshire, 17
Busy Bee, 5–7

California, University of, at Los Angeles, 61
Cambridge University Library, 82, 138
Carnegie, Andrew, 64
Carroll, Lewis
  see Charles L. Dodgson
Carter, John, 69
Caxton Club, 61, 64, 73, 89
Cecil, Robert, 3rd Marquess of Salesbury, 124n
Century Illustrated Monthly Magazine, 37, 41, 137n, 142, 161–64
Century of Progress International Exposition (Chicago), 182
Chambers, David, 6n, 8n, 85, viii
Chaucer, Geoffrey, 46
Chaundy, Leslie, & Co., 57, 114–15, 187
Chicago, 60–61, 64, 89–90
Chicago Tribune, 60
Chiswick Press, 10
Christ Church, Oxford, 27, 37, 42, 96, 123
Christian of Schleswig-Holstein, Prince and Princess, 29
Christie's, 58, 62
Church Association, 4
Church of England, 4
Cicero, 52
Clarendon Building, Oxford, 32
Clarendon Press, 172
Clark, John P., 91, 94
Clary, William W., 83–84
Club of Odd Volumes, 60
Cobden-Sanderson, Thomas J., 20, 181
Cockerell, Douglas, 176, 181–82
Cockerell, Sydney C., 12n, 176
Coleridge, Samuel Taylor, 63
Collins, John Churton, 41
Columbia University Press, 75
Columbia University Library, 67, 74, 187
Colvin, Sidney, 123
Conroy, Tom, 182
Constantinou, Meghan, viii
Corbet, Sir Vincent R., 6th Baronet, 118
Cornell Steamboat Company, 75
Cornell University, 88
Corning Glass Works, 58
Corpus Christi College, Oxford, 30
Cotton, Rev. Richard Lynch, 126
Courthope, William J., 27, 33–34, 59, 116, 127, 133, 135, 138, 144,

[220]

INDEX

147–48, 154, 211–12
Courtney, Miss, 77
Coykendall, Frederick, 74–75
Crane, Lisa, viii
Critic, The, 37
Cruttwell, Wilson Clement, 85
Cruttwell family, 1, 4, 6, 85, 109
Cruttwell, Charles J., 30, 35, 46, 59, 112, 116, 128–29, 138, 144–45, 150, 157n, 217
Cruttwell, Clement, 1
Cruttwell, Maria, 128
Cruttwell, Richard, 1
Cruttwell, William, 1
Cruttwell, Wilson, 144
Crypt Grammar School, 43
Cuneo Press, 182
Cuneo, John, Sr., 173, 182

Daily News, 144
Daniel (Old Testament), 13
Daniel, Rev. Alfred, 1, 3–4
Daniel, Alfred M. G., 1
Daniel, Alfreda G. S., 84–85
Daniel, Charles Henry Olive (*selective references only*), 1–25, 27–32, 35, 38, 41–45, 51, 53, 55–56, 60, 110, 117–18, 187, 189, 197–200
  childhood and youth, 1–8
  early printing, 5–10, 12
  his copy of the *Garland*, 60–62
  letters from, 142, 147, 151–52, 158–60
  letters to, 121–48, 150
  marriage, 14
  photograph, xii
  plans for the *Garland*, 27
Daniel, Eliza, 3
Daniel, Emily Crabb Olive, 10, 14, 15, 16, 20, 21, 23, 28, 32, 38, 55, 58, 70, 76, 90–93, 95, 98–100, 107, 109–10, 113–16, 119, 121, 122n, 131, 134, 146, 150, 159–61, 163–68, 172, 175n, 178–79, 189, 197, frontispiece
Daniel, George, 5
Daniel, George Alfred, 84–85
Daniel, Henry Martin, 21
Daniel, Hilary Martin, viii, 84–85
Daniel, Jane, 85
Daniel, Rachel (afterwards Lee), 15, 23, 27, 28, 32, 34, 35, 39, 46, 49, 82, 91–92, 95, 98, 102–05, 112, 115, 117, 127, 135–36, 140, 142, 145–48, 165–66, 172, 178, 191, 199–217
  photographs, 101, 103, frontispiece
Daniel, Ruth, 13, 15, 21, 23, 38, 67, 92, 102, 104, 106–07, 172, 178, frontispiece
Daniel, Wilson Eustace, 7n
Darmesteter, James, 48, 153
Davis, Herbert, 67n
Davos, Switzerland, 49
Delaware, University of, Library, 97–98
DeZelar-Tiedman, Christine, viii
Dimunation, Mark, viii
Dobson, Alban, 37
Dobson, Austin, 29, 36–37, 41, 49, 76–77, 91, 112–13, 125, 131, 135–36, 137n, 138–40, 144, 148, 151, 162, 164n, 188, 191, 194, 200–01, Pl. 5
Dodgson, Charles L. ("Lewis Carroll"), 16, 27, 28, 37–40, 42–43, 52, 58, 66–67, 75–77, 79–80, 88, 96, 102, 104, 109, 112, 114–15, 121–23, 131, 133, 139, 144, 149–52, 155, 157–60, 168, 185, 187, 189, 205–06, Pls. 2–3
Doheny, Carrie Estelle, 60–63, 194
Donnelley, William, 182
Doves Press, 64, 89
Doyne, Mr., 77
Drinkwater, John, 188–89
Duclaux, Emile, 48
Dundee, 117
Dundee Advertiser, 118, 161n

[221]

INDEX

Earle, Bishop John, 28, 123, 197–98
Eastwick, Edward, 179
Edwardes, Mr.
Ehrman, Albert, 82
Ehrman, John, 82
Eliot, T. S., 71
Ellis, Frederick S., 176
English, Viveca, viii
Erasmus, 125
Estabrook & Company
Eton, 30, 42
Ewelm Collection, University of South Carolina Library, 99–100
Exeter College, Oxford, 27, 126

Fairlie, Capt. David O., 192
Falconer, Charles McG., 44, 52, 58, 72, 91–92, 116–19, 121, 132, 151–59, 161–63, 185–86, 191, 194, Pl. 9
Fales Library, New York University, 66, 83, 89, 114, 189–90
Félix, Rachel, 121–22
Fell types, 9, 10, 12, 31, 55, 122n, 176n, 197
Fell, Bishop John, 9
Ferguson, Stephen, viii
FitzGerald, Edward, 63–64
forgeries, 69
Forman, Harry Buxton, 69
France, 41
Franklin, Colin and Charlotte, viii, 56, 58–59, 70, 86, 112–13, 194
Frazier, Eric, viii
Friends of the National Libraries, 82
Frome, 1–8, 15n, 23, 85, 110, 171n
Furse, Dame Katharine, 77, 168
Furse, Charles W., 77, 169

Garsington Opera, 59
Gee's bookshop, 17, 81, 90, 109
Gehl, Paul, viii
Getty, J. Paul, 56, 58–59, 86, 113, 117
Getty, Mark, viii, 56, 59, 86, 112–13, 115–17

Gifford, William, 144
Gilder, Jeanette L., 37, 77, 91
Gill, Derek J., 1n
Glasgow, University of, 45
Gleeson Library, University of San Francisco, 79
Goffe, Thomas, 130
Goodspeed, Charles, 60
Gosse, Sir Edmund W., 27, 36–37, 40–42, 68–69, 76–77, 89, 110–13, 115, 125, 130, 136–37, 142–44, 151–53, 164, 188, 209
Gosse, Philip Henry, 40, 144
Green, Charlotte, 145
Grolier Club, 57, 60, 64, 73, 75, 87–88
Grosvenor College, Bath, 8
Gutenberg Bible, 64

Haileybury, 29
Hamill & Barker (dealer), 91, 94
Hans Christian Andersen Museum, 61
Hardy, Thomas, 30
Harington, Sir Richard, 36, 38, 42–43, 66, 69–70, 112–13, 116, 133, 139–40, 155–56, 206–07
Harrop, Dorothy, 81
Harrow, 49
Harry Ransom Center, University of Texas, 80, 82, 193
Hart, Horace, 176
Hartshorne, Robert, 87, 191
Harvard University Library, 68
Harvard University Press, 60
Harvey, Arthur Henry, 15n, 22
Hayes, William, & Son, 179
Healy, Sarah McCormick, viii
Henley, William E., 27, 43–44, 49, 72, 76–77, 112–13, 116, 129, 138, 140–41, 148, 151, 153, 188, 210–11, Pl. 6
Herrick, Robert, 89

[222]

INDEX

Hersholt, Jean, 60–61, 192
Hill, Walter M. (dealer), 83
Hoja Volante, 74
Holy Trinity Church, Frome, 1–3
Honnold Library, Claremont Colleges, 83, 192–93
Hookes, Nicholas, 72
Hopkins, Gerard Manley, 32
Hornby C. H. St. John, 8n, 10n, 12, 15, 16, 20, 21n, 176
Houghton Library, Harvard University, 58
Houghton, Arthur A., Jr., 56, 58, 112–13, 116–17, 119, 194
Hugo, Victor, 135
Huntington Library, 55, 71, 112, 114–15, 121n, 127, 134n. 187, Pl. 6
Huntington, Henry E., 71
Hutchinson, Thomas, 38n, 113

Imholtz, August, viii, 96n
Inge, William, 124n
Ingram, Diana, viii
Inland Printer, 73

Jacobi, Charles T., 111, 169
Japanese vellum, 166
Jessop, Augustus, 164
Johnson, John, 67
Johnson, Timothy, viii
Joyce, James, 71
Jutzi, Alan, viii

Kay, Liz, viii
Keats, John, 20, 58, 61, 64, 90
Kegan Paul, Charles, 149
Kelmscott Manor, 17, 175
Kelmscott Press, vii, 10, 12, 19, 64, 73, 82, 87, 89
Kindt-Collins, 88
King's College School, London, 8, 85
King's College, London, 8
Kirkman, Ruth Joanna (*née* Lee), 103, 106, 112, 172

Kirkman, Sidney, 106

Lakeside Press, 182
Lamb, Charles, 63
Lambert, Julie Anne, viii
Lane, John, 17–18
Lang, Andrew, 27, 32, 34, 36, 44–46, 48, 49, 72, 76–77, 112–13, 116–17, 124–25, 135–36, 138, 140–41, 144, 149, 151, 153, 158. 186, 188, 191, 194, 202–03
Langtry, Lily, 46, 126
Lawrence Turnure & Co., 57
Leckie, Marion Robinson (afterwards Symonds), 98
Lee, Reginald, 104
Lee, Veronica, 105
Leicester School of Art, 181
Leopold, Prince, 179
Library of Congress, 58, 61, 87
Lindseth, Jon A., 87–88
Littleton, Sir Thomas de, 129
Locker[-Lampson], Frederick, 27, 46–47, 74–77, 112–16, 132, 134, 141–42, 144, 147, 156, 158, 187–88, 212
London Library, 100
Long, Lisa, viii
Los Angeles Times, 74
Lucretius, 177

Mackenzie, Compton, 13, 107
Madan, Falconer, vii–viii, 7, 8, 10, 12, 15n, 21, 23, 30, 53, 55n, 57, 87, 93, 100, 108–11, 118–19, 122n, 169–72, 178, Pl. 9
Madan, Francis, 109
Madicott, John, viii
Magdalen College, Oxford, 49, 119
Maggs, Bryan, viii
Manchester Guardian, 30
Marillier, H. C., 12n
Marlborough College, 175
Martin, Theodore, 127

[223]

INDEX

Masefield, John, 16, 169
Mathews, Charles Elkin, 17, 18n, 19, 77, 175n, 179n, 188
McNees, Eleanor, 3n
Melbourne, University of, Library, 88
Merton College, Oxford, 27
Michelangelo, 165
Millard, Alice P., 61
Milton, John, 20
miniation in the *Garland*, 28, 85, 95, 113, 115, 118, 146, 163, 178, 193, 197
Moran, Eileen, viii
Morgan Library, 58, 64
Morgan, J. P., 96
Morley & Sons, 28, 76, 86, 88, 98, 106, 175, 179–81, 185, 193–94, Pl. 7
Morley, Henry, 179
Morley, Thomas, 179
Morley, William, 179
Morris, Edward Webster, 180
Morris, Jane, 17, 176
Morris, Leslie, viii
Morris, Lloyd R., 64
Morris, May, 71
Morris, William, 12, 13, 14, 17, 31, 71, 73, 175–76
Morrison, Jane Isabella, 85
Mosher, Thomas Bird, 28, 55, 57, 78n, 90n, 91–94, 118, 160–67, 175n, 191–92, Pls. 4–5
Moss, Lt.-Col. William E., 66–67, 160, 185, 189
Moss, William E., 66–68, 160, 185, 189
Mounteney, Leonard, 90–91, 93, 172–73, 181–83, Pl. 8
Murray, Frank, 162
Myers, Ernest, 47–48, 76, 86, 112–13, 116, 125, 135, 141, 143–44, 153–55, 214–15
Myers, F. W. H., 47
Nash, Paul W., viii

National Gallery, London, 58
National Library of Wales
National Review, 33
Nelson, James G., 18n
New College, Oxford, 100
New Gallery, London, 19
New Sermon of the Newest Fashion, A, 38
New York Public Library, 57
New Yorker, 64
Newberry Library, 55n, 61, 90–91, 191, Pl. 8
Newdigate prize, 33
Newton, A. Edward, 61
Nowell-Smith, Simon, 99–100

O'Day, Alan, viii
O'Shaughnessy, Arthur, 125, 130
Old Westbury Gardens, 65
Onions, John Henry, 133
Oram, Richard, viii
OUDS (Oxford University Dramatic Society), 104
Ould, Martyn, viii, 6, 9, 85
Our Memories: Shadows of Old Oxford, 20
Oxford Bibliographical Society, 119, 170
Oxford Union, 12
Oxford University, 16, 27, 28, 33, 84, 98, 166–67, Pls. 4–5
Oxford University Press, 9, 10, 15n, 176n

Parker, Joanna, viii, 86
Parrish Collection, Princeton University Library, 38, 95–96, 122n, 186–87
Parrish, Morris L., 96
Parsons, Alfred, 28, 36, 55, 99–100, 118, 142, 197, Pls. 4–5
Partridge, Bernard, 77
Pasteur Institute, 48
Pater, Walter, 16, 20, 27, 51, 109, 114,

INDEX

123, 127, 135
Pawling, Sydney, 77
Penny, W. C. & J., 7
Perry, Marsden, 64
Phillipps, Sir Thomas, 193
Philosopher Press, 57
Pickering & Chatto, 135
Pickering, William, 10, 35, 150
Plomer, Henry R., 92, 161n
Plymouth Brethren, 40
Pollard, Graham, 69
Pomona College, 83
Poor, Henry W., 69–71, 80, 92, 168n, 186–87, 194
Pope, Alexander, 33
Portland, Maine, 92
Poynter, Sir Edward, 132n
Poynter, Henrietta, 76, 132
Pre-Raphaelites, 13, 40
preface to the *Garland*, 56, 67, 81, 90n, 170
Price, Thomas, 22
Prideaux, Sarah, 176
Princeton, N.J., 90
printer's device, 13, 55, 99
proofs of the *Garland*, 58
Pryde, Pam, viii
Pugin, A. W. N., 3
Punch, 3
Puseyitism, 3

Quaritch, Bernard, 171
Quinn, John, 64, 69, 71

Rackham, Arthur, 75
Radcliffe Infirmary, Oxford, 98
Randle, John, viii
Ransom, Will, 81
Reading University Library, 18n
Rees, Rev. W., 77
Ridler, Ann, 80–81
Ridler, William, 80–81
Rivière, 173, 182
Robinson, A. Mary F., 27, 44, 48–49, 76, 112, 116, 125–26, 137, 139, 145, 148, 153, 157, 207–08, Pl. 4
Robinson, Edwin Arlington, 64
Robinson, Francis, 116
Rockefeller Foundation, 80
Rogers, Bruce, 64
Rosenbach, A. S. W., 95–96
Rossetti, Dante Gabriel, 12, 73
Rossiter, Anne, viii
Rota, Julian, viii
Rowfant Club, 57
Rowfant Library, 46
Royal Infirmary, Edinburgh, 43
Ruskin, John, 16
Russ, Elsie A., 6n
Ruthven press, 6–8

Saintsbury, George, 149
Saks, John, 64, 194
Samuels Lasner, Mark, viii, 84n, 97–98
Sangorski & Sutcliffe, 177
Saxton, Albert, 23
Scarlet Runner, 108
Schartiz, Arthur L., 12n
Schlitz Brewery, 182
Schneideman, Sophie, viii
School of Art and Design, 181
Scott, Temple, 72
Shakespeare, William, 89, 104, 165
Sharp, William ("Fiona Macleod"), 164
Sheaf, 108
Shelley Society, 68
Shelley, Percy Bysshe, 61, 64, 144, 149
Sherborne, 1, 100
Shorter, Clement, 91–92, 161, 163–64
Shrimpton, Thomas and George, 179
Sialkot, Pakistan, 172
Siegel, Jane, viii
Simmons, Parke Edmund, 64, 190

[225]

INDEX

Sligh, Nigel Archibald, 86
Sloan Foundation, 80
Sloan, Charles H., 91, 93–94, 172–73
Society for Psychical Research, 47
Sotheby's, 177
Spencer, Sir Charles, 3rd Earl of Sunderland, 149
Sphere, The, 161
Spoor, John A., 60–61, 190, 195
St. Andrews University, 45
St. Barnabas, Pimlico, 3
St. John the Baptist, Frome, 3, 4
St. John the Evangelist, Oxford, 108
St. John's Seminary (Camarillo, Calif.), 62
St. Mary the Virgin, Oxford, 52
Standish, Miles, 78
Stetz, Margaret D., 98
Steuben Glass, 58
Stevens, Ellen, 63–64
Stevenson, Robert Louis, 44, 162n, 164n, 165
Strawberry Hill Press, 87
Sunday Times, 41
Surtees, Virginia, 193
Sutton, Sir Richard, 5th Baronet, 118
Swinburne, Algernon C., 46
Symonds, Annie, 98
Symonds, Frederick, 98
Symonds, Horatio P., 97–98, 150
Symonds, John Addington, 34, 49–50, 76–77, 98, 112, 116, 132, 138, 145, 148, 152, 168, 186, 189, 203–04

Taylor, Henry, 127
Taylor, Marvin J., viii
Taylor, Rachel, 91, 94
Temple, London, 53
Tennyson, Sir Alfred, 61, 138
Theocritus, 36, 51
Thomas, Abel Cary, 76–78, 189
Thomas, Martyn, 9
Thursfield, James, 31, 126

Tidcombe, Marianne, 178n
Times Literary Supplement, 57, 100, 109
Times, The, 4, 16, 40, 50, 168
Tomkinson, G. S., 81
Tower Theatre Company, 106
toy press, 7, 21
Tregaskis, James, 66n
Trinity College, Oxford, 53
Tuerk, Laurence, 106
Tuerk, Penny, viii, 95, 100, 103, 105–06, 112, 115, 122n

United State Steel Corporation, 64
United States, 28, 45, 48, 90, 93, 178

Van Gelder paper, 55, 92
vellum, 55, 64, 175, 178, 180, 185–86, 191, 193–95
Victoria, Queen, 179

Wadham College, Oxford, 47
Walker, Emery, 176
Ward, Mary (*née* Arnold), 50–51
Ward, Thomas Humphry, 27–28, 32, 34, 36, 44, 48, 50–52, 78, 109, 112–13, 116, 126, 137–40, 145, 153–54, 188, 193, 195, 213–14
Warner Brothers Pictures, 78
Warren, T. H., 20, 92, 107, 119
Watson, Rev. Albert, 52, 109, 112, 116, 137–38, 150, 152, 157–58, 200
Watson-Smyth, Agnes, 146
Way & Williams, 73
Way, Washington Irving, 45, 73–74, 149, 168n
Weaver, Warren, 79–80
Webb, Edmund James, 177
Weimerskirch, Philip, viii
Whitall, Brigadier-General Samuel R. Whitall, 65
Whitall, William Van Rensselaer, 63–64, 188, 194
Whitbourne Court, 42, 43

INDEX

White, Eric, viii
Whittingham, Charles, the Younger, 35
Widener Library, Harvard University
Wightman, Mr., 139
Wilkinson, C. H., 36, 67, 77, 86, 110, 119, 167–68, 188, 192
Willert, F. P., 27, 33–34, 46, 112–13, 126–27, 133–34, 146–47
Williams & Norgate (dealer), 90–92, 160–61
Wilson Library, University of Minnesota, 72
Wise, Thomas J., 68–69, 89
Women's Guild of Art, 177
Wood, Anthony, 20
Woods, Rev. Henry G., 53
Woods, Gilbert, 53
Woods, Margaret L., 17, 19, 20, 45, 53–54, 77, 79, 82–83, 112–13, 134, 138, 145, 151–52, 167–68, 192–93, 215–17

Worcester College, Oxford, viii, 8, 9, 15, 16, 20, 29, 43, 86, 114, 119, 124n, 126n, 163, 169n, 176
 chapel, 11, 13
 Library, 8, 105, 108, 143n
 Provost's Lodge, 104
Worcester House, 11, 14–15, 17, 20, 32, 39, 74, 102, 104, 176
Wordsworth, William, 61, 118
Wormser, Richard S. (dealer), 87
Wormsley Library, viii, 76, 112, 116–17, 188, 192, Pl. 7
Wrenn, John Henry, 90
Wright, Mary de Diemar, 64

Yale University, 87
Yellow Book, 18
York, University of, 106
Young, Matthew, viii
Young, Timothy, viii

Zaehnsdorf, 116, 186
Zamorano Club, 73